Y0-CBF-404

SANAMU

Adventures in search of African art

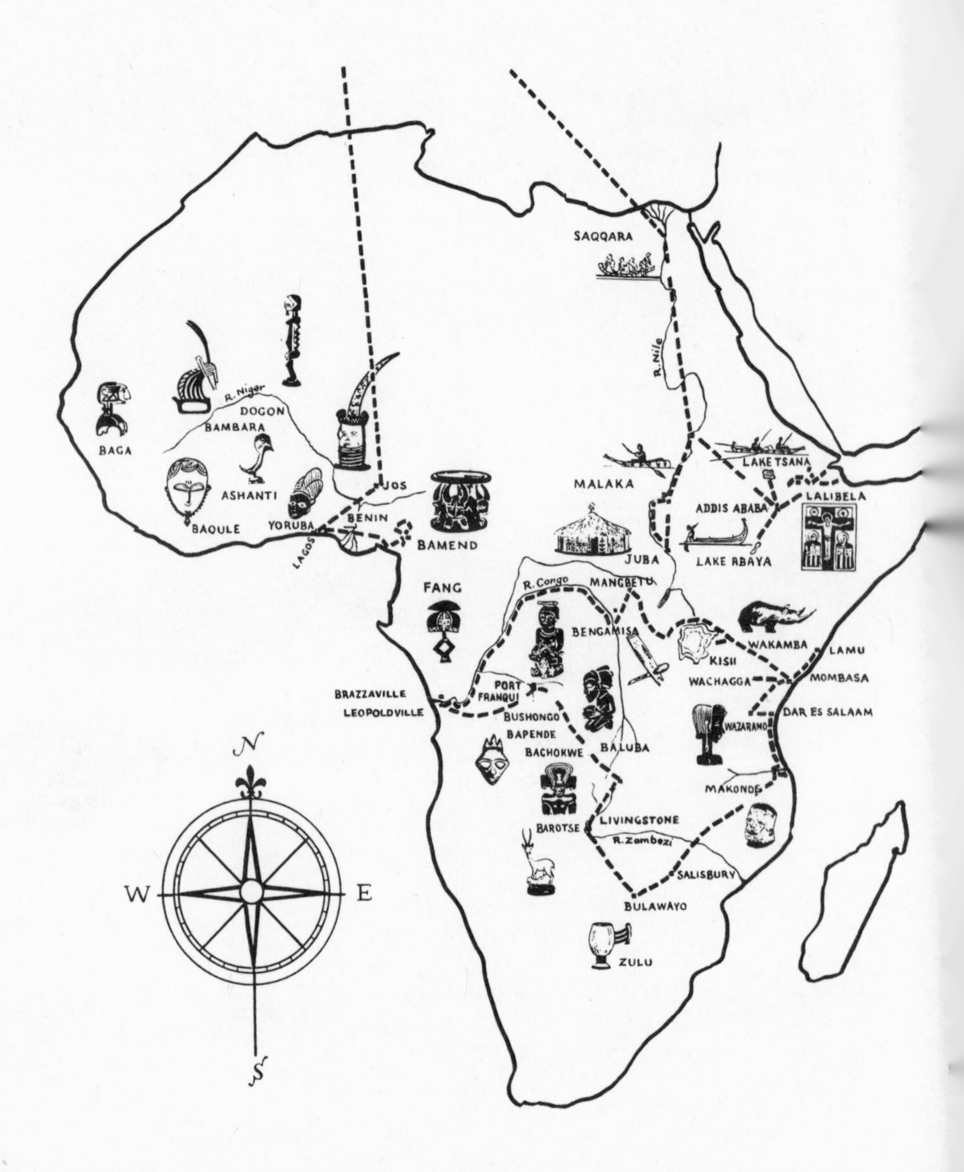

A pictorial map of Africa showing the areas visited by the author

SANAMU

Adventures in search of African art

ROBERT DICK-READ

E. P. Dutton & Co., Inc.

NEW YORK 1964

To my wife Sally

and to my mother, who has complained

that I never tell her anything about my travels

FIRST EDITION

Copyright, ©, 1964 by Robert Dick-Read

All rights reserved. Printed in the U. S. A.

No part of this book may be reproduced in any form without permission in writing from the publisher, except by a reviewer who wishes to quote brief passages in connection with a review written for inclusion in a magazine, newspaper or broadcast.

Library of Congress Catalog Card Number: 64–23217

Contents

 Plates 3 and 4 are by Lewis Morley, and 16-32 are by C. G. Konarski. The remainder are by the author.

Acknowledgements

I owe a great deal to many people who have, at some time or another, wittingly or unwittingly, provided material for this book. But I would particularly like to mention a few who have made a special contribution—Paul Gebauer, who helped me with material on the Cameroons; Armand Denis, who very kindly allowed me to reproduce the painting from the School of Fine Arts in Elisabethville; and Professor M. D. W. Jeffreys and Mm. I. Dugast whose relatively unknown book, "L'écriture des Bamum", provided the material for the passage on Njoya's script.

I would also like to thank Mr. K. C. Jordan for his painstaking work on the maps; and, above all, my publishers, whose criticism, advice, and patience have been invaluable.

Sanamu is the Kiswahili word that signifies any work of art or craft, or a photograph.

CHAPTER ONE

The Opening of "African Art"

"Listen all!" The District Commissioner's voice rang out clearly in Kiswahili above the chatter of the small crowd of Africans squatting beneath the mango trees. "You know why I have asked you to come in to Machakos today. It is to introduce you to Bwana Dick-Read, here. . . ." He paused and turned towards me; and as he did so I was aware of thirty pairs of silent, staring, brown eyes meticulously sizing me up.

"Mr. Dick-Read is going to start a business selling African crafts. He tells me he will have a shop in Mombasa where he will sell carvings to tourists from the mail boats, and he will also sell them to people in other countries—in England and in America—beyond the shores of Africa."

A few dark heads in the crowd nodded their appreciation, and the D.C. went on.

"Mr. Dick-Read has not been long in Kenya. I am sure he will be fair with you if you are honest with him. This is a good opportunity for you to advance the Akamba industries, and I hope you will take it. I will say no more now, but let you get on with the business. Thank you."

I turned and thanked the District Commissioner, and watched him as he strode confidently back to his office. Then, feeling suddenly alone and nervous in this strange company, I went over to join the Boma interpreter who was by then mingling with the crowd.

"Where do we begin?" I said, hoping he would come to my aid and organise everything for me. And the interpreter took my hint and arranged the Africans in a large circle round the edge of the shady clearing.

I had come to Machakos, the District Headquarters of the Wakamba tribe, to purchase my first stock of woodcarvings for a curio shop I planned to open a few weeks later. The people around me were woodcarvers from a village about forty miles into the bush

beyond Machakos. They had gathered today at the D.C.'s request, as the local administrators at that time were doing all they could to establish the Wakamba carving industry as a lasting and valuable source of income for these village people. Now they sat around me on woven mats on which were displayed a vast array of objets d'art great and small for me to sort and choose and bargain over for the rest of that day. There were armies of stiff, upright, wooden warriors holding shields and spears; there were sets of salad servers by the hundred. There were dumpy animals of every description—elephants, hippos, lions, rhinos, buck, zebra, wart-hogs, antelopes, leopards, and giraffes. And there were carvings of people—full length, half length, torso, heads only—carrying bundles on their backs, pots on their heads, sticks in their hands, babies at their breasts. These were the creatures that were destined to people my world for the next few years. And the tribesmen, some sullen, some laughing, who already knew me better than I knew them, and who now began to skin me alive, selling carving after carving at prices they had never dreamed of before—nor ever received again—these were the men who were to become my foes, my friends, the mainstay of my business.

The venture had begun six months earlier when I had come to Kenya from England with no job and not much money to look for a more exciting way of making a living than seemed possible in England. It was January 1953 when I had arrived in Africa, and the Mau Mau troubles had reached new heights in their murderous path. I had travelled out by sea and gone directly to Nairobi where I was staying with friends who happened, at that time, to be playing a leading part in the formation of a private army to combat the Mau Mau terrorists in the forests. And within forty-eight hours of being in Kenya I had been swept up in the vehement settler struggle, and sent off to the Aberdare mountains with a band of English lords, Polish princes, plumbers, lawyers, farmers, mechanics —a bunch of gun-toting brigands themselves—to do battle with the Mau Mau. That was a job that had kept me alive for the time being, and given me a chance to look around for a more regular, interesting, occupation. And it provided me with an opening.

In our camp in the mountains one day a chance conversation with a Nairobi businessman set me thinking about the possibilities of going into the curio trade, selling carvings like those sold on the pavements outside Nairobi's hotels. The man I was talking to told me that he had had several enquiries from American friends interested in shipping African carvings to the United States, where there was a growing demand for such things, as ornaments in contemporary-style interiors, and among the increasing number of people interested in African affairs.

The seed of an idea had been sown, and from then on it rapidly began to germinate. During the next few weeks, whenever I had a chance to slip away from the mountains I made it my business to find out all I could about the carvers; what tribe they were, where they lived, and whether they could produce a worthwhile quantity of carvings. At the same time I started making investigations into the marketing possibilities in the United States and, with the help of the American Embassy, put an advertisement in an official U.S. trade magazine. The response to this advertisement was astonishing, for within a short time I had received over fifty enquiries. I was so encouraged that I decided to take the risk and plunge wholeheartedly into the business—to become a knick-knack merchant, a dealer in the arts and crafts and curios of Africa.

After six months the private army I had fought with was disbanded, and being ineligible for call-up into the regular security forces I was free to go ahead with my plans. From the outset it seemed that the most profitable business to aim for was the export market. But one overriding problem I had to face was a shortage of capital, and to embark immediately on a business solely devoted to export would have needed a great deal more money than I had. It would have necessitated building up large stocks of carvings, and waiting for indeterminate periods before I was paid for them. But I needed something coming in week by week.

I did not want to set up a business in Nairobi; and in any case the high rents and cost of living in the capital would have made this almost impossible. I therefore decided to move to Mombasa on the coast where I could, if necessary, live like a beachcomber, and where rents were within my means. Furthermore, Mombasa was East Africa's main port to which came practically every tourist-carrying liner that sailed up the African coast. It therefore seemed the obvious place in which to open a retail shop aimed specifically at the tourist market. Assuming that the retail business would keep me alive week by week, my plan was gradually to develop the more profitable export trade. So in August 1953, with my car loaded to the roof with the carvings I had purchased in Machakos, and numerous other bits and pieces I had collected elsewhere, I left Nairobi and moved down to the coast.

Mombasa at that time was a quiet town that seemed nowhere near as large as its population figures suggested. Of the sixty thousand people living there, the majority were Africans and coastal Arabs. There were two or three thousand Europeans, and rather more Indians who owned most of the commercial buildings. Though the administration and the more important aspects of commerce were in the hands of the British, the town itself formed part of the Kenya Protectorate—the coastal strip that was owned by the Sultan of Zanzibar. Mombasa's mixed ownership—and its warm, friendly, tropical climate—led to a degree of racial tolerance that was a welcome change after the hypersensitive, knife-edge atmosphere of Nairobi, and gave it a more pleasant social atmosphere than that of any town in the Kenya Highlands.

In appearance, Mombasa was unobtrusive and relaxing. Its buildings—mostly white and seldom more than two stories high—sprawled along a few broad streets shaded by acacias and flamboyant trees. And though only a few degrees from the Equator, and tropical in every respect, the perpetual breeze blowing in from the sea kept the town from becoming unbearably hot.

Now I had arrived in Mombasa the prospect of starting up a business and opening a shop filled me with trepidation. I had not been brought up in a commercially minded household, and my knowledge of finance, book-keeping, and other business mysteries was about as great as that of the wooden warriors I was hoping to sell. I had not the slightest idea how to set about finding shop premises, drawing up contracts, or anything of that sort.

Reluctant to display my complete ignorance of the business world by asking advice, I spent the first two days in Mombasa wandering about the streets, peering in at shop windows, seeking inspiration, and hoping for something to land in my lap. And by a stroke of good fortune that is exactly what happened. Passing a new building in Fort Jesus Road, the main street, I noticed that one shop—a corner shop in a good position—was not yet taken. As I stood looking through the windows a middle-aged Indian in threadbare clothes and down-at-heel sandals came up with a large bunch of keys, unlocked the door, and walked inside. And in a kind of now-or-never fling of courage I moved in behind him and spoke to him.

"Excuse me, do you know who owns this shop?" I said.

"Oh yes," he replied with a heavy Bombay accent, "the shop is my shop!"

But then I was smitten with doubt. Did he mean he *owned* the building, or had merely rented the shop? He hardly looked the sort of person who would own a modern three-storey block of offices and shops. But he came to my rescue as he went on:

"What for you want to know? You want to rent shop? I can rent to you at very good price!" And so in a very short time I had become the proud lessee of a brand new shop with three large windows.

Working as I was, on a minuscule budget, I had no desire to waste a penny on expensive, professionally made, shopfittings. I did not want anything too plush; but I wanted something effective—something colourful, gay and bright—and I felt that I was quite capable of doing this myself with whatever cheap local materials came to hand. So over the next few days I spent my time in the cavernous interior of my new premises brooding over what needed to be done; and wandering around Mombasa's markets, finding out what cheap materials were available.

In the slightly pompous colonial atmosphere of Mombasa it might have been considered rather infra dig. for a European to turn his hands to such menial tasks as I now proposed, so my first move, when the time came to start work in the shop, was to get a bucket of whitewash and slop it over the inside of the windows. I felt that I could then work in peace without having to suffer the inquisitive stares of passers-by.

It was whilst I was whitewashing one of the windows that I looked up to see a wide-eyed black man peering through at me from the other side, with a questioning, expectant look on his face, and waving a scruffy piece of paper in his hand. The fellow obviously had something he wanted to say to me, so I called him inside. The idea of hiring an assistant had not so far occurred to me, but this lad with his fuzzy mop of black hair and happy grin explained that he was looking for work. And as he spoke reasonably good English and seemed clean and intelligent I hired him on the spot. His name was David Otiambo, and I still maintain that David was one of the best assistants I ever had in Africa despite what later transpired. He had a very quick mind and did not care how hard he worked. From the start he willingly pitched into all the chores of shop-fitting. He scrubbed the stone floor, and polished it. He helped me with the painting, and ran errands, and went shopping for me, buying things in the market far cheaper than I would have been able to. And as a carpenter's mate he was invaluable.

Together, David and I made screens of woven palm fronds to divide the shop from the stock-room and packing area. We set up shelves on the walls, and made simple trestle show-tables which we covered with bright yellow fabric bought cheaply in the market. Scouring a scrap-heap one day I found a beautiful old solid mahogany ship's door that had been pitched out; and this, with a bit of shaping and planing, and with the addition of a poker-worked white-wood leg, we made into a desk as elegant as anything in Knightsbridge. The entire bill for fitting out the shop totted up to no more than £12 15*s*. 9*d*. And when all was ready we then set about displaying the collections that I had been building up over the past few weeks.

From the start, it was my intention to keep the contents of the shop entirely African, and to this end I had been scouring the surrounding country for anything and everything that might appeal to tourists. I had written to all the District Commissioners in Kenya, Tanganyika, and Uganda asking if their people had anything unusual to offer, and many of them had made arrangements to send me obscure and interesting objects from time to time. Missionaries —always keen on handicrafts—proved a useful and regular source of supplies, especially of basket-work and beadwork. My network even extended as far as the Rhodesias, Ruanda-Urundi, and Somaliland from which I occasionally received small consignments of carvings in unusual styles, and other goods.

So when the time came to set up the display I had enough knick-knacks and Africana to fill a baronial mansion. There were spears and shields from the Masai, the Karamajong, and other outlandish tribes; drums of every size and shape; soap-stone carvings from near Lake Victoria; beadwork from central Tanganyika; basket-work from Ruanda-Urundi; wooden milk-pots and camel bells from the nomads of Somaliland; table-mats woven from the hairs of elephants' tails; a splendid group of three men in a boat and other carvings from Moçambique; model dhows from Lamu; drinking

gourds from Kilimanjaro; wart-hogs' tusks, hippos' teeth, lion skins, and a mass of other miscellaneous bric-à-brac. All these were in addition to my main supplies—the woodcarvings of the Wakamba.

One final thing now remained—to think up a name and prepare a name-plate for the shop. The name I finally chose was "African Art", and rather than paint this in large letters above the shop front, I decided to carve it in small letters into a piece of poker-worked wood which was then, as every morning thereafter, set up on a large drum on the pavement just outside the door.

The whitewash having been wiped from the windows, "African Art" was now ready to do business, and one Monday morning in September 1953, whilst David busily, but unnecessarily, dusted and re-dusted everything on the shelves, I might have been seen sitting hopefully behind my desk, looking for all the world like a hardened and experienced shopkeeper—waiting.

My first customer, who wandered in nonchalantly at about ten o'clock unaware that he was making history, was a little old Central European professor, myopic as a rhinoceros and without a hair on his head. Rising casually to my feet I greeted him and asked if there was anything I could do for him; but waving me politely aside he muttered that he only wished to look around. As he went from piece to piece scrutinising everything in detail, I hovered nearby ready to rush to his assistance if necessary. Slowly he moved round the tables until at last his eyes alighted upon an object hanging on the wall. This was a kaiamba, a simple grass rattle made of two flat mats of grass with dried seeds between them.

"What eez deez?" he asked, curious; and I explained at length how massed bands of kaiamba players accompanied the exciting dances of the local Wanyika tribesmen.

"Ow much eez it?" he went on. To my horror I suddenly realised I had no idea. I had purchased it only a day or two earlier in the Mombasa market for sixpence; but I had intended it more for show than for sale as, frankly, it had not occurred to me that anyone would wish to buy it. Conscious of a rush of blood to my cheeks, and stuttering in confusion, I blurted out the first figure that came into my head.

"Ten shillings," I said. The price, of course, was scandalous; but the professorial old tourist, without turning a hair, handed me the money and departed. The two thousand per cent profit that I made on this, the first article I ever sold, was I believe the highest profit mark-up that I ever managed to get away with in the whole time I had the shop.

From then on I received a steady flow of visitors, both tourists from visiting ships and Bwanas and Memsahibs from Mombasa who found in "African Art" a novel source of Christmas presents for relatives back home. At first the former were slow to find the shop as it was situated some way from the docks, and many tourists, flagging in the dazzling sunshine, abandoned their explorations of the town long before they reached me. But after a while, growing wise to this, I got David to distribute advertising leaflets in popular cafés, and on the ships themselves, and trade began to pick up.

"African Art" was not without competition from Indian curio dealers, and the Wakamba carvers who clustered on the pavements in the centre of the town. These Wakamba hucksters drew away many of the younger people who were not very particular about what they bought, and who understandably enjoyed haggling for their curios. Thus most of my customers were more selective middle-aged and elderly people who preferred, and could afford, to make their purchases in comfort. Their buying habits I found to be quite unpredictable; some would spend an hour or more in the shop asking questions, scrutinising everything, and buying nothing; others were more like the bluff Texan who stormed into the shop one day wearing a vast stetson, bought three dozen identical paper-knives, and stormed out again. He was "doing the world", and had doubtless been buying paper-knives in every port of call. Some were genuinely interested in African "art"; others, old ladies mostly, gave the impression that by giving their support to African craftsmen they were performing a philanthropic act. All were equally welcome. Customers were invariably a great source of pleasure, with only one exception—a South African who was so rude about the shop and everything in it, including me, that I forcibly removed him from the premises. Nor did I ever discover any case of shop-lifting apart from a woman who, within a few days of my opening, "lifted" my Parker 51 pen!

Some of my most interesting regular visitors were not customers at all, but people who came to sell. The quaintest of these was a middle-aged English couple who lived in Mombasa. I never heard the story of their lives, but they had obviously had a good education and were what one might call "gentlefolk". When I knew them they were absolutely down and out, literally combing a living from the beaches. Both of them walked around in tattered sand-shoes and torn clothes; they were pathetically thin and undernourished. The man, tall and gaunt, spent his mornings catching shrimps which he sold to a local hotel, and sometimes he would bring me a grotesque piece of drift-wood, gleaned from the sand, which he would ask me to sell for him for a shilling or two. She, when she had the energy, used to do embroidery. I never wanted any of this, but periodically I bought a few pieces simply because they so obviously needed money. After a time they stopped coming, and though I never could discover what had happened to them, I fear they may simply have wasted away to dust.

Every few weeks I was visited by a Somali gentleman, himself a curio dealer, from Mogadishu. He used to bring me supplies of beautifully made Somali daggers with ivory and ebony handles, and sheaths made from camel-skin sewn with the hairs from a giraffe's tail; and in return he used to buy a few pieces of ebony carving to re-sell in Mogadishu, though I cannot see how, at the prices he had to pay, he could have made much profit on them. He was one of the finest looking men I have ever seen. He stood about six feet seven; was always impeccably dressed in Somali garb; and his voice, a rich mellifluous baritone, had a strangely mesmeric quality about it. He was a romantic, and I would endeavour to keep him talking as long as possible for the sheer joy of listening to him. Had he been born into a Western society I felt he might have made a fortune as a Casanova of the screen.

One regular gang of visitors I had was a bunch of grimy Arab school-children. They were tiny little kids of eight or nine, and in their grubby white "gelabias" looked like smiling baby ghosts. At

first they were shy. They would pause on their way home from school every day and rub their filthy little noses on the window glass, "ooohing" and "aaahing" at the extraordinary things they could see inside. David used to try to chase them away because it meant he had to clean the windows every time they passed; but I found them entertaining and used to stop him. One day I saw them gaping at my drums, of which I always had a big collection from all over East Africa, and called them inside so that they could get a better look. Then we started playing them; and in a moment there was an uproarious din floating down the main street of Mombasa. The sight and sound of these funny little creatures banging away on the huge drums caused a considerable stir outside, and before long we had a sizeable audience—and loud applause. We used to repeat this treat every week on half-holidays; and I came to look forward to it as much as they did.

One morning David was not at the shop when I arrived at half past eight. This was most unusual as generally he was extremely punctual. But I did not do anything about it as I thought perhaps he was sick and would be sending a message later. Instead, however, at about mid-day a policeman came into the shop and opened the conversation by asking me if I employed David Otiambo. He then announced that David was an escaped convict from Kwale prison near Mombasa and should have been serving a three-year sentence for robbery with violence. David had been picked up the night before, blind drunk, weaving down the road on his bicycle, dressed in a policeman's raincoat! Only after checking his record had they discovered his true identity which I, frankly, found hard to believe. I saw him later that day myself, and a more dejected, downhearted sight could scarcely be imagined. I am convinced that having escaped from prison he had decided to go straight, and I only hope that two more years in prison did not turn him into a lifelong crook. I now had to find another assistant, but I doubted whether I should find one as efficient as David had been.

As in most towns in Africa where there are usually thousands of Africans looking for work, it was not hard to find another assistant in Mombasa to take David's place. Just as I had found David before the shop had opened, so I found his successor who came wandering into the shop bearing a sheaf of references a few days after David's departure. The second lad, a tall, fat-faced, semi-educated Mombasa boy named Rajabu William was slow and dull-witted compared with his predecessor. He was likeable enough, but his slow, lumbering brain found it hard at times to keep pace with what he was trying to do. I felt sorry for Rajabu in some ways. He was a typical mixed-up product of a modern African school, torn between the primitive traditional life of his family, and a mission-influenced education.

This was brought home to me sharply a few weeks after he came to work for me when he asked me for a wage advance. Something in his manner made me ask him why he wanted it. He hedged at first, and in doing so made me all the more curious. He seemed ashamed and very nervous; but ultimately he told me. "Bwana", he said, "I want it for my mother. She must buy a goat. My uncle is sick, and we must get a goat for him to sacrifice to his family ancestor. If we don't get the goat he might die, and my mother, she has no money."

"Rajabu," I said, "why don't you take your uncle to a doctor?"

He looked at me with a pathetically bewildered expression. "Ooh! Bwana. He will not go to a doctor."

"Then tell me, Rajabu, just what does happen if one of your family falls ill?"

"Well." He hesitated, wondering whether to go on. "You see, Bwana, it is like this. Outside our house we have a little shrine in which our ancestor, Kisuka, lives. We must feed Kisuka each day or he will be angry. If somebody is not well, we must give more to Kisuka, or he will be more angry and the man will die. So when somebody is ill we give Kisuka a chicken. Then if he gets no better we must give Kisuka something more . . . a goat maybe. If still my uncle is more ill, well then we must go to make sacrifice to Shetani in the place Msimu where our people in the old days would sometimes kill a baby for Shetani. If no good . . . then a witchdoctor must be found . . . but witchdoctors are expensive in our country. If my uncle is still very ill, and the witchdoctor is no good, then there is a special clan of very strong witchdoctors who live in a place far from here, and if we can pay for it we must go to get help from there. . . . "

Rajabu was silent for a minute and seemed reluctant to go on.

"And what happens if that is no good, Rajabu?" I asked.

He gazed down at his feet sorrowfully. "Then, Bwana . . . then we go to church to pray to Jesus."

I would not vouch for the accuracy of what Rajabu's people do, for I think Rajabu himself was desperately confused with the traditions of his own tribe. But this story of his did seem to be indicative of the mental chaos of thousands of young Africans—of thousands at that very time in the Mau Mau, for instance—rent between two worlds, dragged into the depths of violence, knowing what was right perhaps, but powerless to follow the course dictated by conscience.

As time went on, orders from abroad became more frequent and the export business began to develop. Almost every day there were packages to be wrapped and sent off to shops in Key West, Pasadena, Cedar Rapids, Cincinnati, Santa Monica, Inglewood, Boston, Chicago, and in other American towns and cities great and small. Some of these shops re-ordered, others did not, while a few began to place increasingly large orders. Sometimes orders were so staggeringly large that it was quite impossible to meet them, and I had to turn them down. One import firm, for instance, sent me a single order for 500 carvings at £2 0*s*. 0*d*. each, 1,000 at £1 0*s*. 0*d*., 2,000 at 10*s*. and 4,000 at 5*s*. Even had I had sufficient capital to consider such an order, it would have been quite impossible to obtain the goods from the carvers within a year—and they wanted them by return.

Ninety per cent of the goods I bought for export came from the Wakamba carvers of Machakos district, where I had made my first purchases for the shop. The history of the Kamba curio carving industry is one of the most phenomenal success stories of modern Africa. Before the first world war, apart from several types of stools for different social groups, ceremonial staffs for tribal elders, and household utensils the Wakamba showed no propensity for creative arts and crafts whatsoever. Nor have they until recently ever been looked upon as shrewd businessmen as have their neighbours the Kikuyu. As late as 1948 a British District Commissioner of Machakos wrote: "In general it is fortunate that the Akamba have less business acumen and sense of initiative in trading than most tribes." Had he been writing this report five years later he would have found it difficult to make such a statement. In 1958 an economist (Walter Elkan) investigating the Kamba carving trade estimated that in the peak years of 1954 and 1955, the people of one Kamba village alone —Wamunyu—grossed at least £150,000—possibly as much as £250,000 from the sale of woodcarvings.

The Kamba tribe is one of the largest in Kenya. Ukamba, as their country is called, lies to the south-east of Nairobi and extends almost to the sea. For the most part it is a land of big views, rolling hills, and broad escarpments. It is not Africa's most hospitable land, being dry and none too fertile. The grass is thin; and in summer the countryside is a pale shade of brown. Trees are sparse and stumpy, and the streams are dry except when the rains come, when they rush in torrents through the hills. Pale grey water-worn rocks in the river beds protrude from the scattered pools lending a touch of crisp clean beauty to the harsh landscape. Seen from the air, thousands of dusty tracks worn in the sand by herds of cattle, and smaller crooked paths that link the scattered hamlets and villages, stand out clearly on the arid brown landscape like a veil of loosely woven lace.

The beginning of commercial carving among the Wakamba is attributed to a man named Mutisya Munge who, before the first world war, was known throughout Ukamba for his excellence as a craftsman. Before the war his work was confined to traditional objects such as stools; but whilst serving with the armed forces away from home he began to occupy his idle hours by carving "pictures" from his imagination, for his own amusement. These were of small scenes from daily life, one well-known model being of a man climbing up a tree to collect honey from an African-style beehive hanging from a branch. He found that his officers and other Europeans were intrigued by his carvings, and after the war he devoted more and more of his time to producing them for sale. For the first year or two, reluctant to let others in on his idea, he used to hide himself away in the bush and carve in secret. Inevitably, however, his secret was discovered and before long a number of other carvers in his village had copied his patterns and begun to sell their work in Nairobi.

The market among white men seemed inexhaustible; and between the wars the number of carvers increased. The trade received its first big fillip during the second world war, when large numbers of British soldiers came to Kenya. Then after 1945, with the rapid increase of tourism in Africa, it expanded yet again. By now firms abroad were beginning to take an interest, and the export trade began to develop. The number of carvers was continually increasing, and the street corners of Nairobi and other main towns became crowded with vendors, all of whom did brisk business. There seemed no end to expansion, and in the fifties the industry continued to grow. By 1954–5 there were up to 3000 part-time or full-time carvers, almost all of whom came from Wamunyu village and the surrounding area.

Wamunyu lies far out in Ukamba about seventy miles from Nairobi. As a village there is nothing beautiful about it, nothing romantic. Few people actually live there, for it is primarily a market place to which people come from far and wide to sell their produce every week. It is a simple, open-ended rectangle of tin-roofed, semi-detached, single-storey shops and stores, shoddily thrown up in pale brown brick. There are one or two shops where cheap coloured cotton, beads, and flashy trinkets can be bought. There are butchers' shops where fly-covered meat hangs in the sun. And there are several flourishing beer shops. But most of the buildings belong to the woodcarvers, and it is from here that they have organised their trade since it began.

Though most of my buying was done in my shop to which craftsmen regularly brought basket-loads of carvings, I occasionally travelled up-country to see the carvers at work. It is always a joy to watch a craftsman who has complete mastery of his tools and materials, and I found I could easily sit for hours watching and listening to these Kamba carvers. Generally I would find them sitting beneath the spreading branches of a huge fig tree—fifteen or twenty of them—chipping at chunks of ebony and muninga and a dozen other species of timber. The muted rhythmic thwacking of the steel blades biting into the wax-smooth wood, and the subdued murmuring of their soft deep voices breaking from time to time into ripples of casual laughter, blended well with the sweet smell of resin and sap in the heat of the day. For them it was a gentle life, unhurried and dreamy. They were a happy bunch; but as motley in their tattered shorts and khaki shirts as the sunlight that filtered through the leaves and fell about them in scattered pools of light and shade. Chip, chip, chip, chip,—they wielded their adzes in unhurried, accurate strokes, sending slithers of timber flying through the air, to fall upon the springy carpet of wood-chips beneath them.

Not far away, under the rusty iron eaves of huts from which the whitewash peeled in flakes, sat their wives and children, labouring too, with more zest than their menfolk, papering and polishing until the feel of the wood was as smooth and sensual to their fingers as it was to their big brown eyes.

Despite their vast production the methods of manufacture employed by the Wakamba remain today identical to those used by craftsmen before Europeans came to Kenya. Excepted here, of course, is the use of sandpaper and boot polish which are now used for finishing the carvings. Their tools consist of a variety of home-made adzes and a scalpel-type knife. All the carvers I have ever known spurned such European innovations as carborundum stones. As they have done for centuries, they gather their sharpening stones from an outcrop of quartz-basalt in the hills about forty miles from their homes.

Amongst the Wakamba carvers I made many friends. Moses, for instance—a tall, lean, sensitive man always smiling and laughing but with a better eye for business than for art, who invariably took me to his home when I came to Wamunyu to drink tea with his wife, and to show me with pride his two delightful children, his garden with newly planted banana trees, and the extension to his house with its shining new corrugated iron roof And there was Wambua, small, rotund, always trying to pull a fast one, but a ball of fun. Wambua had once taken his tools and a load of carvings across Africa to Léopoldville in the Belgian Congo. When the Mau Mau broke out all Kenya Africans' passports were cancelled, but Wambua refused to leave the Congo—he was making so much money from the rich Belgians—and eventually he had to be forcibly extradited. It was Wambua whom I met in Salisbury, Southern Rhodesia, a year or two later. I was walking down the street past Meikle's Hotel when I suddenly heard someone behind me muttering in Kiswahili—"Eh! Bwana Sanamu . . . "—"Mr. Picture" as they came to know me. I turned round and there was Wambua once again fifteen hundred miles from home, confident and cocksure in a foreign land though he spoke not a word of English.

The Wakamba have always been great travellers, even in the days before the white men came, when they used to penetrate as far south as southern Tanganyika on elephant hunting expeditions. But perhaps the most enterprising and widely travelled of the post-war generation of carvers is a man named Mwambetu Munge, the son of the founder of the industry, Mutisya. By 1953 Mwambetu, who like Wambua could speak not a word of English, had hawked his carvings as far afield as the Union of South Africa, to Léopoldville, and as far north as Khartoum in the Sudan. On one trip to Khartoum, having run into some trouble with the authorities, rather than return to Nairobi, he took a 'plane and flew to London. Here he took to carving African curios in English oak, and learned to speak the language. Two years later, still in London, he wrote to the District Commissioner of his homeland in Kenya, on headed notepaper and in good English, asking him to "see to it that those who make the carvings at Wamunyu get a chance to send them to London". He enclosed a leaflet he had written on the "Art of the Kamba People", in which he set out his version of the history of the trade; and he asked the D.C. to give him complete proprietorship of the whole carving industry on the grounds that his father, after all, had begun it! The District Commissioner refused.

Such are the men who make up the Kamba carvers. They were quick to realise that it was to their advantage if we could develop our own export lines, and they knew too that I was doing business on a shoestring. There were many occasions when, to fill an order rapidly, they let me have carvings on account, and there were times when I was in debt to them to the tune of a hundred pounds or more for a month or six weeks.

Buying carvings from the Kamba was always treated as a game. They would try to get away with anything if they could; but if they failed they accepted it with good humour. Very few of them had any education or could speak English; yet they were as sharp as cheesewire. They used to bring their carvings into the shop in huge baskets, and we would go through the work piece by piece on the floor. A high percentage always had to be rejected on account of quality, and these they would take back to sell from their street-corner stands.

There were moments when they displayed a delightful sense of humour. I had one excellent carver named Daudi, a young boy of sixteen or seventeen. Daudi was a dour character who rarely spoke, and seldom, if ever, laughed. I had asked him on one occasion to carve me a dozen figures of the local Giriama women (these are a coast tribe whose women wear no more than a short kilt-like skirt). He brought the carvings into the shop, and in the normal way stood them all up for me to check. At first glance everything seemed fine. They all stood firmly upright with one arm raised holding a pot on their heads, and the other arm extended stiffly down their sides. Then I noticed that one of them, instead of having her right arm down her side, had it thrust rudely down inside the front of her skirt. I looked up at Daudi; and I believe it was the only time I really saw him laugh. In fact he could not stop laughing. He stood shaking for several minutes, utterly overwhelmed by his joke.

As soon as "African Art" was firmly established, and whenever the opportunity arose, I made brief explorations to look for new material in parts of East Africa other than Wamunyu. One of these journeys was to Lake Victoria to visit the people of Kisii where there is a small group of craftsmen making curios from soap-stone. Most of the Kisii curio merchants are primarily farmers, tilling the rolling green hills around the shores of the lake, carving only in their spare time. As with the Kamba industry, the Kisii carving also has a traditional background inasmuch as these people have long made tobacco pipes from the soft pink and white streaky stone. These days the industry is devoted almost entirely to the production of little fishes and frogs which sell rapidly to tourists, and flower

vases of ghastly European design, which disintegrate in water unless they are properly sealed—a thing the carvers seldom do.

I also welcomed any opportunity to slip away from the humid heat of Mombasa to the cool dew-laden slopes of Kilimanjaro, not only to breathe the fresh mountain air for a change, but also because there were a number of interesting craftsmen among the Chagga tribe that live on the slopes of the mountain. These craftsmen, like the Wakamba, worked in wood; but their products were entirely different. The crafts of Africa, as elsewhere, have more often than not developed along lines dictated by the raw materials at hand. Most African tribes use pottery in their homes because the raw earth is handy, and suitable for the job. The volcanic earth of Kilimanjaro makes poor pottery; but in place of it there is plenty of excellent timber growing up the slopes of the massive mountain. Thus, until they were able to buy cheap pots and pans in the shops, most Chagga people made their household utensils out of wood. These included huge bins in which to brew beer, and an assortment of trays, bowls, spoons and stools. It was their wooden bowls that sold best in the shop—objects that were made on an interesting mass production basis. The carvers, working with the same tools as the Wakamba, would take a long straight branch of a tree in which they would shape six or eight bowls joined to one another by an arch of timber. These were then cut off either singly, or in pairs, or sometimes in threes making elegant multiple dishes not unlike some contemporary Scandinavian designs. All the bowls were made in fig-wood, not only because it was easy to work, but because it was virtually tasteless and did not taint the food. Other Chagga products that caught the eye of customers were their large beer gourds, holding about two pints each, covered in quaint symbolic designs of the sun and the moon, and various creatures, weapons, and huntsmen, burned into the yellow gourds with a red hot needle.

Unfortunately most of the Chagga crafts were rapidly dying out. The farmers on the slopes of Kilimanjaro produce some of the world's finest and most highly priced coffee, and the per capita income of the Chagga is higher than that of any other East African tribe. It is not uncommon to see a brand new Mercedes sheltered in an umbrageous grove of bananas and wattles outside a mean grass hut half-way up the mountain; and people who can afford that sort of luxury are not going to be bothered with making their own household utensils. Tom Marrealle II, the enlightened, highly educated Paramount chief of the Chagga was making strenuous efforts to encourage local artists and craftsmen to keep going, and had formed a craftsmen's co-operative where their products could be sold. But is was an uphill struggle, and the volume and quality of work was in steady decline. I visited Tom Marrealle on a number of occasions, and once—as a house-warming present for his new European-style mansion—I presented him with one of a set of cups I had carved myself in English Oak, after a Zulu design. The work, in some respects, was not unlike that of his own craftsmen; and though I was careful to explain its origin, either the confusion of influences was too much for him or he thought I was trying to pull a fast one on him, and his gratitude was only lukewarm.

One easy safari from Mombasa that was always interesting if not always worth while from a business point of view was to the small Arab island of Lamu, 150 miles to the north. Lamu island, not much larger than Mombasa island and, like it, separated from the mainland by a narrow sound, is one of those few remaining corners of the earth that have been completely forgotten and bypassed by time and progress. For several centuries, until the Indian Ocean fell under the control of European fleets and East Africa became a zone of influence for colonial powers, Lamu, like Zanzibar, was an important entrepôt of Arab trade from which ivory and slaves and mangrove wood were exported from Africa to the thriving cities of the Trucial Oman coast and the Persian Gulf. Lamu was nourished on lucrative trade, and the rambling Arabesque palaces of merchant princes that line its water-front to this day testify to a past era of wealth and splendour. Palm trees spring up from the high-walled courtyards of houses clustered along streets barely wide enough for two donkeys to pass, and in the narrow waterway that leads to the open sea, noble Arab dhows from Aden and Kuwait swing lazily on their anchors with the tide. Along the docks shouts ring out from Bajuni porters with powerful glistening backs as they hump and heave mangrove poles and sacks of dates—the romance of Sinbad the Sailor and the Thousand and One Nights seems to breathe over every nook and cranny of the seething, spicy town. Lamu was the first port of call in the Arab's annual journey south, and among the rugged sailors with their henna-dyed beards Lamu's women, purdahed, but peeping coyly through their jet black bui-buis, gained a reputation as lovers unexcelled in any other port.

Although they say that a young boy may yet be carried away at dead of night to be sold into slavery in Arabia, the banning of the slave trade was the first step down the ladder of decline for Lamu. Then the ivory market came under rigid government control in East Africa and most of this valuable commodity went, by law, to the official auction rooms of Mombasa. After the war the only trade that supported the people of Lamu was the export of "boritis"—mangrove poles—which, because they do not rot, were valued as building materials in the treeless wastes of Arabia. But with the oil-rich countries of Arabia now using reinforced concrete for their building, even that trade is diminishing, and Lamu today is little more than a dejected shadow of what it used to be.

But despite—or perhaps because of—the sensual air of decadence that hangs over the crumbling remains of Lamu, it still exudes a vibrant and enticing feeling of history that makes it one of the most attractive, if least known, towns in East Africa. I used to go there whenever I could, not to buy products from modern craftsmen, but to look for relics of antiquity. At one time, in its brighter days, Lamu's merchants used to import porcelain and pottery from Europe and China—Chinese junks have even been known to visit the port—and though most of these valuable imports have long since been broken and thrown on to the sands, where one can still find chips of Ming ware glistening in the sun, a few antiques survive.

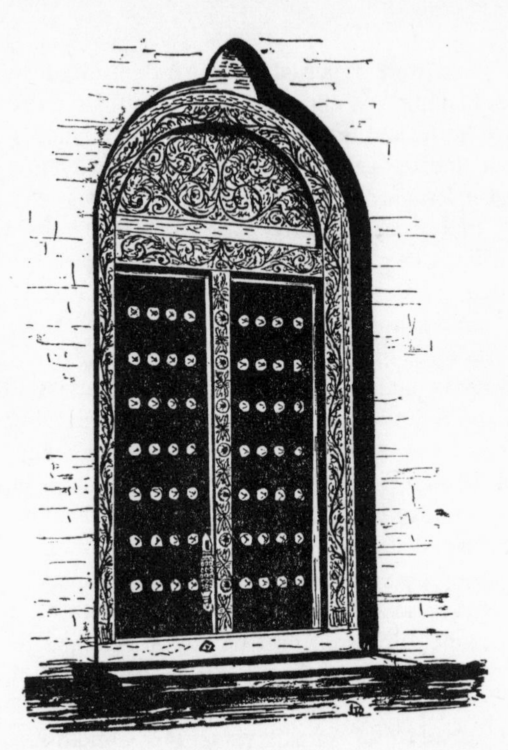

On my visits I used to wander round the streets, peering into old houses and seeking, if I could, an introduction to the owners. The inside walls of many of these houses were often beautifully constructed, with a mass of tiny arched alcoves formed in plaster in which, in days of old, knick-knacks from all over the known world might be displayed. Most of these little alcoves were now empty but just occasionally it was possible to find something of interest in them that the present poverty-stricken owner would willingly sell.

Once, having wheedled my way into an old house, as I sat talking to the ancient shrivelled Arab who owned it, I spotted amongst a conglomeration of other junk, several objects of a type that I had not seen before in Lamu or anywhere else, that looked more like local products than imports. One was a bowl made of African hardwood deeply carved with the traditional Arab floral design that can be seen on the old carved doorways of the large houses. Apart from this there were several pots, crudely made, but with a beautifully delicate duck-egg green and blue faience on the top half of the pot. I knew these were rare pieces when I bought them for a few

shillings each; but I did not discover until later that they were very probably unique—the sole remaining examples of an ancient potter's craft that had once been carried on along the East Coast of Africa. Nobody in Lamu—or later in Mombasa or Nairobi—was able to tell me anything about them with certainty, so I sent them to the British Museum for identification. There, for a time, they were shuffled back and forth between the Department of African Ethnography and the Department of Oriental Antiquities—the former declaring they could not be African, a glaze of that type being unknown in Africa—the latter, on grounds of style and design, saying they could not be oriental. In the long run they came to the conclusion that they are probably the only known examples of 13th–17th-century Swahili pottery, showing a fascinating mixture of influences from both Africa and Arabia.

I did not have occasion to do much business with Arabs along the coast, but when I did, it needed more time and delicacy than dealing with less wary Africans. On one occasion I had an order for some carpets from the Katikiro of the Baganda. The Katikiro is the Prime Minister of the powerful Baganda tribe in Uganda, and he and his cabinet were shortly moving into their fine new Parliament building in Kampala. In typical African fashion the Ministerial offices of the Baganda were somewhat larger than any of their counterparts elsewhere in the British Commonwealth, and I was asked to purchase six "of the largest oriental carpets to be found in East Africa".

I was at liberty to search in Lamu, Zanzibar or Dar-es-Salaam if I wished, but it seemed that I would do no better in these towns than in Mombasa, for as the carpets came down from Arabia by dhow, and as most of the dhows these days make Mombasa their first port of call, the dealers here have the pick of the bunch.

There were two Arab merchants in Mombasa with whom I was dealing at the time; and two more diametrically opposed people would be hard to imagine.

On the one hand there was Sharif Shatry, member of the Kenya Legislative Council, nobleman and intellectual; and on the other, Sheikh Mohammed, a wily bearded ruffian, armed always with a dagger, who kept his cash in a sea-chest in the cellar, and owned most of Mombasa's whore houses.

With Shatry I would sit for hours, politely sipping coffee and discussing politics and Islam, before the conversation veered to the question of carpets. Then we would sit for hours more as he and his henchmen expounded the relative merits of a Kurman or a Tabriz.

With Mohammed I would sit for a long time too; but with him the talk turned to the relative merits of women or boys, and his efforts to sell me his daughter, Amina, surpassed his interest in rugs.

Shatry's carpets were laid out to view in a spotless warehouse down by the Dhow harbour. Mohammed's were bundled amongst casks of reeking, fermenting dates, up a squalid alley in the Old Town.

The rugs they had were much the same; and having played them off for about a month I finally chose the safest course and bought three from each at a total cost of about £300, all of which now adorn the Lukiko building in Kampala.

Though the shop paid its way and kept me alive from day to day, it never looked like making me a fortune. There were usually two or three days in each week when no tourist ships were in the harbour, and on these days business was very dead. Even when the town was thronged with tourists not many of them spent much money on curios. However, the retail business had served its purpose in enabling me to develop the export trade, the pattern of which, having started with numerous small orders from many different shops all over the United States, gradually began to change. After about eighteen months, almost all these small orders had been discontinued, and ninety per cent of my business was going to two Americans in New York.

These two Americans, Al Kizner and Nat Karwell, were originally together, running a store in the Bronx named "African Modern". From our very earliest contacts it was obvious to me that theirs was the business I wanted, as they were interested not only in vast quantities of identical goods, but also in a wide assortment of individual pieces—for they too were both wholesalers and retailers. Most of my correspondence was with Al Kizner, and glancing through the bulky files I often felt that our relationship was nearer that of pen-friends than business acquaintances. Al, no mean poet and a philosopher, wrote me lengthy letters on the problems and frustrations of life in the big city, harking always on his desire to break away and come roaming in Africa; and in mine I would ramble at length on the strange habits and customs of the "people of the wilds" amongst whom I was living. After a while Al and Nat split up and formed two separate companies, and though I was sorry that their partnership had been broken, the rift was beneficial to me as we mutually agreed that I would supply each of them on an equal basis.

In the post one morning I received a gift from Al—a book on African art with a large number of photographs of magnificent pieces of traditional African sculpture. Though unquestionably a generous gift, there was no doubt in my mind that there was a secondary motive in Al's choice of this present for in an accompanying note he remarked that it would be good to receive a few consignments of the type of work shown in the book. What I believe he had in mind was that I should have the photographs copied by Kenya craftsmen; but this, I knew, would be impossible, for very few Wakamba craftsmen were capable of reproducing anything accurately. However, Al's remark set me thinking along different lines.

When I went into business and opened "African Art" it was never my intention to stand behind a shop counter for the rest of my life. It had its moments of interest and amusement, but on the whole its horizons were somewhat limited. Ninety-eight per cent of the goods

I dealt with, though I sold them under the heading "African Art", were essentially curios with little artistic merit. I had for some time had a desire to travel to other parts of Africa where the quality of traditional African art far excelled anything to be found in East Africa. And now, suddenly, I saw a way in which I might possibly be able to do this. If I were to hand over my East African business to someone else, and embark on a long safari across Africa in search of art from other parts of the continent, would Al and Nat agree to purchase any collections I might make en route? I put the idea to them, and presently received replies from both saying that they would willingly support me on such a safari. We had been doing business together long enough to have developed an understanding of the types of goods required, and they were willing to trust my judgment on quality and price.

Such a safari would occupy a good many months and was not an undertaking to be rushed into. Suitable people in East Africa had to be found to supply Al and Nat with Wakamba carvings while I was away, and I wanted to find out more than I knew at that time about the famous art-producing tribes of Africa, and African art in general. So over the next few weeks I set about reading any books that I could lay my hands on that told me of the history, the distribution, the motives and the techniques of the famous artists of Africa.

Over the past half-century African art has not only become the most popular of all so-called "primitive" arts and the most sought-after by serious collectors, but it has also found a permanent place among the great classical arts of all time alongside those of China, India and Greece. But the elevation of African art to a place of greatness has only recently come about; and the history of its "discovery" is of some interest.

From the beginning of the age of discovery of Africa in the late fifteenth century right up to the present century, the few Europeans who ever bothered to think twice about the carvings of "wild savages" dismissed them as crude, rough, and entirely lacking in artistic merit. This attitude towards the art of Africa was no doubt conditioned by the naturalism which had dominated European art since the Renaissance. In the late nineteenth and the early twentieth centuries, however, the world of art in Europe began to undergo a revolution that is still going on to this day. All the avenues of purely technical development in art had been explored and re-

1. "African Art"
2. Koli and Moses at work with their adzes in Morogoro

3. *Far left:* Modern Makonde ebony carving

4. *Left:* Mzaramo ebony carving

5. *Below left:* Curio carvers in a Makonde village, Mozambique

6. *Below:* Makonde women fetching water from the wells below the plateau

7. *Right:* Working mother—Bushongo woman making "velue de Kasai"

8. *Far right:* The children can be quite a handful!

9. *Below:* Gogo and friends

10. *Below right:* Prelude to the dance—Makonde drummer

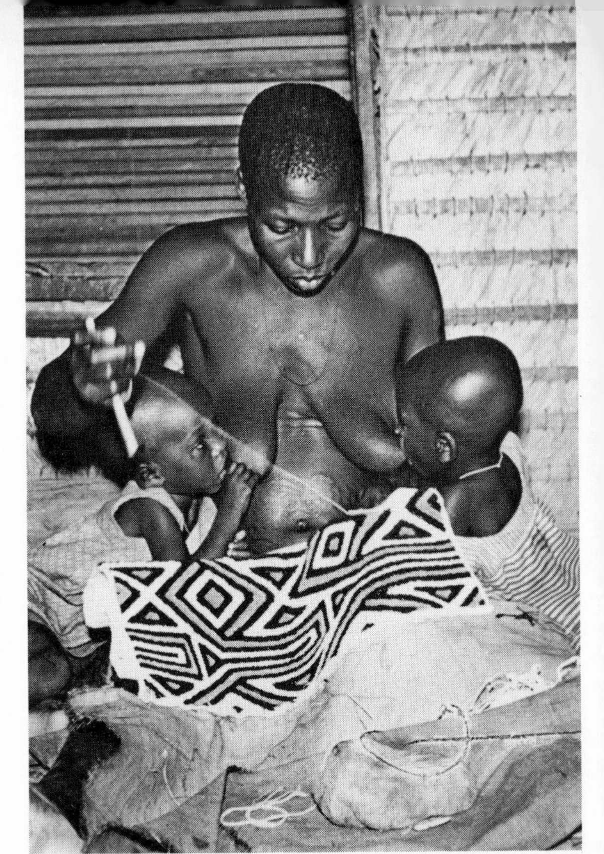

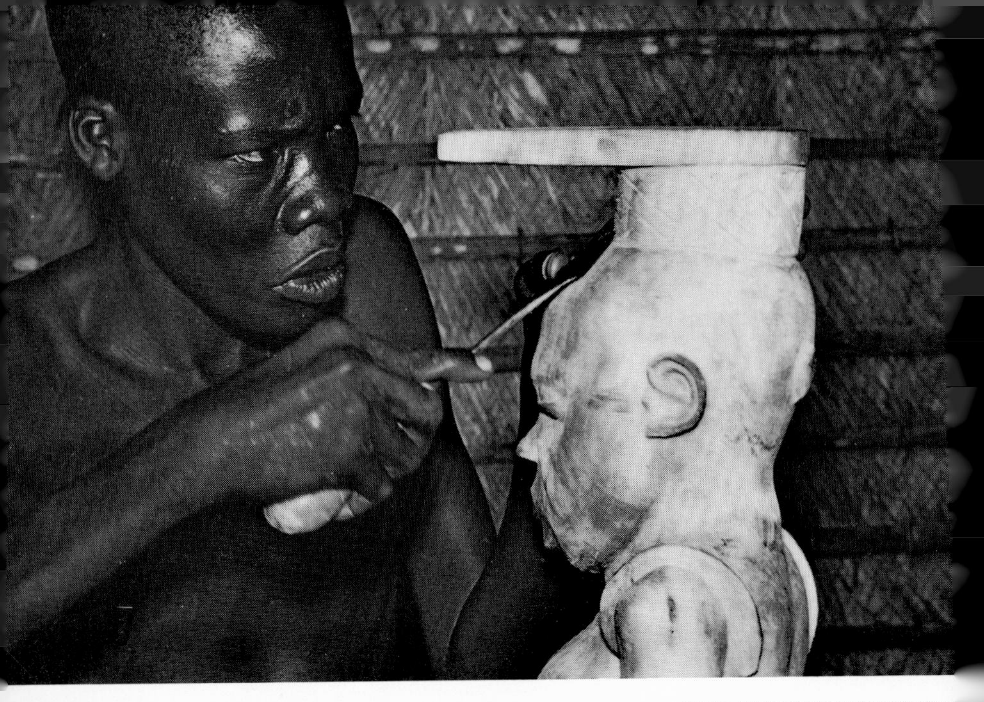

11. Carver and King–Bushongo carver at work on a statue of Bopey Mobinj
12. Lokele trader of the Congo in his house-canoe

13. On the Congo river

14. Crossing the Rovuma

15. The Bamanga spearmen
16. Hobolos in harbour

explored, and artists began to seek greater freedom in their work. And so the trends in art began to turn away from naturalism, towards expressionism, cubism, and other means by which the inner emotions of the artist might be expressed rather than the faithful image of his subject.

In the intellectual climate of this twentieth-century artistic revolution it was, perhaps, not surprising that many European artists began to look at "primitive" art in ways that their predecessors had never considered. And in the forceful, direct simplicity, and the architectural strength of African carving, they began to find just the sort of emotional freedom for which they themselves were searching. To them, in their studios in Paris, it appeared that the African sculptural form was wholly successful in releasing an intense aesthetic power. And from that time on, from the days of the young Picasso, Modigliani and others, African art has played a significant role in the development of contemporary European painting, sculpture, and even architecture.

The art for which Negro Africa has become famous—the traditional art that has its roots centuries back in antiquity—all comes from a relatively small part of the huge continent.* Geographically, the limits of the major art-producing tribes of Africa extend around the West coast, from Guinea to the Congo, north to the Sahara desert, and east to the Great Lakes of Central Africa. This means that huge parts of the continent—including the Union of South Africa, almost all of the Rhodesias and Portuguese Africa, Tanganyika, Kenya and the Sudan—have no great historical art traditions at all.

Just why the people of some parts of Africa should apparently be so much more artistic than others is something of an enigma. In some cases it may simply be that certain Africans are basically inartistic, just as the English do not sing so well as the Welsh. Also, some pagan societies and religions, for reasons that remain obscure, have developed in such a way that there has been no call for much artistic activity in their tribal systems. With yet other tribes it may be that Muslim influence has suppressed the visual arts, as it is forbidden by the Muslim religion to reproduce images in the human form. And probably a major reason for the lack of art in some

* A map at the beginning of the book shows the major art areas of Africa with examples of different styles of the more important tribes.

areas is that many African societies are too young and unsettled. South Africa, for instance, only became settled by Bantu people within the last few hundred years, and tribes continually migrating and subdividing may have lacked the stability essential for the establishment of great artistic traditions, becoming instead famous warriors like the Zulu and the Swazi. Whatever the reasons are they do not seem to have any racial basis; for some of Africa's finest artists are racially akin to neighbours whose supreme achievement with the adze has been to chop down trees for firewood.

The motives behind the production of works of art in Africa, and the various uses to which they are put, are multifarious; but as in other forms of art they all fulfil a definite function. This may be a religious function—effigies of ancestors or tribal deities to be set up in family or village shrines; or they may have a magico-religious use as that of many masks and statuettes representing demons of the forest or other spirits that are produced for the strange rituals of secret societies. Or their function may be purely social—elaborate stools, tobacco pipes or staves that are status symbols of noblemen and chiefs.

But though the famous traditional arts of Africa—the high-priced collectors' pieces, the "classical" arts—are confined to certain parts of the continent only, that is not to say that other areas are entirely devoid of artists and craftsmen whose achievements have been in less important fields. Between the two worlds of classical art and mass-produced curios there is an intermediate field which includes many traditional arts and crafts produced for purely practical purposes, such as weapons of war and day-to-day household objects. Though having no aesthetic pretensions on the one hand, and though not produced for the tourist trade on the other, these nevertheless frequently have considerable artistic merit. In my shop, "African Art", I had in fact been dealing almost wholly in curios. Now that I was developing an interest in the classical African arts I found myself in danger of becoming an "art snob", wanting to pursue nothing but valuable collectors'

pieces. To set out across Africa, however, on such a search would have been decidedly risky, as I had no idea whether or not I should be able to find a sufficient quantity of traditional work to make the journey pay for itself. I decided therefore to widen my approach to cover the arts and crafts of Africa on a much more catholic level, embracing everything from classical art to curios.

I christened my safari "Sanamu", a Kiswahili word covering all types of arts and crafts, and having by now found other traders to supply Al and Nat with Wakamba carvings, and made all the other necessary preparations for the journey, I was ready to set out. All my remaining stocks I shipped to America, and having done that—not without regrets after two years' hard work—I closed the doors of "African Art" for good.

CHAPTER TWO

Masks of the Makonde

Having decided to go off on expedition "Sanamu", I now had to make up my mind in which direction to head. Looking at maps that showed the distribution of the richest art areas of the continent, the most obvious place to go seemed to be West Africa. From Nigeria to Guinea, throughout a region a thousand miles long, almost every tribe seemed to be renowned for its artistic prowess. In Nigeria there were the Bini, creators of some of the most famous African works of all—the Benin bronzes; and the Yoruba, said to be the most prolific traditional woodcarvers anywhere in the world. In Ghana there were the Ashanti, well known for small brass castings of people and animals used for weighing gold in olden days. Then there were the Baoule of the Ivory Coast, who produce delicate and beautiful masks, and in what is now Mali there were the Bambara and the Dogon, producers of amazingly powerful woodcarvings, and in Guinea the Baga tribe, makers of huge masks with protruding beak-like noses. Turning the pages of books on classical African art, this area seemed to be the gold-mine at which to aim.

But there were numerous objections to trekking all the way across to West Africa. In the first place, it was a journey of nearly three thousand miles from Mombasa to Nigeria—a journey that would be extremely costly. Secondly, I had been unable to find out with any degree of certainty how much traditional art, if any, was still produced in West Africa; or whether I would be able to buy it economically even if there was plenty available. I could not afford to risk any capital on this expedition. If I was going to go at all, it had to pay for itself as I went along. So, tempting though the rich fields of West African art appeared to be, I reluctantly decided that a trip there would not be an economic possibility, and I therefore turned my attention to areas nearer home. As traditional artists many people of the Belgian Congo—the Bushongo, the Baluba, the Batchokwe (on the Angola border) and the Bapende—ranked as equals to the sculptors of West Africa. So I finally decided to go to the Congo following a route that would take me through Tanganyika to Portuguese East Africa, across Nyasaland and the Rhodesias and eventually to the Belgian Congo itself. I felt that here I might make a valuable haul, but even if not, I could quite easily escape back to Mombasa and financial security if necessary.

I had no intention of rushing this safari. I did not mind if I was away for six months, a year, or even longer—so long as I was paying my way as I went along. It was with this in mind that I chose to spend a considerable length of time in Tanganyika on the first leg of the journey. I had previously been to Tanganyika on a number of occasions—to Kilimanjaro—and liked what I had seen of the country. Though Kenya is scenically one of the most sensationally beautiful countries in the world, Tanganyika does not lag far behind; in fact, for richness of African character, both in its topography and its people, it surpasses Kenya. These considerations might have been sufficient temptations on their own to dally in Tanganyika; but in addition, I had a ready-made excuse in that one or two of Tanganyika's tribes produce curios that vie for commercial value with those of the Wakamba in Kenya. Foremost among these tribes is the Wazaramo who live in the hinterland behind the capital of Tanganyika, Dar-es-Salaam.

It occurred to me that if I was going to stay in Tanganyika for several months, reaping the benefits of the Wazaramo craftsmen, I might just as well augment my profits whilst I could, by retaining some links with the Wakamba. From the heart of Tanganyika it would have been impossible to continue buying large quantities of work from the Wakamba; but this did not worry me—it was quality I now wanted. Accordingly, I suggested to two of my best carvers in Kenya that they might come along with me for a few months to set up their workshop wherever we might be. The two carvers were Moses Molu, whom I had frequently met at Wamunyu, and another named Koli Ngwatu. They were both excited by the proposition, and readily agreed to come.

Koli and Moses were both good friends, but completely different in character. Moses was congenial and loquacious, a proficient worker and good businessman, and a pillar of the Church—as his name might imply. He was a proud father, and a good husband—in fact a clean-living and sensible person in every respect.

Koli, on the other hand, was the nearest thing to an African beatnik I ever met. He was one of the few Wakamba carvers whom I would call, without hesitation, an artist. To watch Koli working was a joy; his adze would flick through a chunk of wood as though it were butter, deftly bringing to life a roaring lion, or an old man crouching pensively on a stool—"sanamu" that were always full of individual character, and often outstanding. But if Koli was an artist at his work, that same free-flowing artistic streak found expression also in his private life. He was impetuous and completely unreliable, and one never quite knew what he might do next. Still in his early thirties, he was well built and good-looking with soft, sympathetic eyes and sensual lips. He was an insatiable womaniser, and an evening of fun for him meant an evening whoring and boozing. He drank away most of his earnings which sometimes amounted to sixty pounds a month; and he treated his wife and children, whom he seldom saw, abominably. He had married his wife, I should say, for her physical attractions which were considerable and despite her husband's blatant infidelity she worshipped him. But for all his irresponsible, easy-going ways, Koli was one of the most likeable people I met.

When the time came to leave Mombasa, we packed all our belongings into my new long wheel-base Land Rover, and early one morning amid touching farewell scenes from dozens of other carvers and their families, we drove out of town to the south on the first part of our journey to Tanganyika.

When we left Mombasa I had no precise idea where we were going. I had no hotel accommodation booked anywhere, and no house rented. We were heading somewhat vaguely for an area marked on the map "Central Tanganyika". I had a large tent in the Land Rover big enough for all three of us if necessary, and a crate of emergency food supplies. Then, as on subsequent journeys, I was reluctant to commit myself to any unchangeable destination lest, on arrival, it proved unsuitable or insalubrious. Though I intended to do business with the Wazaramo I did not wish to live in their country as I had heard from my carvers that it was dry and inhospitable. I had only one uncertain pointer as to where we might go first, and that was to a town called Morogoro. From my map I knew that it lay at the foot of a range of mountains; and I had seen enough of Africa's highlands to feel sure that the countryside and climate there would be attractive. The contrast between the freezing peaks and the hot and sticky plains, between the dewy pastures high up on Africa's mountain slopes, and the brown flat bush-land thousands of feet below, is invariably beautiful and stimulating. And furthermore Morogoro lay only ninety miles from Dar-es-Salaam, within easy reach of the Wazaramo.

It was a long day's drive to Morogoro from Mombasa, and it was already dark when we arrived. Koli and Moses preferred to find a room in an African hotel, and I booked into the Savoy—a Greek hotel which reeked of ouzo—near the centre of the town. It was too dark to see what sort of place we had come to, so I waited until the morning before taking a stroll around.

When I saw Morogoro I immediately took a liking to it. It was a Provincial Headquarters town with a mixed population of white civil servants, Greek and Indian traders, and several thousand Africans who lived in shanties around the outskirts. There was a club with a cricket field, and a number of cumbrous-looking administrative buildings. But despite these there was nothing pretentious or smart about the place. Morogoro was the epitome of "Africa", its atmosphere being derived more from its dusty streets, its scrawny palm trees, and the macabre flocks of evil-looking vultures that hovered over the native quarter, than from the neat dwellings of the government officials.

The town lay in the plains; but above it, like a mighty wall, rose the great green massif of the Uluguru mountains, whose weather-worn peaks towered to nearly nine thousand feet. I am not mountain-mad to the extent that I must climb to the top of every molehill I set eyes on, but the Ulugurus were an impressive, alluring spectacle, and I had no second thoughts as to whether or not Morogoro would be a good place in which to stay. I did not like the Savoy, however, and I decided I would have to find some other place to live in, if I was to remain here.

As I stood in the town on that first morning looking up at the mountains, I noticed a thin track zigzagging and winding up a spur. At the top of the track, just visible about three thousand feet above the town, was a little red-roofed house perching like a bird on the edge of the forest. I thought to myself what a magnificent view there must be from this house—what a marvellous place to live in. I had no idea who owned it, or what went on up there; but, on impulse, when I returned to the hotel, I asked the manager if he knew anything about it.

"Morningside?" (that seemed to be its name). "That belongs to old Mrs. Willis," he said. "She's lived up there for nearly forty years. She and her husband built it, way back. He was a settler. He wandered all over the country looking for gold and never finding any he finally settled on the mountain and opened up a mica mine there. He died. Then she ran the place as a rest house for a time, but now she's old and rheumatic, and just lives up there on her own."

This "old Mrs. Willis" stayed in my mind, and I wondered, as Morningside used to be a rest-house, whether she would consider putting me up. If I was prepared to look after myself, she might conceivably let me a room or two. I felt at least there was no harm in asking, so in the afternoon I drove up there to see her.

Three thousand feet above the plain it was even more beautiful than I had expected. The house was built between two cool clear streams that cascaded down beside the garden and irrigated flower beds packed with roses, canna lilies, poinsettias and primulas, in fact every sub-tropical and temperate flower imaginable. Jungle trees, hung with green-grey moss, encroached to the edge of the garden, and honey-birds, their bright colours glistening in the sun and their long curving beaks protruding deep into the flowers, hovered in front of showers of fuchsias.

"Old Mrs. Willis", rheumatical and charming, was surprised to see me. When I said I wanted to stay in Morogoro for a time, and told her what I was doing—that I was living off the earnings of two woodcarvers—she was even more surprised. She would hardly have been more incredulous, in fact, had I told her I was living off the earnings of two immoral women. For, to her, a tough old prospector's wife, my occupation seemed a queer and eccentric sort of thing for a young man to be doing. But when I broached the subject of staying in Morningside, she was immediately delighted. She was obviously hard-up and could do with the money; besides which I think the poor old lady was rather lonely. There was only one snag—she was going away after a few weeks and would be away for several months; but she saw no reason why, if all went well, I might not stay on and act as her caretaker.

Mrs. Willis even went so far as to offer to find a room in the servants' quarters for Koli and Moses; so with them I moved up to Morningside the next day. This arrangement was short-lived, however, for after only one night they asked to be taken back down to town again! They were used to the dry air of Wamunyu, or the hot

humid air of Mombasa, and up in the mountains they could not stand the biting night air, or the cold damp mist that penetrated their steaming blankets in the early morning. And frankly I do not think they liked the idea of being so far from the town with all its varied attractions for these two very different characters. Back in Morogoro again they found themselves a hut, rented from an Arab. It was no larger than a dog-kennel, but they seemed happy enough with it, and were prepared to stay there as long as necessary—though within a few days Koli had fixed himself up with a voluptuous and vivacious mistress, and eventually he moved in to live with her. Koli's pastimes made not the slightest difference to me, so long as he took time off occasionally to do a bit of carving. As soon as they were settled we went together to a local timber merchant to lay in stocks of mahogany, and other hardwoods from the bush. Then, as they already had a good idea of the sort of carvings I wanted, I left Koli and Moses to their own devices, and let them get on with their work in their own time.

Meanwhile, from Morningside, I laid plans to visit the country of the Wazaramo to place an order with their carvers that would keep them busy over the next two or three months. I was already familiar with the carvings of the Wazaramo, as much of their work finds its way to Kenya where it is sold by Wakamba middlemen. They carve almost entirely in ebony, the black heartwood of several different species of slow-growing trees that abound in the lowlands throughout East Africa, as far south as Nyasaland. Though one of the best carving woods of all, ebony is extremely hard, and to work it requiries a considerable degree of skill. As they chose to use this wood rather than many others easier to work, I expected to find the Wazaramo energetic and go-ahead people; but when I arrived in their country I was sorely disappointed, for they struck me as being about the laziest, most lackadaisical lot on earth. Never once, even in Dar-es-Salaam only a few miles away, did I meet a Wazaramo man selling his own work. Instead, they all prefer to put their carvings in the hands of middlemen from other tribes who hawk them at considerable profit on the streets. And needless to say, despite their reputation back in Kenya as unbusinesslike people, all these middlemen are Wakamba, who, with an eye to the main chance, have travelled hundreds of miles from Machakos and Wamunyu to make their living in Tanganyika.

The Wazaramo carving, so far as I could gather, has no traditional background whatsoever. Originally, after the first world war, a few schoolboys were taught to carve by a German missionary whose hobby was woodcarving. The industry, such as it is, has developed entirely from those small beginnings. Having from the start taken the commercial approach to woodcarving, it is perhaps not surprising that there is very little artistry in their work. Yet it seems one cannot generalise about anything, particularly in Africa, for just occasionally for some unpredictable reason, the odd carving appears which is outstandingly beautiful. There was a time, later on, while sorting out five hundred identical ebony heads of Masai warriors, when I suddenly came upon one which, though basically of the same design as all the rest, was in a class entirely of its own. It was as though the carver, after a good meal with plenty to drink, had fallen into a trance that had enabled him suddenly to put some emotion into his work, thus accidentally creating a work of art in a jungle of otherwise crudely mass-produced tourist junk. It was occasional discoveries such as this that saved curio collecting from becoming an unrewarding drudge.

Having seen Uzaramo—the land of the Wazaramo—I was glad I had not decided to stay there while in Tanganyika. It was as dry and inhospitable as I had been told; and the people, living in squalid thatched huts, were boorish and dull. It was good to get back to Morningside, high up on my mountain ledge. There, time went by rapidly. Mrs. Willis went away and left me in charge; and whilst Koli and Moses carved out my livelihood in the town below I sat back and luxuriated in this lotus-eating life. In the mornings I breakfasted out on the verandah beneath a canopy of honeysuckle, rising early to watch the morning mists that stretched out below me in a carpet of silver as they rose with the heat of the day, swirling and eddying up the steep gullies in eerie phantasmagorical shapes. In the afternoons I walked in the forests of podo and camphor behind the house, hoping to catch glimpses of the black and white furry colobus monkeys that swung chattering high in the trees; or I wandered among the farms on the precipitous hills below. It seemed so peaceful in these farmsteads; yet even while I was there, there were riots among farmers who refused to obey laws and terrace their fields to conserve the soil, and people were killed in the riots.

Life at Morningside was easy. I had two gardeners and five acres of strawberries that produced two crops a year in this perfect climate; in the house I had a kitchen boy, who chopped the wood for the antiquated kitchen range; and in addition to Mrs. Willis's staff, I had my own servant whom I had hired locally, a Mluguru named Rashidi, who was one of those old-world manservants that are now almost impossible to find. He was about forty and a Muslim, and he wore the flowing white garb of his faith. As a servant he was everything he should be and more. He washed and ironed superbly and was a passable cook. He looked after me from dawn till night as though I were his own property. He was complete master of the household: the other servants ran to his bidding. And when I had guests for the night he was a model of discretion and tact. He was, besides, an excellent companion.

For the first few weeks carvings flowed from Koli and Moses. But then Koli started drinking. He spent less and less time in the dog-kennel, and more and more behind the darkened shutters of his woman's hovel. He began to acquire that dull-eyed look of over-indulgence, and output dropped. Moses grew worried about Koli's health. He thought he was taking bhang, the African marijuana. But every now and again, when things seemed at their lowest ebb, Koli would reappear, healthy and bubbling with energy, and carvings would once more begin to emerge from baulks of timber with renewed fluency and individuality.

Meanwhile I had other problems to cope with. When the time came to leave Morogoro I planned to travel south to the Rovuma river, and from there across the border into Portuguese East Africa to visit a tribe called the Makonde. I had a friend in Southern Tanganyika who had for some time been sending me consignments of Makonde carvings. Unfortunately, this man Jock had fallen foul of the law, and now the poor fellow was serving a prison sentence not far from Morogoro. I visited him in prison a number of times, endeavouring to keep up his spirits by smuggling in the occasional bottle of whisky. As the Makonde live in very remote country I had been hoping that he might have been able to come with me on this expedition. But though he was able to give me a lot of useful advice from his prison cell, in the long run it was I who was to help him rather than vice versa. He had left his home at very short notice, and there had been no one to take care of his possessions. And he wanted me, when I arrived in Southern Tanganyika, to inquire into the state of his house, and do what I could to preserve anything of value.

We stayed in Morogoro for five months. At the end of that time I returned to Uzaramo to sort out and pay for the ebony carvings I had ordered when I arrived, and these together with the lorry-load of carvings from Koli and Moses, were then packed with wood-shavings in large wooden boxes and handed over to a shipping agent who arranged for their despatch to New York. Good as their word, as soon as they received my invoices, Al and Nat cabled me the money for them; and I was then ready to move on to the next leg of expedition "Sanamu".

It was never intended that Moses and Koli should accompany me any further. In any event Moses was getting restless for his wife and family, so he packed up and caught a bus back to Kenya. Koli, unfortunately, was really going to the dogs, and, a withered remnant of what he had been five months earlier, he chose to remain with his mistress in Morogoro. Months later I heard that he eventually moved to Dar-es-Salaam where he found himself another woman, took to drink even more heavily, gave up carving, and stopped sending any money to his wife. Despite all efforts of mine, and Wakamba friends, he refused to go home, and what happened to him in the end I do not know. His degeneration was very sad; for when I first met him he was one of the most amiable and creative people I knew.

Rashidi by now was part of my existence and I had no desire to leave him behind in Morogoro. When he heard that I was thinking of leaving, he of course took it for granted that he would be coming too, and when I asked him if he would come he gave me a look as though to say, how the hell do you think you could keep yourself alive without me?

But when I told him we were going to the Makonde it was almost possible to see his expression fall from his face and surge like a jelly round his knees. The name of the Makonde was known far and wide even amongst people in Kenya, and most Africans were convinced that they were nothing less than dangerous cannibals. Rashidi himself had told me a story of how some Makonde sisal workers were said to have been found one day eating a new-born baby that had been drowned and then matured in a bin of maize beer. And with such horrors in mind, poor Rashidi was now dumbfounded. But he had already committed himself and there was no backing out now.

So leaving Morningside in the care of one of Mrs. Willis's relatives, Rashidi and I now came down from our mountain paradise for good, and set off on a three-day drive to Newala, the frontier post for Moçambique.

We spent the first night in Dar-es-Salaam, and the second in an old German building overlooking the ancient port of Kilwa, where our only visitors were bats. Along the foreshore in front of this building I was surprised to see hundreds of tons of ebony logs that had obviously been lying there a long time. Ebony is valuable wood —this lot must have been worth a fortune—and I was curious to know why it was there. Apparently it belonged to an Indian timber-merchant who had hoped to ship it from Kilwa and save the expense of transporting it overland to a bigger port. The old port of Kilwa is now silted up and, as large vessels no longer go there, the only way in which he could get it out was in a chartered Arab dhow. Ebony is dense, very heavy wood, and each of these logs weighed several hundredweight. The only way the Arabs could load them was to drag them through the shallow water and heave them bodily into the boat. Unfortunately, when they lifted the first baulk over the side, it crashed straight through the bottom of the dhow! After that no one would touch it, and the wretched Indian was left with an expensive problem on his hands.

If Morogoro had struck me as the epitome of Africa, Newala, which we reached on the third day, did so even more. This little administrative town is perched high on the edge of a sandy escarpment with one of the grandest views on the continent. Far below, cutting through a brown and misty valley that stretches for twenty miles to distant hills, flows a silvery thread, the Rovuma river. It flows through history too. Along this valley for hundreds of years passed Arab caravans with their booty of human beings, shackled, often dying, wrecks for the slave markets of Kilwa and Mikindani on the coast. Along here, also, came Livingstone, with his camels and water-buffaloes and mules, when he set out hopefully for the interior on his last fateful journey of discovery.

There are no green fields around Newala that are "just like England"; no huge eroded chasms that are "just like the Grand Canyon"; no crisp panoramas to be likened to the land of the Jackaroos. The snakes that rustle the leaves of Newala's mango trees are green mambas; the marauders that steal the local fowls are leopards; and the ugly market women with ungainly discs in their lips could come from nowhere else but Africa.

Looking down from the crenellated German fort that crowns the red escarpment in Newala, I gazed across at the Rovuma. For five hundred miles of its length, from where it rises not far from Lake Nyasa, there is neither a bridge nor ferry on this broad stream To cross it would be a problem; but beyond lay the plateau of the wild Makonde, luring us on.

Newala was the township in which Jock had been living, so one of the first things we did when we arrived there was to look for his house. We found it easily enough; but never in my life have I seen a place in such an incredible state. It had been empty only about three months, but in that time Africa had moved in, lock, stock, and

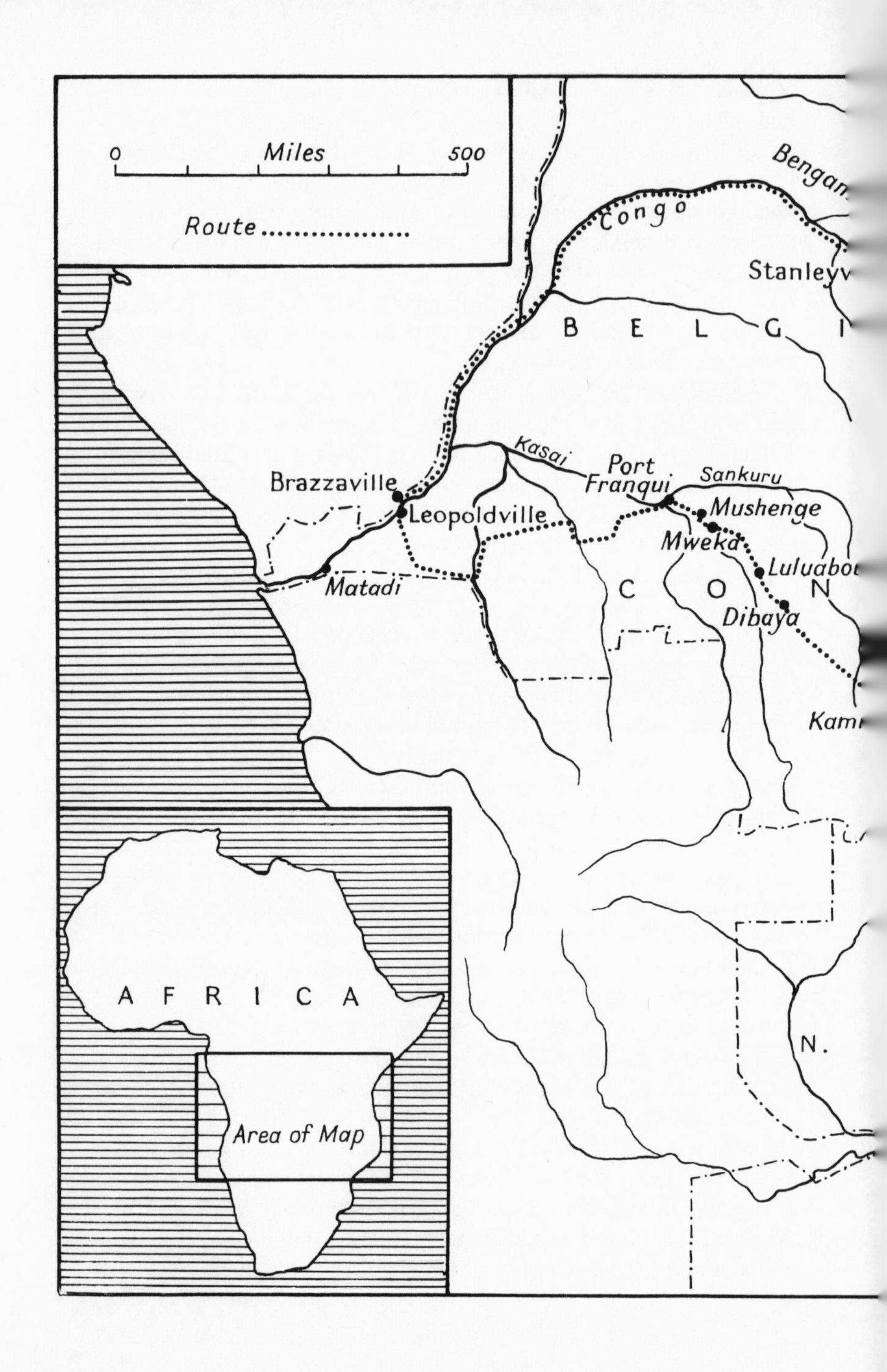

0
Miles
500
Route
Congo
Bengam
Stanleyv
B E L G I
Kasai
Port Franqui
Sankuru
Brazzaville
Leopoldville
Mushenge
Mweka
Luluabo
Matadi
C O N
Dibaya
Kam
N.
A F R I C A
Area of Map

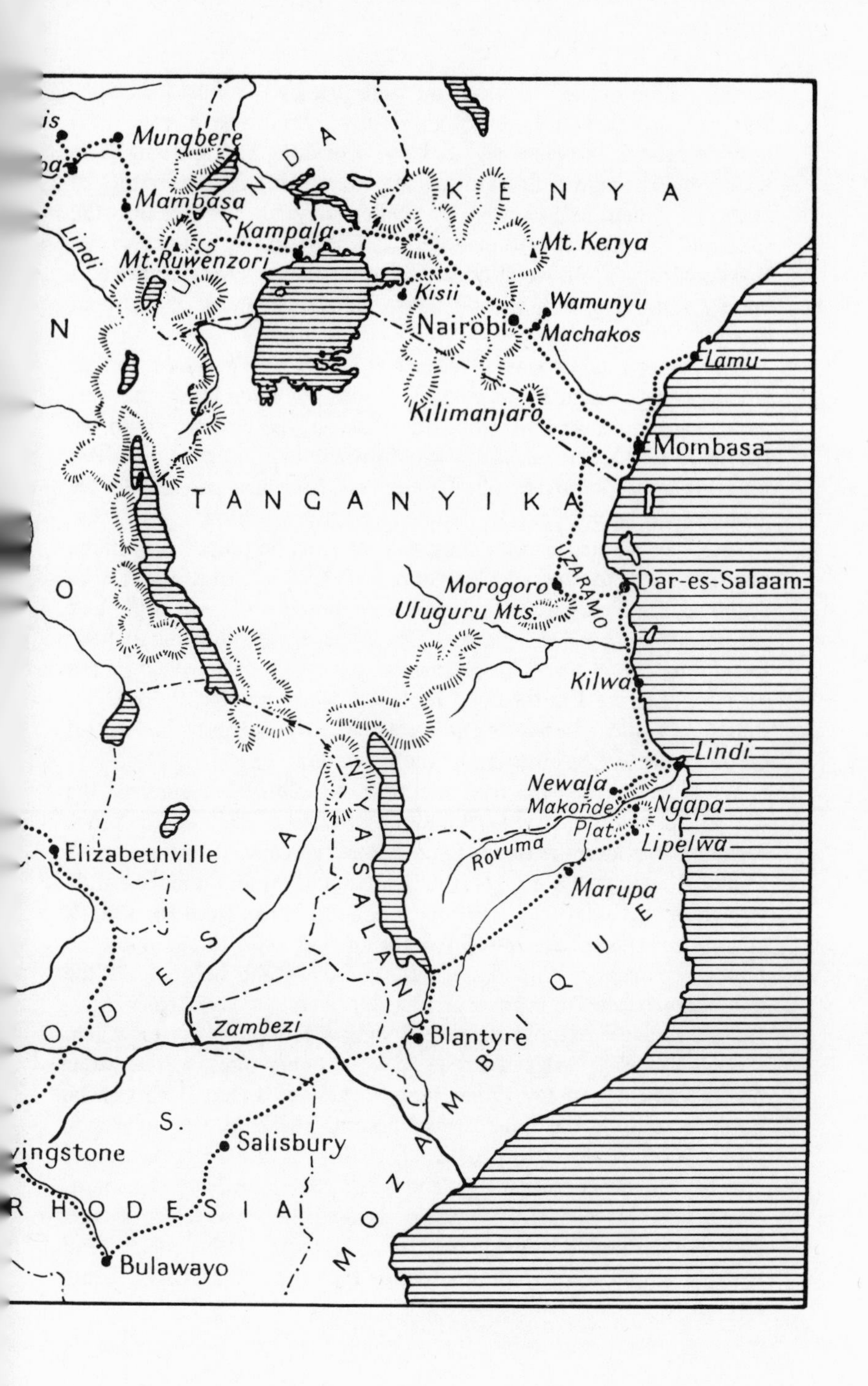

Mungbere
Mambasa
Lindi
UGANDA
Kampala
Mt. Ruwenzori
KENYA
Mt. Kenya
Kisii
Wamunyu
Nairobi
Machakos
Lamu
Kilimanjaro
Mombasa
TANGANYIKA
UZARAMO
Morogoro
Uluguru Mts.
Dar-es-Salaam
Kilwa
Lindi
Newala
Makonde
Plat.
Ngapa
Lipelwa
Rovuma
Marupa
NYASALAND
Elizabethville
Zambezi
Blantyre
MOZAMBIQUE
S.
RHODESIA
Salisbury
Bulawayo

barrel. As we opened the door we were met by the most indescribable sound. The house seemed to be alive. From end to end, from floor to rafters, the place was ticking, squeaking and scraping. The wicker chairs were disintegrating into dust; little inch-long bits of cane had fallen, half-chewed by beetles. Dry rot had got into the roof, and the plasterboard ceiling folded despairingly at the corners. Powdered dust from wood-borers hung in the air. Every corner and cranny was alive with ticking fleas. The house stank of rats and decay.

One of our tasks was to gather up Jock's large collection of woodcarvings which he wanted me to sell for him. When this was done, and when we had tidied the place up as best we could we hurriedly turned our backs and closed the door. I do not know how long his house survived; but I imagine Africa had eaten it to the ground long before the poor fellow came out of prison.

Jock had warned us that we would have to be prepared to make our own ferry to cross the Rovuma into Moçambique. I therefore searched the local shops in Newala for bundles of sisal rope, and several strong builders' planks. The latter proved difficult to find; but ultimately, at a shocking price, we managed to hire them on the promise that we left them by the river when we had finished, so that they could be collected later. Then early one morning we set off down the twelve-mile trail to the Rovuma.

When we reached the river the news rapidly spread amongst the riverain people that we were planning to cross. This was to prove fortunate for many reasons. Even before we came to the water we found it impossible to get the loaded car across the half-mile stretch of soft sand that separated the flood banks from the water's edge. The wheels just spun in the sand and sank to the hubs. So finally we had to unload the car, and with the help of all the onlookers, hump the baggage across the river.

Now I made a stupid mistake. I took a look at the river which, though about a quarter of a mile wide, was very shallow. The water barely came up to my thighs, and I calculated that it should be possible to drive the Land Rover across. The bank the other side was a sheer six-foot drop of sand, so first of all we crossed over and hacked out a track to get the Land Rover up from the water. When that was done I once again checked the route I would take, and re-measured the height of the vital parts of the engine. But being a stupid idiot, I didn't realise that the Land Rover, being rather heavier than me, would sink in the sand. I should have learnt my lesson on the soft dry sand; but under the water it seemed hard and firm.

So I drove the car straight into the river. We went about twenty or thirty yards out and all was well. But then we suddenly hit a soft patch, and the trouble began. At first it only slowed us down. I tried to change gear to keep up speed. Then—woomph! As I changed gear the car momentarily halted, and nothing I could do would make it move again. Instead, the more throttle I gave it, the more it chewed its way down into the sand. The water rose rapidly over the engine. Somehow I had to keep the motor running. If that stopped, I would be in dire trouble. Furthermore, if it had been raining in the hills upstream, at any moment the level of the river might rise a foot or more; and I began to have visions of my home, my transport, my worldly belongings, and my entire safari being washed away to the sea.

From behind the wheel I shouted at Rashidi to get everyone round the front of the car. They refused. They just stood and looked. I shouted at them and cursed them. They wanted money. How much money? I offered them fifty cents each. They refused. Two shillings, they said. Ridiculous, I shouted. Meanwhile the engine was getting perilously near to drowning, and the wheels were being washed deeper into the sand. You bastards! One shilling. O.K., they agreed to one shilling. But they wanted the money first. I called them every name under the sun. I look very funny when I get angry; and this did it. They burst into laughter and gathered round the car. Now I told Rashidi to get a couple of our planks, and as everyone lifted, to push the planks under the wheels. But the wheels were down to the hub-caps. They couldn't lift them high enough. They tried to scrape out the sand, but as fast as they scraped, new sand was washed into its place. They tried to lift again, but failed. There were no more people. I was getting blue in the face with worry by now. I just had to keep that damned engine running at all costs. They tried a third time. No luck. O.K., I thought; there's only one thing to do. Don't lift the wheels above the level of the sand, but lift them enough to put the planks down under them, even if at a sharp angle. I hoped that I might then be able, in low ratio reverse gear, to drive the Land-Rover up on to the planks. They got the planks in; and very gingerly I put the car in gear and let out the clutch. For a moment the wheels skidded on the wet planks; but they gripped just enough to push them a fraction further underneath, and slowly—very, very slowly—they climbed up on to the wood. Taking no chances, we laid a track back to the bank with the other planks, and drove the car to safety. Never was I so relieved to feel soft dry sand under my wheels.

After that I called together some of the local boatmen; and at a cost of six pounds, over and above Lord knows how many shillings for carrying baggage and retrieving the car, we got four of the largest available dugout canoes, lashed them together, and floated the car safely across to Moçambique.

Once over the river, we had to cross about a mile of bush and mud, pot-holed with the tracks of elephant and hippo, before we reached a small village and a track that led up to the Makonde plateau. The road was rough and rocky. It twisted and turned through densely thick bush and forests of bamboo, occasionally breaking out across a small clearing in the forest where local Africans were lazily hoeing plantations of cotton.

About twelve miles up the track we came to the Portuguese Administrative post of Ngapa. Ngapa was the opposite number to Newala, and like the Tanganyika frontier post, was perched high on a ridge overlooking the Rovuma valley. The District Commissioner at Newala had advised me to stop here and make my presence known to the Portuguese officials.

The reputation of the Portuguese administrators was not the best. I had heard people say that they disliked stray Englishmen wandering around their territory; that they were frightened that we would write derogatory articles about them in the press. It was only later on that I got to know something of the Portuguese colonial system. In the meantime I wondered what sort of official would greet me at Ngapa.

Armando Mendes da Silva, the Chefe do Posto, was a little man who wore a topee a size too large for him. His big nose gave him a bird-like look. He was very quiet; in fact he seemed to be half asleep. When I arrived, he was inspecting a platoon of dishevelled policemen, and until he had finished he seemed not even to have noticed my presence. He was not being rude, but he was so dreamy by nature that even if I had been Salazar himself I don't think his reaction would have been any different. When he did finally come over to me he was so bewildered by the fact that we had no common language that he began to relapse again into his dream-world.

Eventually we had to converse through a Swahili-Portuguese interpreter.

I got to know Armando Mendes quite well later, and often used to visit him, spending hours with his family at Ngapa. His house, a dapper little bungalow decorated with potted plants, ebony and ivory trinkets, and a bidet in the bathroom, was a small piece of Portugal transplanted. It was, in fact, the object of his dreams; for Armando Mendes was an outcast in a far-flung province who longed for nothing more than to be at home in Portugal. Of all the Portuguese administrators I met he was by far the most gentle and pleasant. I felt rather sorry for him, for he obviously loathed the vicious administrative system of which he was part; but being a very junior officer he was powerless to do anything but go along with it and profit by it where he could.

Having had our passports stamped we set out on the last lap of our journey to the Makonde country. Now if the north bank of the Rovuma had been known for centuries, the south bank, and the Makonde plateau in particular, remained unknown to Europeans until relatively recent times. There are several reasons for this. First, there are no natural harbours on the coast immediately south of the Rovuma, so the south bank never became an Arab or African trade route. Secondly, as the Makonde plateau lies well over a thousand miles from the capital of Moçambique, Lourenço Marques, and as it contains no natural riches, the Portuguese colonisers have never had much interest in it; and thirdly, the plateau is waterless—the women have to walk ten miles into the valley below to fetch water—and people have found it hard to live there. Finally, the Makonde tribe who inhabit it have long been recognised as some of the most savage people in East Africa. More powerful neighbours such as the famous Angoni, unable to defeat and absorb the Makonde, were content to pass them by—just as were the Arabs and the Portuguese. The latter made no attempt to bring this wild region under administrative control until after the first world war, and there was no permanent white occupation there until 1923.

In books on classical African art the Makonde are the only tribe in the Eastern part of Africa that are ever mentioned, though they are generally considered to be of minor importance compared with the great artists of the West coast. They are always erroneously described by anthropologists as living in Tanganyika; but although there is a Makonde tribe north of the Rovuma river, they are a relatively recent offshoot of their more interesting relatives in Moçambique. The Mocambique Makonde are frequently referred to as the "Mawia" tribe, but this is no more than a nickname meaning "the angry people" given to them by their neighbours.

The Makonde have a fable referring to their origin which bears directly on their skill as craftsmen. In the beginning, so the fable goes, there was an old man, half-creature, who lived alone in the wilds. He never washed and his hair was long and greasy; his skin was rotten with sores. One day he took up his knife and a piece of wood, and from it he carved a figurine. He stood the figurine outside his rude shelter, and during the night it came to life, so that when the old man awoke in the morning he found in its place a living woman. For some time he lived with this woman down by a river, and presently she had a baby. But the baby was still-born. Interpreting this as a bad omen, he moved his shelter over the hill, and settled down near another river. Soon the woman had another baby; but again it was still-born. So once more he uprooted himself and his home, and this time went to live on top of the plateau. A third baby was born, and this time it lived. Thenceforth all his offspring were enjoined to live on the plateau in the thick, thorny bush that was called "konde". So there came into being the people of the "konde", or the Makonde.

And now Rashidi and I, as soon as we had left the Chefe do Posto at Ngapa, began to pass through Makonde country. As we did so Rashidi grew more and more silent. With visions of being boiled in a pot and torn to shreds at a cannibal feast he was scared stiff, poor man; and as groups of semi-naked savages shouted at us, flashing their filed teeth and waving their bows and arrows, he closed his eyes and slumped down in his seat. A little ashamed of his fear, he said he was tired after the trouble we had had crossing the river, but it was quite surprising how he came to life as we left each village behind us.

We were heading now for a little village called Lipelwa, where there was a mission station run by the Montfort Fathers, and we had an introduction to the man in charge from Jock. He was an old Dutchman, short and bent, with long white hair, named Father Vloet. Father Vloet had been the first white man to settle in Makonde country, five years after the first world war had ended. For the first seven years he had toiled in vain amongst the proud and primitive Makonde people, and it was not until 1930 that he made his first convert to Christianity. Since then his flock had grown to sizeable proportions, and scattered throughout his district he now had eight other missionaries to help him. One of these, Father Van Bergen, lived with him at Lipelwa, and between them the two missionaries found plenty to keep them occupied. Father Vloet was the Evangelist and Builder, spending his non-praying hours making bricks for the church he had been building for fifteen years. Father Van Bergen was the Provider, who, though he too prayed occasionally, spent most of his time in the bush hunting elephants.

The missionaries were kind to us, and invited us to stay with them. Though neither Rashidi nor I spoke Portuguese, Dutch, or Simakonde, we were able to converse with them through a Makonde servant who spoke Kiswahili. I told them why I had come—that I wanted to make a collection of masks and other carvings—and they promised me all the help they could give. They told me that being English would make things easier for me amongst the tribesmen; had I been Portuguese I would have found it very difficult, for the Makonde loathed their colonial masters like poison.

Life at the mission station was austere but not uncomfortable. As eggs were threepence a dozen, and chickens a shilling each, these formed the basis of the missionary diet. But as Father Van Bergen, the Provider, was not the sort of person to let us think he was no good at his job, he saw to it that there was always a plentiful supply of wine. He himself drank wine—for breakfast, elevenses, lunch, tea, and dinner. He washed it down with Bols after dinner and fumigated his insides with revoltingly pungent Dutch cheroots.

I spent the first few days visiting neighbouring villages, putting the word about that I wanted to buy masks and any other carvings. Rashidi remained behind at the mission station on these occasions at his own request. He had no desire to stick his neck out any further than necessary.

One of the first places I visited was a small village called Mboo, a few miles from Lipelwa. None of the Makonde villages lies actually on the sandy roads that criss-cross the plateau; but they are easy to spot as all are linked to the highways by paths as straight as arrows cut through the thick bush, and often neatly planted with rows of sisal or flowering shrubs. I had never before seen such paths in Africa, as few Africans have an eye for a straight line and even fewer care about flowers. When I came to

Mboo I left my car on the road, and walked up the path to the village at the far end. This consisted of two concentric circles of well-built rectangular thatched huts around an open space planted with mango, orange, and lime trees. Like most other Makonde villages it was spotlessly clean and in the centre of the open space was a small grass shelter where the villagers could meet to smoke and chat.

Beneath the shelter several men were busily at work, carving. One had an elephant's tusk on which he was incising miniature scenes from Makonde life—people hoeing, women carrying water-pots and other pictures—in high relief. Another was chipping at a chunk of ebony with an adze, forming a beautiful head with a tall, mitre-like head-dress. When I strolled in alone, these carvers looked up at me with some surprise. Thinking that I was Portuguese they fell silent, eyeing me suspiciously, wondering why I had come. When I spoke to them in Kiswahili their surprise was even greater, and they were delighted when they discovered I was English. Except for "Bwana Kazi" (Mr. Work—whom I later discovered was Jock) they had never before seen an Englishman in their country. The babble of excitement caused by my arrival brought people running from their huts, to the shelter, where most of them stood in silence staring at me curiously as though I was some strange wild animal.

Their spokesman was one of the carvers, a fearsome-looking man named Gogo whose incisor teeth were filed to a point, and whose face and torso were covered in cicatrised tribal markings. I told him why I had come, and that I wanted above all to buy some masks—"mpiko", as they are called. At the mention of mpiko a deathly hush fell over the crowd. Gogo looked around him nervously, then all of a sudden he jumped up and with a frightening yell chased all the women and boys away from the hut. One or two of the men looked at me reproachfully, nodding their heads and clicking their teeth, saying that it is not good to mention mpiko in front of women or small children who may only see or hear about masks when they are being used in a tribal dance. But their anger was short-lived, and after a few minutes they led me away to where the mpiko were kept.

The mask-house was a small thatched hut hidden in a dense piece of bush two minutes' walk from the village. At the entrance to the path leading up to it were two sticks, signifying that only full-grown men were allowed beyond this point. Yet, despite this rule, which no one would dare break, voices were lowered when we neared the hut, and the mpiko were mentioned in hushed, awe-stricken tones. Now that we were going to look at the masks, Gogo, who seemed to be a man of some authority in the village, posted a guard by the path to make doubly sure that no unauthorised person followed us in. Then he led me inside. Though there were no windows, sufficient light filtered through the doorway for me to see that the hut appeared to be quite empty. I had expected to see racks, or pegs, with masks hanging from them; but no—the place was absolutely bare. For a moment I wondered whether I was being fooled, or thought perhaps that I had misunderstood them. But then Gogo, reaching up under the darkened eaves brought down a bundle wrapped in several layers of black cloth, and unravelling this with great care, he revealed a mask. It was an extraordinary, helmet-shaped object, rather terrifying, and ugly beyond belief. It represented a man obviously of Gogo's own tribe, for its yellow-ochred face was overlaid with ribs of black wax depicting the elaborate patterns of the Makonde tribal markings; and its hair was human hair, pressed into the soft white wood from which the mpiko was made.

As their masks appeared so sacred to the Makonde I wondered whether or not they would be willing to sell them. Though most of them were so gruesome that I could not imagine that any European or American would want them to hang up as wall decorations, I wanted to buy quite a large number for Al and Nat to distribute to various museums in the United States. But when I suggested buying them to Gogo, he willingly agreed. Furthermore, after consultations with the other men, the price he asked was astonishingly cheap—only five shilling per mask. The reason for this was that, being made of very soft "njala" wood—the wood of the cotton tree—they were easy to make, and their antiquity was of no importance to the Makonde. They were hidden away not for the sake of preservation, but to keep uninitiated people from seeing them. Indeed sometimes they did not hide them in huts at all, but in particularly dense patches of undergrowth. There was an occasion later on when we were looking for a mask hidden in the bush when it took the man who hid it twenty-five minutes to find it. So I bought that mask at Mboo, and several others besides.

The dance for which the masks are used is the central feature of

Makonde ritual life. Whilst in their country I saw this dance performed on numerous occasions, and it was like no other that I ever saw elsewhere in Africa. The whole village, men, women and children, were assembled in an open clearing out in the bush, arranged in a horseshoe around the arena. At the open end of the horseshoe were the drummers beating out a fantastically rapid, high-pitched rhythm like the sound of hailstones pattering on sheets of corrugated iron. For some time the drummers played while the women around the arena clapped and sang to their rhythm. Suddenly into this cacophony of sound, clothed from head to foot in strange garments, sprang the Lipiko—the dancer with the mask—who rushed in from the bush, beating his feet upon the ground, prancing round the line of women who now cowered away from him in silent fear. For several minutes, while the drums beat on incessantly, the awesome figure of the dancer charged the terrified crowd, stopping short as he appeared about to strike them. Then as the drums beat faster and faster to a climax, a signal was given to the crowd who, with one accord, turned on the dancer, shouting and yelling, chasing him ignominiously from their midst—back to the bush from which his spirit form had leapt.

Though the precise meaning of the Makonde dance was difficult to establish, it was, according to Father Vloet, originally a war dance. Most of their masks portray people other than men from their own village, and used to represent an attacking enemy. The powerful "enemy" charges into the arena and at first terrifies the villagers; but finally he is vanquished and chased back into the bush. Father Vloet told me that in times gone by villagers used to hurl stones at the dancer and beat him with sticks during the last part of the dance, and it was not unknown for a dancer actually to be killed. Destruction of the "enemy" in this spirit form was supposed to give the Makonde power to defeat him in real life. Such magic is quite common throughout the primitive world, and is called "sympathetic magic". It is this sort of thing that can be seen in the most ancient cave paintings, thousands of years old, in which wild animals are being "killed" by the arrows of hunters.

Since tribal and internecine battles were stopped by the Portuguese, the Makonde dance has lost its point as a war dance. But it would seem that with a deep psychological twist there was no reason why the sympathetic magical powers of the dances should have ended there. I saw dances that suggested that its magical powers were being used for many other things, some of which were beneficial to society. For instance, I saw one dance in which the lipiko, dressed as a girl, was scattering corn from a basket. This appeared to be directed at ensuring fertility and good crops during the coming season. There was another of a very different nature, obviously directed at a homosexual member of the village—homosexuality being rare and strongly frowned upon in most African societies. There were two dancers, one of whom was miming the motions of buggery on the other. Yet another involved a man and two small boys dressed as girls whom he was attempting to "rape", getting frenziedly excited in the process. This was obviously addressed to a "cradle-snatcher" in the village, and the idea in both these dances was that by making a public example of the culprit in spirit form, they hoped to shame him into giving up his activities in real life. In that way, venting their wrath indirectly, the Makonde could clean up their society without being forced to take any direct

punitive action on the individuals concerned. I saw similar types of dances among the Makonde of Tanganyika also; though here the dance form is different, and the lipiko performs on enormous stilts for reasons that no one seems to know. This stilt dancing, though not as exciting as the dancing in Moçambique, showed a remarkable degree of acrobatic skill, and it was strange to see the dancers at rest, sitting casually on the roofs of houses as though they were stools.

The most extraordinary example of sympathetic magic I witnessed was on an occasion when a lipiko came prancing into an arena wearing a mask of none other than "Kwini Elizabeti Yapili wa Waingilesa"—Queen Elizabeth the Second of England. The Queen was referred to by name, and though the mask itself was no flattering work of art, there was no doubt whom it was supposed to represent from the crown on its head. The dance that Her

Majesty performed was as fast and furious as any of the others, but they treated this mask with particular respect, and everything about it indicated that the Makonde wished they were her subjects. By translating their desire into this magical being they hoped that sooner or later they might bring about a change of rulers. In another village I saw a similar dance performed in which an "American sailor", heavily ornamented with Makonde markings, was the central figure. This occurred shortly after a U.S. naval ship had put in at Mtwara on the Tanganyika coast; and no doubts were left about the lipiko's meaning when one of the audience came up to me and asked pathetically, "When are the *Americans* going to take over from the Portuguese?"

All these masks, whether the Queen, an American sailor, missionaries, ugly Portuguese policemen, or neighbouring tribesmen, were treated with the same reverence and fear by the Makonde people. This was made clear on countless occasions as I watched the precautions they took to hide them from those who were supposed not to see them. One such instance concerned Gogo who, after our first meeting, acted as an agent for me, collecting masks from other villages which he then used to bring to the mission station to show me.

Outside my room at the mission was a small balcony with a low wall along the front, beyond which was an open garden stretching nearly two hundred yards to the nearest forest. Standing at my window one morning I caught sight of a figure moving furtively about the bushes on the edge of the forest. Suddenly, as though stung by a scorpion, the man broke cover and raced across the garden towards my room. It was Gogo, and under his arm was a bundle wrapped in the familiar black cloth. As he pounded across the clearing he glanced over his shoulder to right and left to make sure that no one was watching him, and when he came to the house—though there was not a soul in sight—he hurled himself down behind the verandah wall where for a moment he lay, oblivious that I was watching him, panting from exhaustion. Then slowly, and cautiously, like a soldier under fire, with only his backside visible above the wall, he crawled along the verandah towards my room, finally jumping through the window with a heavy sigh of relief.

Only when he had got his breath back did he look up at me

triumphantly and whisper, "Mpiko!" And from under layers of cloth he produced the mask.

The Makonde sincerely believed that if a woman were to set eyes on a mask, when not being worn in a dance, her "eyes would roll in their sockets till only the whites showed", and she might go mad, become sterile, or even die. With some of the more primitive amongst them their belief in the power of the mask went even further. When I asked one gorilla-like man whether white ants ate the mpiko when they were hidden in the bush, he replied emphatically "No! They are afraid, for they know that if they eat the mpiko they will die!"

Before I left the Makonde plateau I collected between forty and fifty masks of different types; but ironically, after all those weeks, traipsing around the bush, the best "mpiko" I ever found was not within three thousand miles of Moçambique. Two or three years later, in London, I was browsing round the shelves of one of the leading primitive art dealers in England when, high up on a shelf, almost out of sight, I suddenly noticed a very unusual mask. To me it was unmistakably Makonde, for it had the same facial markings and other characteristics. It was particularly unusual in that it was neither a face mask such as those worn by the northern Makonde,

nor a full helmet mask worn by the southern Makonde. It was what is called a "half-helmet mask" which covers the face but has a piece extending backwards over the crown of the head; and it was the only one like it I had ever seen. I asked the dealer if he knew anything about it, but until he had checked his lists he was not even sure it was Makonde. In any event he had no idea it was particularly unusual, and as, like most Makonde masks, it was not particularly beautiful to western eyes, it had been sitting up there on the shelf for years, unsold. The price he had on it was rather high, but after a bit of bargaining I persuaded him to let me have it for rather less than half the list price—just to get it out of his way. He wrapped it; I thanked him and, jumping into a taxi, drove straight round to the British Museum. Within half an hour I had sold it to them (at a handsome profit) and a few weeks later it was published as the frontispiece of the Royal Anthropological Institute's magazine *Man*—one of the finest and most unusual Makonde masks known.

The elaborate markings with which the Makonde decorate their masks are exactly the same as the designs that they frequently "cicatrise" on their bodies, from forehead to thigh. The Makonde are the supreme masters of this art on the African continent, and though the effect is sometimes similar to tattooing, cicatrising is a

very different process. Whereas tattooing is done by injecting a pigment under the skin, cicatrising is done by cutting the flesh, rubbing powdered charcoal into the wound, and allowing it to heal over to form a black scar. Both men and women are cicatrised, and the designs used may at one time have had some symbolic significance, but if this was ever the case, their meanings have now been forgotten.

If cicatrisation makes the Makonde look grotesque, the lip-plugs that their womenfolk wear make them even more so. The lip-plugs of Makonde women in Tanganyika, though nowhere near as large as those of some tribes in western Africa, are sometimes two or three inches in diameter. Those of the Portuguese Makonde women are smaller but from them protrudes a spike which presses against their noses giving even the most attractive amongst them a strangely pig-like look. In one village I discovered a very old man wearing a lip-plug decorated with coloured beads. I was told that many years ago all the menfolk used to wear them; but when I was there only two such men survived, and by now they are doubtless both dead.

It is not known for certain why the Makonde mess their bodies about as they do, but there are two theories. One is that they feel it genuinely enhances their beauty. The other is that in the olden days it made them less attractive to slave dealers. There is probably some truth in both theories, though today, more and more young children are refusing to be cicatrised, as they rightly believe it will make it more difficult for them to find good jobs when they grow up. Their extraordinary appearance is probably the reason why other Africans believe they are cannibals. There is certainly no other evidence that they eat people, and even Rashidi, when he had overcome his initial fears, was forced to admit that the Makonde were not only pleasant people, but also that they were more hospitable to "foreign" Africans such as himself than most other tribesmen he had met.

Even if the Makonde do not eat people, some of the things they do eat are certainly curious. They love snakes—not only python which is eaten in many places, but small grass-snakes as well. They go delirious over elephant and hippo, and rave over a crocodile steak (which, having tried myself, I can genuinely appreciate). And they also eat mice and rats.

Walking through the bush one day I came upon a little hut outside which was a small boy, eleven or twelve years old, sitting in front of a fire, cooking. He was totally absorbed in what he was doing, and took no notice of me even when I sat down near him to watch. On the ground beside him he had laid out two sticks, and upon these was the object of his attentions, a pile of rats. With great care he took each rat in turn, stuck a stick through its body, end to end, and roasted it over the flames. When the rat, which had had neither skin, entrails, nor anything else removed, was cooked to a crisp brown, he sprinkled it with salt and replaced it on the sticks. There were eight or ten rats in all, and he was cooking them for his chums just as a Boy Scout might sit down casually and cook "twists" with flour and water.

The hut outside which he was sitting was the boys' initiation hut in which all the boys of initiation age in the neighbourhood spend five or six months learning the secrets of manly existence. Tribal initiation is still very important amongst the Makonde. During the long initiation "term" they are not allowed to visit their homes, nor receive any visitors. With the help of only one "master", they have to look after themselves entirely. It gives them tremendous confidence and makes them feel and behave like men. If they are not considered adult enough after their six-month course, they go back again the next year; and sometimes one comes across boys of eighteen and nineteen who are still not initiated.

I came in for the final initiation celebration on one occasion at which everyone greeted the new initiates at a three-day party in the village. Initiation generally accompanies circumcision and marks the attainment of manhood sexually as in every other way. These celebrations were marked by one final ceremonial blessing before the boys went out into the world. The ceremony, which seemed to be the climax of the whole affair, was marked by considerable modesty, bashfulness and humour. The boys were instructed to take their clothes off, and in front of the whole village they filed past one of the elders whose job it was to perform the blessing. In a bowl beside him was an oily black liquid, and as each boy came past he first daubed his forehead with the liquid, then, dipping an instrument like a ring spanner into it, passed this several times over each boy's penis. I must have shown my surprise, for the crowd suddenly started laughing at me, whereupon the old man came up to me and asked if I too would like to be blessed. Apparently this was an infallible prophylactic against venereal diseases, impotence and lack of virility. I declined hurriedly.

In three or four weeks, besides buying the masks, most of which were more of ethnographic interest, I paid out about £80 for ebony carvings which had a more general appeal and which I was able to sell at a very good profit. Though these included a few traditional pieces such as clubs with heads carved in the form of faces, gourd-bungs, and carved powder-horns, most of them were curios covering the same range of subjects as those of the Wazaramo and the Wakamba. The quality of the Makonde carving was far superior to that of the other tribes, and significant features of the classical tradition were worked into their designs. Now the time came to pack them up as before, and get them to the coast to be shipped to New York.

Armando Mendes da Silva had told me there was a high export duty on native crafts; and with the amount I had, I would have had to pay about £60 in duty. I was damned if I was going to do this if I could avoid it, so I decided to smuggle them across to

Tanganyika, and ship them from there duty free. The snag was that to get to the river I had to go right past Armando Mendes's house, and he had asked me to let him know if ever I was going down to the frontier. I wasn't particularly keen to see the inside of a Portuguese prison, and I had learnt by then that they had no compunction about putting visiting English inside if they had half an excuse. There was only one thing to do, and that was to drive past his house and hope for the best. I had two things on my side. First, his house was on a hillside, and the road sloped quite steeply past it. Secondly, like every good Portuguese, I knew he always, unfailingly, took a long siesta in the afternoon. With careful timing, I planned to arrive at Ngapa, with my Land Rover stacked to the roof with crates, at the siesta hour. To make sure I didn't wake him I would coast down the hill past his house.

But, when the time came, luck was against me. As I free-wheeled down towards his house a burly African policeman stepped out into the road and waved to me to stop. If I stopped he would certainly see my load and become suspicious. But I guessed that if I drove straight past we would surely have time to get the load across the river before Armando Mendes had a chance to wake up and catch up. So I put my foot down, and sped on down the Rovuma road, leaving the policeman gaping after us, shaking his fist with fury. I parked the car in the little village about a mile from the river, and hastily collecting up all the men and women I could find, we head-loaded the carvings down to the frontier on the first leg of their journey to New York. I had sent a runner ahead to an Indian merchant in Newala to get him to meet me at the river, and we carried the cargo across without mishap.

When I got back to Ngapa I found Armando Mendes sipping a glass of wine in his dressing-gown. He hadn't heard I had been past. The African policeman had obviously felt it was less trouble to say nothing.

When I was out collecting, I used to spend many hours talking to Africans about the Portuguese. They loathed them; and from all I ever discovered (and corroborated) they had every justification. The Chefe do Posto of one of the Makonde villages was a particularly unpleasant man in their eyes. If an African failed to salute him as he drove down the road, the Chefe would have him put inside and given twenty-five or fifty strokes of the "balamatola", this being the local word for that pernicious form of torture, the bastinado, with which the palms of the hands and soles of the feet are beaten until they are raw.

These frontier Africans were in a particularly frustrating position. Across in Tanganyika, goods in the shops were as little as a third of the price of equivalent goods in Moçambique. Conversely, wages in Moçambique were far lower than in Tanganyika. (A Moçambique African, after *six months*' compulsory labour on a nearby sisal estate, came away on average with seventy shillings in his pocket.) The obvious tendency was to shop in Tanganyika twenty miles away. Penalties if caught taking produce or bringing goods across the river were severe, involving prison sentences, and up to a hundred strokes of the bastinado. It was very difficult to stop the Makonde, however, for only they knew the bush paths.

It often astonished me how little the Portuguese knew about Africa or the Africans. I never met a single Portuguese administrator who could speak any local language, and most of them seemed utterly callous about the people, selling their labour for personal profit to Portuguese estate owners, and treating them like slaves. It was their ignorance of the local language that eventually brought about my own departure.

One day Father Van Bergen came into my room, and in place of the usual smile his face was like a stone wall. He spoke to me somewhat sharply, simply saying that he was very sorry but that I would have to leave immediately. Would I go after lunch, or if not, early the next morning. I was completely bewildered. He would give me no explanation for this; he was severe, yet at the same time he seemed rather sorry having to talk like this. He said something about it being a rule of the mission that no one could stay longer than a certain period; but this, I knew from earlier conversations, was completely untrue.

Father Van Bergen had that morning been in the district headquarters talking to the administrators for the Makonde, and judging from a conversation I had with his driver, I am pretty sure I know what happened. It was simply that the Portuguese did not like an Englishman wandering about from village to village, talking to Africans in a language that they could not themselves understand. They knew as well as anyone that the Africans loathed their guts; they knew too that many of their own Africans were already members of TANU, the Tanganyika political organisation. They distrusted my presence and simply wanted to get rid of me.

As there was no hotel within sixty miles where I could stay, there was only one course for me, and that was to leave Moçambique altogether.

I had no desire to make things difficult for the missionaries, so early the next day Rashidi and I packed up the remains of our collections, loaded everything into the Land Rover, and rather sorrowfully said good-bye to them. Being Dutch, they were already in a tricky enough position with the Portuguese, and I am quite certain they were sorry to see us go in this way.

My original plan, on leaving the Makonde, was to drive down through Nyasaland and Southern Rhodesia, and from there to go up into the Congo. There was therefore no need to re-cross the Rovuma into Tanganyika, and we set off down dreadful roads across the northern part of Moçambique. Nyasaland lay only four hundred miles to the west, but this was a two-day journey.

When darkness fell on the first day we came into the small town of Marupa. I knew there was no hotel or rest-house here, but I hoped we might be able to find a bed somewhere and not go to the bother of putting the tent up. To be quite honest, I was fully prepared to scrounge off the Portuguese if I could. It turned out to be easier than I expected, for as we drove past a row of houses the front door of one of them opened, and a tall young man came down the path towards his car. I drew up behind him.

"Pardon, monsieur . . . " I always tried my French on the Portuguese first as more of them seemed to understand that than English. "Can you tell me, please, how I get to the hotel?" A blind opening, as I already knew there was none.

The young man replied in English. "Ah! You are English man, no? So please let us talk English language, as I speak it very very well. But Sir, pardon me, and accept regrets; there is no hotel in Marupa."

"Oh dear . . . " My jaw dropped in mock bewilderment. The young man saw my evident distress and thought hard for a moment, anxiously wondering what to do.

"But people back in Montepuez told me there was . . . " I went on, lying outrageously. But there was no need to worry. The young man suddenly drew himself up to his full height, clicked his heels, and addressed me as though I were an important ambassador on an official visit.

"Sir. Please to introduce myself as the Portuguese Chefe do Posto of Marupa. It is the policy of my government to be hospitable to English persons. You will therefore kindly stay with me!"

Another click of the heels, a little bow, and we drove off to his house. My host was very pleasant. Indeed, he was showing me a side of the Portuguese colonials that is undeniably charming. On the surface they are the most hospitable people. They ply you with wine to saturation point, and make it their business to see that you are comfortable. On more than one occasion I met Portuguese who seemed to consider it part of their duty to provide me with an African woman; and in that lay a hint as to their character. Africans to them are chattels. They consider it part of their "civilising mission" in Africa to make the able-bodied men work, with or without pay; but as they have a genuine disregard for skin colour they have no qualms about taking an African mistress. There is no colour bar in Moçambique, and Africans can achieve full Portuguese citizenship if they are considered "civilised" enough. If they are not "civilised", (and in Portuguese eyes only a handful are), then they are animals and are treated as such. The country is ruled by force, as I saw clearly the next day when I was taken to the Administrator of Marupa. On a table beside his desk lay a loaded submachine gun.

Tens of thousands of Africans have migrated from Moçambique into neighbouring British territories—400,000 alone to Nyasaland. The effect of this mass migration became astonishingly clear the day we left Marupa. For over two hundred miles Rashidi and I drove through endless forest. This was land occupied by two great tribes, the Ngoni and Yao. Yet we scarcely saw a soul. We went through scattered villages in which a few dispirited and thin figures rose to salute us as we passed. Then, when we came to the Nyasaland border, we passed through a gate in a stone wall and suddenly entered a totally different world. On one side hundreds of miles of empty forests; and on the other, every square inch of land under cultivation—thriving villages through which lorries raced, scattering pigs, chickens and children. From a dead land to a land of the living. Yet, only a hundred years ago, Livingstone had found this part of Nyasaland ravaged by poverty and disease, and sparsely populated. There is little wonder that the Portuguese are worried about their "overseas provinces", as their colonies are known. There is little wonder they are frightened by the ogre of revolution that hangs perpetually over their heads. Bullets will be their only hope; but ultimately they cannot succeed.

Rashidi and I drove straight through Nyasaland, down to Salisbury in Southern Rhodesia, where I arranged to spend a week or two with some friends. Rashidi was, of course, quite out of his element here, and as we were beyond the fringes of Swahili-speaking Africa I was the only person with whom he could talk. Yet, determined neither to let me down, nor give a bad impression of Tanganyika's people, Rashidi came into his own. It was Christmas time, and my friends had a sizeable house party. Undeterred, Rashidi put on his cleanest raiment, and plunged straight into the kitchen. There he took over control. He was appalled by the way the cook was dishing up the dinner; so showed him how to do it. He was disgusted by the houseboys' slovenliness when serving at table; so without a word he took over. My hosts were highly amused; but more than that—they had never before thought it possible that an African servant could be so well trained. This delighted Rashidi, but he greeted the compliments with the impassive look of any good Jeeves.

But sadly my time with Rashidi now came to an end. While in Salisbury he had a letter from relatives in Morogoro saying that his son was seriously ill, and asking him to go home. Very reluctantly, therefore, I put him on a bus back to Tanganyika. I greatly missed him when, after a week or two, I packed up once again and continued my journey to the Congo.

CHAPTER THREE

Woodcarvers of the Congo

I set out on the next part of my journey with high hopes. Travelling via Bulawayo and the Victoria Falls, I planned to visit an area considered by some experts to be once the richest of all the art areas in the continent of Africa. This was the vast territory that was then the Belgian Congo and I intended first to visit Léopoldville and Brazzaville. Then, coming up the Congo River, I would head back across the whole width of Africa to Mombasa having, I hoped, scooped up a valuable haul of treasures en route. This would be a safari of over five thousand miles from Salisbury.

In the Rhodesias there was not a lot to be found either in the way of curios or art. With the exception of one or two areas, in the far north-west where the Batchokwe tribe spread across the borders from Angola, and in a few parts of Barotseland, there has never been much traditional work produced here, so I decided to head directly towards the Congo. I did, however, spend two days in Livingstone where I packed and despatched several crates of Barotse curios. Barotse, or Lozi, carving is not unlike that of the Wakamba, and the carvers of this area have risen to fame and fortune in much the same way as their brethren in Kenya—on the recent tide of tourism. But both Al and Nat had asked me not to send too much from here as they were already receiving regular supplies from other people.

From Livingstone I drove on, across the frontier, to Elisabethville, the capital of Katanga in the southern Congo. A friend in Southern Rhodesia had suggested that when I reached Elisabethville I should call on a Belgian named Laurent Moonens who ran an art school for Africans. So as soon as I arrived I went along to the Académie des Beaux Arts where I understood Laurent was to be found.

Laurent Moonens, himself an artist on the way to becoming quite well known in Belgium, had originally come out to the Congo for

a short period, on a commission from the Belgian government to paint a number of official pictures. While out there, however, he had been appalled by the lack of interest shown by colonial educationalists in the encouragement of art among African children. And there and then he decided to stay in the Congo to set up an experimental "school" to encourage aspiring young African artists.

When I found Laurent—a quiet and unassuming man in his thirties—he was just off home, so he invited me back with him for lunch. During the meal he told me the history of his Académie, and how he was trying to run it. When he started, only two or three years before my visit, he had no more than three young pupils in their early teens whom he had found in one of the schools run by the Union Minière mining concern. From the start one of the basic features of his experiment was to avoid giving the children any technical teaching. To set them down in front of a model and teach them to draw would, he felt, be inviting disaster in that it would kill the spontaneity, imagination, and feeling that he hoped to get his children to express. So what he did was simply to give them paint and paper and let them do whatever they wished.

The first Académie was an open grass shelter on the outskirts of Elisabethville, and the artists' drawing boards and tables were old wooden boxes. And the results were astonishing. He found that the children, sons of Bushongo and Baluba tribesmen, had an amazing natural ability to express themselves in a remarkably coherent way. Before long, as news of the exciting "discovery" of painting spread amongst other children, he found his Académie inundated with budding artists who came voluntarily not only from school in Elisabethville, but from other areas hundreds of miles away. When the Académie grew too large for grass huts, he was eventually able to move it, with official backing, to a fine modern building where it became a fully-fledged school, providing its young artists with a general education in addition to art facilities.

In his home, Laurent had a collection of over four hundred paintings from the Académie. So when lunch was over we moved into the next room to look through these, and they turned out to be some of the most extraordinary and colourful pictures I had ever set eyes on. Inevitably a certain style had developed within the school, and all the paintings had some fascinating things in common. Given a range of colours far greater than anything available in the bush, the young Africans had shown astonishing colour perception. No attempt whatsoever was made to depict a third dimension, yet despite this lack of perspective they achieved a tremendous feeling of depth by the interplay of objects and colours used. The subjects were mostly taken from the world that the artists knew best—the bush. There were animals and birds of all descriptions; snakes entwined round jungle trees; and violent, fantastically lively tribal dances. One of the favourite subjects was men fishing, or carrying their day's catch on poles along the water's edge with fishes clearly visible under the water at the bottom of the painting.

The effect in these "water" scenes was identical to reliefs in many Egyptian tombs, in which boats float over myriads of fishes and reptiles depicted underneath. I asked Laurent if they could have seen reproductions of these Egyptian reliefs; but he was sure they had not. A few paintings were of towns—one which depicted an ambulance rushing to the scene of a road accident was dramatic and packed with humour and observation.

When we had done with this feast of colour and imagination I asked if I could buy a few paintings. As a special concession Laurent let me have a dozen; but generally he did not sell any at all. He was terrified that his pupils would discover the commercial possibilities of their work and begin churning them out by the thousand for sale to tourists. This he rightly felt would be the beginning of the end of the Académie, as was in fact the case with another art studio I visited later, on this safari.

As I left Laurent I could not help reflecting that, given the opportunity and encouragement, there might well be a very interesting rebirth of art in Africa. This school in Elisabethville was not unique on the continent, but nothing of its type existed in East Africa. In fact, apart from an over-sophisticated art school at Makerere College in Uganda, art teaching in East African schools was non-existent. I think the lack of official interest in Kenya, Tanganyika and Uganda stemmed from the fact that the East African territories had no traditional arts upon which to draw, and it was therefore considered that the people themselves were inevitably inartistic. But it occurred to me now, that just because East Africans had no previous experience of visual forms of expression, there was absolutely no reason to suppose that they had no latent talent which should be encouraged in every way. Pondering over these facts gave me ideas that I later followed up when I returned to Kenya.

Leaving Elisabethville, I drove north into the town of Kamina in the territory of the Baluba. I had been given an introduction to an English missionary couple here named Womersley, who were said to know more about the Baluba tribe than anyone else. They, if anyone, I had been told, would be the people to put me in touch with the best Baluba artists.

One of the great things about travelling in Africa is that you need never find isolation or loneliness unless you are looking for it. There is barely a corner of the continent where mission stations have not been established, and I found very early on that far from being considered a nuisance when I drove up to a mission station and asked for a bed, I was usually welcomed. Most missionaries lead a somewhat isolated life, and almost all of them enjoy and appreciate meeting a new face, especially if their guest is interested in the people amongst whom they are working. Their hospitality is usually frugal, as one might expect, but always sincere and enjoyable. So it was with the Womersleys whom I found living in a modern house on the outskirts of Kamina township. These two had been living amongst the Baluba for forty years, but in that time they had lost none of their characteristic north country English habits and hospitality. Their house was as English as they could make it; and the food we ate was good old Yorkshire duff.

The Baluba tribe, one of the greatest in the Congo, live in a huge area extending north from Elisabethville. Since the Congo gained its independence the Baluba have acquired a reputation of being cruel and vicious people. They are in fact no more prone to violence than most other Bantu of Africa. But one or two stories that I heard about the Baluba while staying in the Katanga do perhaps give a good indication of the sort of traditional attitude towards violence from which these people are endeavouring to free themselves. The first of these stories was told me by Mr. Womersley who was present at the funeral of the last great Paramount Chief of the Luba, King Kabongo, in 1948.

In the olden days, Luban kings and chieftains were always put to death violently whilst there was still life in them. There was good reason for this; for if the king died a natural death, the "King spirit" was thought to die with him. To the Baluba this would have been an unimaginable catastrophe for what then would happen to his successor? If the "King spirit" was dead, it was thought inevitable that the power of the tribe would collapse.

The death of the king was, to say the least of it, about the most unpleasant death imaginable. When it was seen that he could not live for long, his chief councillors were called upon to do the deed. They sneaked up on him at night, and having first stuffed his mouth with powdered wood both to keep him quiet and to stop his spirit escaping, they twisted his testicles until the last breath of life had departed from him.

Then came the burial; and this I quote from the journal of the explorer Cameron written in 1875. (Cameron dedicated his journal to Queen Victoria, and it was probably out of deference to her that he omitted any account of the king's death, which I heard from Mr. Womersley.) First, the chief's head is severed to be preserved with the heads of other great chiefs from past generations. The next "proceeding is to divert the course of a stream, and in its bed to dig an enormous pit, the bottom of which is lined with women. At one end a woman is placed on her hands and knees, and upon her back the dead chief, covered with beads and other treasures, is seated, being supported on either side by one of his wives, while his second wife sits at his feet. The earth is then shovelled in on them, and all the women are buried alive with the exception of the second wife. To her custom is more merciful than to her companions, and grants her the privilege of being killed before the huge grave is filled in. This being completed, a number of male slaves—sometimes forty or fifty—are slaughtered, and their blood poured over the grave; after which the river is allowed to resume its course. Stories were rife that no fewer than a hundred women were buried alive with Bambarre, Kasongo's father; but let us hope that this may be an exaggeration."

Kasongo, to whom Cameron refers, was succeeded by his son Kabongo who did not die until 1948. Familiar with the local custom, the Belgians took great care to see that Kabongo was allowed to die a natural death. He was, in fact, the first chief of this great tribe ever to do so. Furthermore they were determined to ensure there was no slaughter at his burial, and that he was not first decapitated according to custom.

Though the police were alerted for Kabongo's funeral, the Belgians wanted to avoid any action that might be provocative. They therefore agreed to have just one representative present: and for this, knowing he was respected by the Luba, they chose Mr. Womersley.

Now the entire manner of Kabongo's death had infuriated a large number of the older members of the tribe. The "King spirit" was dead, and this was a calamity that surely spelt doom to the whole tribe. But many of them felt that if the funeral were traditional, the tribe might be reprieved, and they had made plans for a last minute take-over of the funeral proceedings. Word of this had leaked out, and when Mr. Womersley entered the hut where the dead king lay in state, he was suddenly besieged by dozens of women who beseeched him to come to their rescue. Womersley told the police what was going on, and extra precautions were taken. The funeral went off without incident; but who knows what took place in the bush once the security was relaxed?

Although things went peacefully in the long run, the Belgians again had reason to fear trouble when the time came to choose Kabongo's successor, for many of the Baluba elders were in favour of the traditional methods of accession. These involved even more bloodshed than the death of the king, for by tradition, all the king's sons would fight for the throne.

When Europeans first settled in Baluba territory they found it a sparsely populated land. One of the reasons for this was that the country had not yet recovered from the slaughter that followed the death of the Luba king, Ilunga Kabale. Knowing what would follow their death, it was customary for Luba kings to drown most of their sons at birth, retaining only three or four of the strongest babies. Ilunga Kabale, however, a soft-hearted man, had let all sixteen of his sons live. Thus the inter-tribal battles that followed his death practically annihilated the entire tribe.

In these battles, in which each son with his own followers fought the rest, there were certain rigid rules of war. When one of the princes saw that he had lost the fight, his code of honour forbade him to run away. Instead he allowed himself to be captured. Following his capture he was treated to a tremendous party that lasted for several days, during which he received full honours of the king himself, and even his victorious brother would pay him homage befitting a great chief. But he knew his time had come, and as a point of honour it was up to him to give the command for his own execution. Seated on a throne amid thousands of hushed warriors, he raised his hand as a signal to the executioners. Holding a twisted leather thong between them, the two executioners moved up close to the prince who now tilted his head backwards, baring his neck. The executioners then sawed through his neck with the thong until his head was completely severed.

Such stories of wilful brutality among the Baluba greatly surprised me when I first heard them, for they seemed so out of keeping with their tremendously sensitive and delicate art style. When I arrived in the Congo I was already acquainted with Baluba sculpture not only from books, but also from the superb collection of woodcarving housed in the museum in Bulawayo, which I had called in to look at on my way through. This collection, the Codrington collection, had been captured from the kraal of a Baluba chieftain named Kazembe during a punitive expedition in the last century. At that time a few outlying groups of Baluba lived on the Northern Rhodesian side of the frontier, though these later moved into the Congo. In the Codrington collection I had seen some very fine wooden caryatid stools, in the form of a woman holding the seat above her head; and also a number of magnificent carved ceremonial paddles that used to be given to ferry-boatmen by the chiefs when they crossed rivers during journeys in outlying parts of their territory. It was carvings of this sort that had spread the fame of African sculpture throughout the world; and now that I was in Lubaland it was these that I was after and I asked the Womersleys where the best places to search would be.

Mr. Womersley looked at me glumly and fidgeted for a moment before answering, as though he did not quite know how to put the reply. But at last he spoke:

"I am afraid you are going to be very disappointed. I know of not one single Baluba artist in the whole of this huge territory. In the olden days, of course, there were certainly some excellent artists and craftsmen. But I fear that since the coming of this civilisation of ours, all that sort of thing has gone. In fact, let me tell you the story of a thing that happened to me when I was running our mission at Kabongo. Kabongo was then the capital of the Luba king of the same name, so if there were any artists anywhere in Lubaland, that is where they would have been living. The great chiefs, the paramount especially, were always the ones who sponsored the arts, as you know. Well, there *was* one artist, an old man who is dead now, who used to live and work in a small village near Kabongo. One day he came to see me at the mission in a dreadful panic. Some people, he said, had tried to kill him, and he wanted me to protect him. The old chap was very distraught, and I thought he was exaggerating his story, so I quietened him down, and sent him back to his village. I couldn't really see any reason why anyone would want to kill him. But not long after that, exactly the same thing happened again; but this time he resolutely refused to leave the mission. He said he was lucky to have escaped as it was, and if he went back to his village he would surely be killed. So I gave him a bed, and over the next few days made some enquiries as to why anyone should want to kill him. What I heard was this. A number of young men in his and a neighbouring village, seeing him sitting outside his hut whittling away at his wood, began to wonder where this man got his knowledge and skill. The only conclusion they could come to was that he must be in league with the devil; and those in league with the devil deserved to die. We kept him in the mission for several years, and he did some excellent work . . . here, take a look at these. . . ." Mr. Womersley went over to a cupboard and took out a headrest, some combs, and several elaborate hatpins such as Luba men used to wear. They were beautifully carved in the old tribal style. "But as far as I know", he went on, "he was the last Luba artist or craftsman in the country." So it looked as though any search in Lubaland would be a waste of time.

I stayed with the Womersleys for a day or two; then, feeling very depressed, once again got back on the road and headed north toward the land of the Bushongo where I hoped my luck would be better.

En route to the Kasai Province, where the Bushongo live, I had an encounter that raised my hopes again. I spent a night at a small hotel in the town of Dibaya, and in the public rooms I noticed a few fine pieces of Bushongo carving, an elaborately decorated drum, a mask, and a figurine. I remarked on these to the Belgian hotelier, and seeing that I was interested, he beckoned me through to his private rooms in the rear. There he proceeded to show me his incredible collection of carvings. Scattered all over his sitting-room floor, on shelves down the narrow passages, under the beds, and even in the dirty-clothes basket beneath the bathroom basin, were carvings of every variety the Bushongo ever produced, many of them quite beautiful and some unique. Furthermore, he told me,

he had about double this quantity stored away at his home in Belgium. The hotelier had worked on the railway that runs through the Kasai to Port Francqui on the Kasai river, and he had built up his collections over the many years he had spent wandering through the different villages in the bush. I was particularly struck by one carved figure that stood nearly two feet high. Tentatively I asked him if he would sell any of the carvings. He was a bit dubious, and asked me how much I would be prepared to pay. As I knew I could sell that one statue for practically anything I asked, I offered him the equivalent of fifty pounds. I thought the sum might be sufficiently large to shock him into selling it. But he merely looked at me and laughed. "I have already been offered twice that," he said; "but I would not even sell it for five hundred pounds!" Just what his collection was worth I do not know. But he had a small fortune stacked away there, and he knew it.

So I now drove, through Luluabourg, deep into the heart of the Bushongo country. Having as yet made no purchases in the Congo I was getting slightly worried about my finances. If the Bushongo offered nothing, I began to wonder whether I should be able to continue the safari right across to Léopoldville as planned.

Not many miles from Mweka, the headquarters town of the Bushongo, I had a strange encounter that gave me a financial relief for a day or two if nothing else. I was driving down the road through a stretch of gigantic forest, when I saw ahead of me a cavalcade of people like an army of tiny ants against the enormous trees that towered on either side. As I came close I noticed that all the people, twenty or thirty of them, were running as fast as they could, most of them sweating profusely and clearly exhausted. In amongst them, almost dropping to their knees, were four stalwart, semi-naked men bearing upon their shoulders a very large—but quite empty—palanquin. For a moment I was bewildered by this strange sight. It seemed almost as though it were some tribal "rag" to raise money for the witch-doctor by seeing how far the porters could run with an empty palanquin in a given period of time. For there appeared to be no reason whatsoever for such unusual haste.

Some way ahead of the main party, I then spotted a lone figure pedalling furiously away on a bicycle with two young men prancing along on either side. Judging by his spectacles, pith-helmet, white shirt, and his corpulence, this man was obviously someone of considerable importance. And, equally obviously, he and his small party were part and parcel of the sweating cavalcade that struggled along behind. Curious to find out who the cyclist was and what was going on, I drew into the side and waved him to stop. My excuse was that I wanted to take a picture of the palanquin.

The gentleman introduced himself as Chief Albert, chief of an outlying district of the Bushongo tribe. He spoke French quite fluently, and as he appeared to be a friendly sort of person, I felt I could ask him, without causing embarrassment, why he travelled with both palanquin and bicycle.

"S'il vous plaît, monsieur, when I am on the road I ride my bicycle because it is faster and my men carry my palanquin. But when I am on the forest paths that are very bumpy my digestion is upset, so I ride in my palanquin, and my men carry the bicycle." This seemed very reasonable; but Monsieur Albert was clearly quite oblivious to the discomfort he was causing everyone!

My curiosity having been satisfied I then took a photograph of the palanquin, and turned to thank the chief and say good-bye. But to my surprise I saw that he had wandered over to the Land Rover and was now peering in at the back looking with amazement at the contents. Suddenly he started clapping his hands and crying with delight. "Ah, monsieur! Un lit de sangle! Un lit de sangle! Sensationnel!" His eyes had alighted upon one of my camp beds. At the time I had two such beds in the car, one of which, with a wooden frame, was broken. It was this one that he now dragged from the car asking me pressingly if he could please buy it from me. For him, the camp bed, like his bicycle, would be the greatest status symbol he could dream of, elevating him to the very peak of grandeur when he went on tour round his district. I pointed out to him that it was broken; but this made not the slightest difference. He wanted desperately to have it. The trouble was that I was not sure if I wanted to sell it. So in the hope that it would put him off I said gravely that it would be very expensive, and quoted the equivalent in francs of about five pounds. But to my astonishment Chief Albert immediately whipped out a bundle of notes and before I could have second thoughts, thrust it into my hands.

Chief Albert was heading for his home village five or six miles down the road. So, thinking that I might give his exhausted entourage a rest, I gave him a lift in the Land Rover. I dropped the Chief without further excitement; but as I was about to leave his compound he stopped me and told me to wait, as he wanted to give

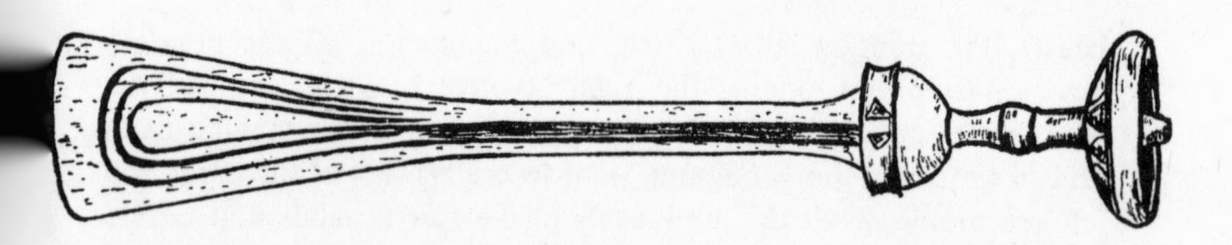

me a present. And from his house he brought out a fine old Bushongo cutlass which only later did I discover was a rare piece to find in the Congo at that time.

So now I had arrived in the country of the Bushongo, one of the greatest tribes of central Africa with the most ancient and fascinating history, and once some of the most prolific woodcarvers of the Congo. Many African tribes have lengthy and complex mythologies and oral histories; but perhaps those of the Bushongo are amongst the most interesting of all. The first European to whom they were divulged was an ethnographer named Emil Torday who visited their country soon after the turn of this century.* Their mythology is of particular interest in its similarity to Genesis, though at the time when Torday recorded it it would have been impossible for any knowledge of the Old Testament to have been imparted to the Bushongo people by Europeans. In Emil Torday's words, it begins as follows:

"In the beginning there was darkness and the earth was all covered with water; in this chaos, Bumba, the Chembe (God), reigned alone. Chembe was of human shape, but of enormous size, and white of colour. One day he felt great pain in his belly and began to vomit; first he vomited the sun, then the moon and then the stars; thus there was light. Then, under the influence of the sun, the water began to evaporate, and sandbanks appeared on the surface; but these sandbanks, like the waters from which they had risen, were devoid of all animal and vegetable life. Then Bumba vomited again, and originated the leopard, the crested eagle, the crocodile, the minnow, the tortoise, the lightning (an animal like a black leopard with a fiery tail), the egret, a scarab and the goat. Then he vomited men innumerable, but only one of them was white like him, that was Loko Yima.

"The animals he had created now bestirred themselves to people the earth: the egret vomited all the birds (except the hawk); the crocodile all the snakes and the iguana; the goat all the horned

* And wrote *On the Trail of the Bushongo*, London, 1925.

beasts, the minnow all the fish, and the iguana all the hornless beasts. After that, one of the men, Nyonye N'Gana, vomited the white ants, but such was the effort he had to make that he died. Out of gratitude the white ants went to the bowels of the earth and fetched mould; with this they covered the sterile sands and buried their creator in it. Chonganda vomited a plant from which all vegetable life sprang; another man, Chedi Bumba, tried to create something new and vomited the hawk, but nothing else.

"Thus was the world we know today created."

The mythology continues at some length, explaining how the lightning animal became troublesome and was banished to the sky; how Man procured Fire from the trees it struck; and how Bumba the God called together his best men, appointing tasks to each, making Loko Yima, the only white man, the supreme chief of humanity. Many other African mythologies are similar to this; and in particular it is surprising how many look upon the Supreme Being as a white man. Many early European explorers were to benefit from this, their sudden presence in a village leading the inhabitants to believe instantly that God was come among them. Perhaps this is why we hear so little about mythology from present-day Africans.

As Emil Torday sat listening to Bushongo elders recounting their tribal mythology and history, prompting and correcting each other if they so much as spoke a wrong word, he made a fascinating discovery that strongly suggests that there may be far more validity in oral histories of African peoples than many believe. For he was able, with some certainty, to date the reign of a certain king who lived nearly three hundred years ago. At the time when he made the discovery, the tribal historians were recounting the great events of various reigns.

When, in Torday's words, "we came to the ninety-eighth chief, Bo Kama Bomanchala, they said that nothing remarkable happened during his reign, except that one day at noon the sun went out, and there was absolute darkness for a short time."

Emil Torday's reactions were immediate. "When I heard this I lost all self-control;" he wrote "I jumped up and wanted to do something desperate; the elders thought I had been stung by a scorpion! It was only months later that ... the date of the eclipse became known to me; but I may just as well mention that there was no doubt left that it was the 30 March, 1680, when there was a total eclipse of the sun, passing exactly over Bushongo, the conjunction being at 10.33, Greenwich time, which makes in our longitude, 11.58, two minutes before noon! There was no possibility of confusion with another eclipse, because this was the only one visible in the region during the seventeenth and eighteenth centuries."

The list of Bushongo kings, numbering one hundred and twenty names, with their full titles, takes a tribal historian over forty minutes to recite; and they date back probably eight hundred years to the time of their most famous mortal ancestor, Woto. By far the greatest king, however—and surely one of the most remarkable men that Africa has produced—was the ninety-fourth ruler of the Bushongo, Shamba Bolongongo, who reigned about A.D. 1600. Shamba was the Confucius of the Bushongo, the ultimate in wisdom and knowledge, and creator of parables and epigrams that are quoted to this day.

"A man had two dogs," so Shamba said, "and every day when

he had finished his meal he divided the remains into two equal shares and gave them to his pets. One day he had a bone so big that he could not break it. 'Well, let them gnaw it together,' he said and threw the bone to his dogs. They both went for the bone growling furiously, and soon began to fight over it so viciously that both dogs died from their wounds. Only then did the man see his mistake. Let every dog have his bone, and every woman her husband, and there will be peace in the village."

And again: "Fresh sap collected from a palm tree tastes sweet and has no strength. But day by day its sweetness decreases and the liquor becomes stronger, until at last the wine becomes potent and harsh and devoid of all sweetness. Man is like a palm-wine: sweet youth lacks wisdom, wise old age lacks sweetness of character."

Shamba was a good man. He banned warfare except for self-defence, and laid down laws by which his people should live. Many Bushongo attribute the seventeen "commandments" that are taught to boys in their initiation school to Shamba Bolongongo.

These include such commandments as "To avoid obscene language"; "Not to gamble"; "Not to kill, even in war, but to defend yourself with valour"; "To respect other people's wives"; "To respect women's modesty"; and "If your father's clothes are in disorder, tell him; if your mother's, leave it to your sister to do so; you must not make your mother blush."

The great Shamba travelled far and wide, and brought back many new ideas to his people. He introduced the art of weaving, and taught people to make soft raffia clothing that superseded the ancient bark-cloth. He encouraged arts and crafts in every form: embroidery, metal-working, and above all, wood-carving. Strangely the Bushongo, great craftsmen though they are, do not make any pottery. It is thought that, having become renowned far and wide as woodcarvers, some King forbade them to make pottery lest it detracted from their prowess with wood. (The Bushongo use pots; but all are purchased from neighbouring tribes.) Wood, however, sufficed to provide them with all they needed in the way of boxes, bowls, spoons, and the beautiful cups for which they have become famous. These were the sort of things I was hoping to purchase when I arrived in their country.

I drove first of all not to the administrative centre of the Bushongo country, but to their tribal capital, the Mushenge, a few miles further to the north. I had heard from the hotel-keeper in

Dibaya that this was where most of the Bushongo craftsmen lived. He had advised me also to try to arrange an audience with the present King whom he felt would be able to help me obtain the sort of things I wanted. There was nowhere for me to stay at the Mushenge, so when I arrived I pitched my tent in a copse of giant trees on the edge of the village.

Almost as soon as I started to erect the tent I was surrounded by one of the most unruly gatherings of young Africans that I have ever come across. If the Bushongo are artistic in some respects, they are anything but musical. And the gang of onlookers that came to peer at everything I did would soon have driven me to distraction with their raucous cackling and jabbering had not an old man (obviously of the polite Shamba Bolongongo school) arrived on the scene to rebuke them fiercely and send them home with a barrage of insults and curses for being so rude to a stranger.

By a lucky chance I discovered that this old man spoke both some French and some Swahili. The latter was rare among the Bushongo—in fact he was the only man in the Mushenge whom I heard speaking it—but it was extremely useful; for it welded an immediate link between us of which he was inordinately proud, and he remained with me wherever I went over the next few days, looking upon it as a great privilege to interpret for me.

With the old man's help I was able to arrange to see the King the day after I arrived. I had met numerous tribal chiefs before, in East Africa, but all these had either been such small chiefs as to be unimpressive, or the products of European schools, and thus lacking any of the primitive splendour that I had always associated with powerful tribal overlords. The Bushongo had been one of the last tribes of the Congo who had submitted to European rule, and being immensely proud of their great past, they had continued to live, even into the nineteen-fifties, in the same traditional way as their ancestors. Almost all the older men still dressed in the tribal fashion, and the Mushenge, although many of its houses were dilapidated, was still pervaded with a rich atmosphere of power and pomp. Thus, when I came to visit the King, I did so with some awe and trepidation.

Early in the morning a group of functionaries from the King's palace came down to my tent with my old man to conduct me to the audience chamber. My camp was some way from the palace, necessitating a long walk through the village, down broad streets, past the ornate court-house with its woven cane walls and finely carved verandah posts, and into the palace itself. This consisted of a maze of courtyards, one leading into the next through narrow doors, surrounded by the thatched houses of the King's wives, concubines and courtiers.

We came at last to a small gatehouse where I then had to wait for almost an hour with two of the functionaries who spoke not a word throughout the whole period. Suddenly, as we sat there waiting, an imperious woman with an attendant swept through the gatehouse like a queen. Those with me bowed low, and clapped their hands in obeisance to her; and I was told by my old man that this was one of the royal sisters, a woman of great importance in the land, indeed almost a queen. It seemed that she had wished to talk to the King at short notice, and that it was on her account that we had to wait so long, for now almost immediately we were shown through yet another yard into a dingy little hut which I could not at first believe was the audience chamber. Here I was asked to take a seat; and here we waited for another twenty minutes. Then suddenly there was a commotion outside, and the courtiers in attendance backed obsequiously towards the walls. And with as much grace as he could muster Bopey Mobinj III, Nyimi of the Bushongo, Lukengo of Bakuba, Chembe Kunji, the Lord's own Lieutenant, entered the room and slid deftly into a huge and very rickety chair.

Bopey Mobinj III was a man of enormous stature who weighed nearly twenty-one stone. Upon his head he wore a conical cap held in place by carved wooden pins. His legs, from ankle to knee, were enclosed in huge coils of solid brass. His vast stomach protruded and from well below his navel hung an impressively voluminous kilt with a leopard-skin sporran. The "throne" upon which he now sat was of European make, very cheap, and falling to pieces. Above it, on the wall, hung a gaudy painting, from Port Said or Cairo, and doubtless given to him by a European visitor, of an Arab Sheik sitting upon a camel far out in the desert beneath a virulent blue sky.

Suddenly, face to face with this grotesque mixture of primitive splendour and ersatz junk my vision of the powerful Majesty fell to pieces. Poor Bopey Mobinj. Though there were things about him and his court that were the epitome of power and greatness, in the last resort he was a great big figure of fun. He, whose ancestors held power of life and death over thousands, who were considered so sacred that their feet might never be allowed to touch the ground (God help the slaves who would have had to carry Bopey Mobinj!), descendant of the fabled Shamba Bolongongo, son of warriors feared throughout the Congo—he, the Nyimi of the all-powerful Bushongo, became in an instant no more than a gross shadow, a man deceived by modernity, a mere puppet whose every act was manipulated by a young Belgian sitting a few miles off in an air-conditioned office. Suddenly I felt desperately sorry for him. Here before me was an elderly man who had known the great days of his tribe before the coming of the white man; but the world of his ancestors had been torn to shreds by the "nouveau" ways of foreigners, and as surely as darkness follows the setting of the sun, when Bopey Mobinj died the spirit of the Bushongo would depart from this world forever.

Through my interpreter I now asked the Nyimi if he could help me in my search for Bushongo works of art. The poor old King hardly moved as he spoke, and on his face there was an expression of utter despondency. Though I learned later that he got along well with his European masters, and did all he could to encourage his people to accept European teaching and to go to school, I could not escape the feeling that he was distressed by what he now had to tell me. Today, he said, the only place in which I could buy Bushongo works of art was in the Belgian Government crafts centre a few miles away in Mweka. That is where I should have gone. Was there nothing in the Mushenge, I asked, that I might be able to purchase? "The craftsmen live in the Mushenge, certainly," he replied; "but they send all their work to Mweka as they are not allowed to sell it direct to Europeans in case they ask unfair prices." But then the old King turned to a courtier and muttered something I did not understand. Speaking to me again, he said he would make a special concession as I was interested in the Bushongo crafts, and sell me one or two things from his private collection. And a minute or two later the courtier to whom he had spoken arrived bearing a bundle of woven raffia cloth and a beautifully made knife.

The knife was about sixteen inches long with an unusual leaf-shaped blade called by the Bushongo an "ikula". In the olden days no Bushongo would have been seen without such a knife hanging behind his right hip, and some of the older people can still be seen wearing them even now. Though it is only meant for show, on dark

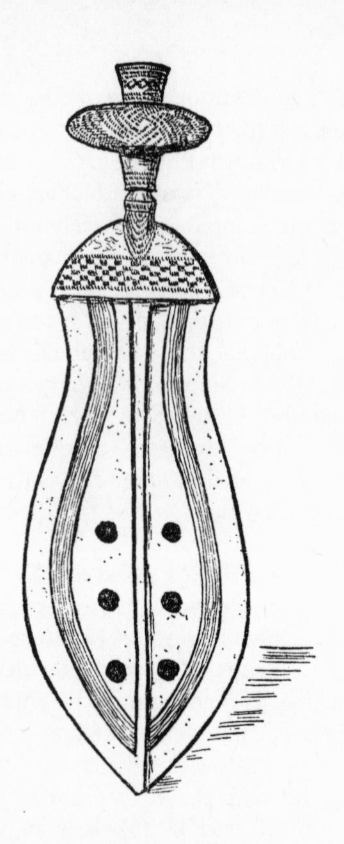

nights the ikula has to be replaced by a wooden replica so as to avoid brawls or accidents. Knives of various types feature prominently in Bushongo culture. The very name of the tribe is taken from a vicious weapon—a four-bladed throwing knife—that was known to fearful neighbours as the "shongo" or "lightning"—hence the Bushongo, the "People of the lightning knife". Three hundred and fifty years ago in Shamba Bolongongo's reign, the shongo was banned along with shields and bows and arrows, and the only weapon of war then allowed to the Bushongo was a knife known as the "ilondo". It was now that I discovered that it was an ilondo that Chief Albert had given me, and that it must be a weapon of considerable antiquity. In Shamba Bolongongo's day no one was allowed to wear the ilondo in peace-time; and when it was transported from place to place it had, by law, to be wrapped carefully in cloth—such was the desire of the mighty Bushongo in ancient times to avoid any act of aggression. It is astonishing that

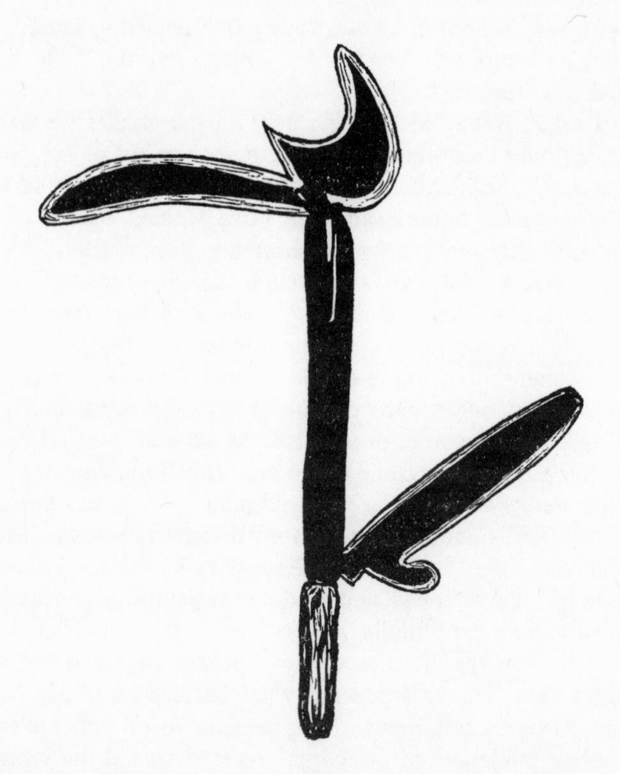

despite their peace-loving nature they held power over such a wide area. But so great were the reprisals that would follow any act of aggression upon one of their people, that it was sufficient, so they say, for a Bushongo merely to state his tribe when travelling in a foreign territory, for people to fall down upon their knees in respect.

The other pieces that Bopey Mobinj now showed me were squares of raffia embroidered like velvet with a soft pile. Embroidery of this type, which is used on dance dresses to this day, once again had its origins in Shamba Bolongongo's time. He himself had brought the art from further west in the Congo. But embroidery had become all the rage when the great King had chosen as one of his wives the most proficient needlewoman in the Mushenge. Later I saw several embroideresses in the village sitting, as at a sewing-bee, beneath the eaves of their houses, chatting whilst they worked. The raffia that they used, red, black, and yellow, had been dyed in natural vegetable dyes, and the traditional designs that they worked, often very beautiful, all had names that related to famous ancestors such as Woto, or other familiar objects like the "wild pine-apple" and the "tortoise".

I asked Bopey Mobinj the price of the articles we were looking at. Without hesitation he quoted the equivalent of five pounds each for the embroidered squares and three pounds for the knife. The knife was an antique and the price seemed reasonable; but the squares were modern and I felt certain he was guilty of overcharging. Later my suspicions were confirmed, but although in retrospect I am sure he expected me to bargain with him, for some reason I felt that to enter into the common practice of haggling, with a King, was somewhat undignified. So I took the easy way out and purchased just one square of embroidery, and the knife, to keep for myself as mementoes of the visit. As we were completing the transaction a messenger came to the door to tell the King that one of his daughters was sick. The poor old man became very perturbed, and with scarcely another glance in my direction he was helped from his chair, and the last I saw of him was as he squeezed his vast frame through the doorway and waddled urgently off across the palace yard to visit his ill child.

That was before the Congo became independent, and often, since then, I have wondered what became of Bopey Mobinj and his powerful but peace-loving people. In all probability the disruptive influences of "freedom" have shattered the remains of his proud empire more convulsively than they have disrupted the less proud, more primitive world of the neighbouring riff-raff.

When Emil Torday first came into Bushongo territory half a century ago he described a village thus:

"Stepping out of a lovely grove of palm trees we faced a long street, at least thirty feet wide, as straight as an arrow. It was bordered by oblong huts, each standing alone at an equal distance from its neighbours; they were all the same shape and differed only in their walls, which were made of mat work ornamented with beautiful designs in black; their conventional patterns varied from house to house. The houses were as spick and span as if they had just been finished; the road was swept clean. Though the day was still hot the village was as busy as a hive. Everybody was working, the looms of weavers were beating, the hammers of smiths clanging, under the shields in the middle of the street men were carving, making mats or baskets, and in front of their houses women were

engaged in embroidery. The very children were bent on some task, some working the smith's bellows, others combing the raffia for the weavers, or making themselves generally useful. The whole place was a picture of peaceful activity."

Fifty years later the description still fitted the Mushenge of the Bushongo well, with the exception that the quality of the housing was now poor in comparison to the beautifully ornate buildings of ancient times. Weavers, needleworkers, smiths and carvers worked peacefully away at their tasks. But today their products were being made less and less for their own use and more and more for sale to tourists. I spent a day or two in the Mushenge just to watch these craftsmen at work—to see, for instance, how they prepared the raffia fronds for weaving by pounding them in troughs of water, then spreading them over the roof-tops to dry, and later splitting them into threads as fine and soft as cotton. I was interested, too, to see some of the traditional techniques of the woodcarvers—how they darkened light wooden objects by burying them in a bog, and how they "sand-papered" them with a certain oily leaf covered in spines like the rough skin of a shark. I had once had a bitter argument with one of my American customers who described in a piece of advertising, how the "primitive tribal Wakambas of Kenya smoothed their carvings with leaves like sand-paper gathered from the forests." This, of course, was utter bunkum about the Wakamba, who used nothing but the best English glass-paper; but I saw now where he had got the idea.

When I left the Mushenge I went directly to Mweka to visit the Belgian Administrator and make arrangements to purchase a consignment of goods for the United States. Most of the objects on sale were copies of traditional work—various initiation masks, and masks of so-called "secret" societies either carved in wood and painted, or made of raffia cloth and ornamented with beads and cowrie shells; half-moon shaped cosmetic boxes to hold powdered red camm-wood for rubbing on the body; cups and bowls of various designs; and effigies of past kings, each one holding his traditional emblems of office—such as Shamba Bolongongo whose emblem was the "Lela" board, a common game in Africa. The work was depressingly clumsy and bad compared with original pieces I had seen in the hotel and museums; and the prices, fixed by the co-operative who ran the shop, were exorbitant. So I spent a day or two going carefully through the stocks selecting the best I could find and packing them into crates scrounged from a local merchant in Mweka. These crates I then stacked into the back of the Land Rover to take them to a shipping agent in the nearest Congo river port, Port Francqui, from there to be shipped to New York.

Whilst in Mweka packing up my purchases I learnt that there would be little point in dallying in the country of the Bapende and the other tribes that live in the vast open grasslands of the Southern Congo through which I would now be passing on my way to Léopoldville. A Belgian ethnographer, Dr. Maesens, had recently spent two years wandering about their country making collections for the Tervuren museum. During those two years he had found some superb pieces of traditional work. However, not only had he had the time to search, but also the authority of the Belgian government behind him, and the wherewithal to pay for interpreters and other money-consuming adjuncts necessary for a successful expedition. Although it seemed from his experience that the traditional arts of the south had not entirely disappeared, it was clear that any trip that I might make would inevitably be uneconomical. I therefore decided, when I left Mweka and the Mushenge, to drive straight across to Léopoldville, a dreadful journey of over 500 miles along bone-shaking roads, through the dull rolling grass plains of the Southern Congo.

The journey was without incident, except for the occasion when I was accused of being a cannibal. The night after I left Mweka, I planned to stay in a remote mission station a little way off the road. The Congolese roads were not well signposted, and I was none too clear where I should turn off. It was already growing dark, so seeing an African bicycling down the road, I stopped to ask him the way. To my surprise he took one look at me, jumped on to his bicycle, and pedalled off as fast as he could in the opposite direction. A bit odd, I thought; but no matter . . . A few miles further on I came into a small village. There were many people around, by the roadside and outside their huts. I drew up, got out, and was going over to the nearest group when with a shout and a scream every single man jack in that village disappeared into the bush. Just one little three-year-old boy stayed behind, who though he sucked his finger and gazed at me benignly, was too small to help.

There was nothing for it but to try again. The next bit of "civilisation" I came to was an oil-nut processing factory. Lights were on, and boilers were burning, so guessing there was a night shift at work I drove up. There was indeed a night shift; about a dozen Africans in overalls clustered round a boiler. I hailed them. They looked at me. They looked again. And . . . oh *no*! . . . they took to their heels and *ran*.

I was getting very frustrated and angry by then. The whole business was totally inexplicable and utterly ridiculous.

I eventually found the mission station, though it was very late, and when I arrived I asked the missionary if he could throw any light on the extraordinary goings-on.

For a moment he looked bewildered; then suddenly he smiled.

"Which sort car you have, Monsieur Read?" he asked in his broken English.

"A long wheel-base Land Rover."

"Ah! that is it, that is it!" he laughed. "Let me explain! This is very funny. Not many weeks ago we had a fellow-Belgian—an artist—who came through here in his Land Rover. He was making portraits, and in the back of his Land Rover he had a bust of an African.

Some Africans saw his car, saw the likeness of their people, and the word went all across the country that the gentleman was coming to capture Africans, cut them up, and sell them as tinned meat. And you, monsieur! You are just another cannibal in a Land Rover!"

Though I had done a fair amount of business in the southern Congo, I was somewhat disappointed in the quantity and quality of the work I had found. The country had been scoured by local collectors, from Emil Torday (who collected most of the superb Congolese material in the British Museum), to such people as my hotelier friend in Dibaya. The old, beautiful, and really valuable pieces were not being replaced, and only in isolated regions were the native craftsmen interested in producing commercial carvings.

CHAPTER FOUR

A Forest of Canoes

I did not intend to spend more time than was necessary in Léopold-ville or its twin city across the Congo, Brazzaville. After several weeks in the bush it would no doubt have been pleasant to while away a few hazy evenings in the chi-chi continental nightclubs of Africa's "petite Bruxelles", or loll back idly sipping Pernod under the gay umbrellas of Brazzaville's "bistros". But these two cities were among the most expensive in Africa and business had not been sufficiently good to allow for such luxuries. Nevertheless I was eventually compelled to remain there for nearly three weeks, as space was not immediately available on any of the river steamers that plied up the Congo river to Stanleyville. So during this enforced stay I endeavoured to do what business I could.

The big cities of Africa are never the best places to buy anything that has come originally from the hands of village craftsmen far out in the bush. Having passed through numerous middlemen en route the prices of the goods are astronomical by the time they reach the gold-lined boulevards of the capital. In Léopoldville this was more noticeable than in any other city I had visited. For some strange reason, despite the latent ability of Congolese craftsmen to create a curio industry of their own, almost all the goods on sale in Léopoldville had either come originally from Nigeria, or been produced by Wakamba carvers in Kenya. And as the hucksters who did the rounds in the hotels and bars were some of the sharpest businessmen in Africa—Hausa traders from the far distant "Soudan"—the prices of most things were far beyond my limits.

There were, however, a few exceptions to this. In a missionary establishment in Brazzaville I unearthed two or three boxes of soft-wood carvings by Bakongo craftsmen making their first tentative exploration of the tourist market. And from the pavements of both Brazzaville and Léopoldville I was able to purchase a large number of locally produced African paintings at the favourable price of two shillings each.

The painting business in this part of Africa had originated in an art school run by a bearded Frenchman named Pierre Lods. Like Laurent Moonens in Elisabethville, Pierre, having scoured the back streets of Brazzaville to find his first few pupils, had unleashed an astonishing explosion of artistic talent. Many of his pupils were artists of the highest order; but most of them were older than their counterparts in Elisabethville, and they had been quick to discover the commercial value of their work. Though they were able to sell their own paintings at high prices, they had, early on, imparted their techniques and ideas to friends and neighbours at home, who had then proceeded to flood the pavements with a hailstorm of cheap reproductions. These street paintings, executed on coloured paper in a spiky style, humming with life and movement, were immediate best-sellers among Europeans. For me they were a godsend, as the mark-up I was able to put on them was more than sufficient to cover my expenses in the twin cities of the Congo. Nevertheless I was thankful when the time came to load the Land Rover on to the river-boat and head once again into the wilder regions of the great Congo forests.

Stanleyville lies a thousand miles from Léopoldville, a journey of six days by steamer. Upstream from Léopoldville the river first passes through open savannah; but soon the grasslands recede and the only sight that meets the eye is the oppressive wall of blue-green jungle that surges down to the water's edge, struggling for light and air. The Congo is a sombre river, deeply mysterious and quiet. When Henry Morton Stanley first paddled down it, the natural savagery of the forests was equalled only by the savagery of the natives he encountered. Seventy years later the people may have been at peace; but on the river itself, nature was still untamed. As we fought our way upstream against the current it seemed that we did so only by the grace of the gods of the forest; that at any moment a clap of thunder and a flash of lightning might signal the end of the truce, and the matted, twisted jungles would bear down on us from all sides and crush us into oblivion. It was powerful and frightening, yet the river was intensely beautiful. Brightly coloured birds flitted low over the water's edge, and in the trees on the banks monkeys chattered as they crashed, unseen, from branch to branch. As the sun set each night it did so with a fierce intensity, deep red and

purple, sharpening the outline of the forest giants, turning the rippling water into pools of blood and fire. Deep in the undergrowth the bullfrogs roared their greeting as the night fell. The cicadas, whose incessant chirruping had stirred the air throughout the day, fell quiet, hushed by the falling darkness. The powerful searchlight of our boat came on, and all through the night swept back and forth across the wall of green, fearful of the spirit of the jungle.

As though the power of Africa alone was not enough, the Congo river was threatened by another encroaching peril. Three years before my journey, an American missionary in some distant station up a remote backwater had brought from the United States a sprig of pretty blue water-hyacinth for his wife's water-garden. In three years, under the tropical sun, that sprig had multiplied beyond imagination until now it formed a menace of colossal magnitude to the Congo. Washed downstream it had lodged beneath every root and branch on the myriad islands and miles of bank, there to multiply and send its offspring floating on towards the sea. Even at that time, so soon after its introduction, it was estimated that it would cost £4,000,000 to clear it, if indeed it could ever be destroyed. In fact it was not destroyed and never will be. Instead, it has spread to other rivers. Its seeds, carried by birds and the wind across the narrow watersheds in the centre of the continent, have found their way to the Zambezi and the Nile. And today it still costs hundreds of thousands of pounds a year to keep these three great waterways clear of the weed and open to navigation.

As we moved upstream we passed many villages large and small. Sometimes we could see a village far ahead, marked by a pillar of dense smoke that rose above the forest from the chimney of an oil-nut factory. With a "whoop . . . whoooop" our sirens would burst on the still air, and the foreshore would thicken with a mottled pattern of faces, black and white, come down to collect their weekly mail, or unload a cargo of beans and flour.

Sometimes men and girls on the banks would hail us and perform a cheerful erotic dance for our pleasure until we passed on out of sight; and sometimes fleets of canoes, black men paddling furiously, would emerge from the jungles and fight their way alongside our boat. Many of these carried traders who came on board with bundles of dried crocodile meat to sell to meat-hungry townsmen upstream.

In one of these fleets of canoes there was a white man. He was big and burly, and at first I took him to be a forester. But when he came on board I found he was a missionary, called John Carrington. He had made a name for himself, not as a Baptist preacher, but a musicologist and linguist whose special study was the drum language of the people around Stanleyville. Like all other traditional arts the drum language was rapidly falling into disuse among young Africans, and John Carrington, himself an expert, was worried that it would soon die out altogether. So with the backing of tribal elders this English missionary held classes every week at which he himself taught the younger generation the secrets of the "talking drum".

There was another use to which John Carrington put his knowledge of the drum language. If, when preaching a sermon, he noticed his congregation dropping off, he would suddenly, without warning, switch to the language of the drums, beating it out on the front of the pulpit. This never failed to captivate his startled congregation with the result that people from all over the jungle flocked to church, if only to hear him preaching in the drum language.

John was a great help to me when we reached Stanleyville, and told me of a number of places in the neighbourhood where I might be able to do some good business. One of the first places he suggested I should visit was a small village called Bengamisa on the banks of the Lindi river north of Stanleyville. Here, he told me, a certain tribe called the Bamanga had, since time immemorial, made chairs of an interesting design, from the sides of old disused canoes. So as soon as the car was unloaded from the boat, I drove north, up a red laterite road that ran for most of the way along the jungle-clad banks of the Lindi.

The chair-makers of Bengamisa, like the carvers of the Bushongo, had been organised into a co-operative by the Belgian Administration, and they worked in a large shed near the centre of the village. It was late evening when I arrived, and the craftsmen were about to go home; but as soon as they saw that I was interested in doing business they stayed for a while to show me the chairs.

The design of the Bengamisa chairs must be unique; they are like solid wooden deck-chairs made of two boards, one of which is slotted through the other. They are not the sort of things that many Europeans would buy, but as this was my only chance to get any, I decided to lay in as large a stock as possible. The price of the chairs had been fixed by the co-operative at £2 each so no time had to be wasted over the somewhat tedious business of bargaining. I asked the head craftsman how many chairs he had in stock. He did not know off-hand, so we went into the store to count them. There were forty-eight. Right, I said. I would have the lot. And I brought out a thick bundle of Congo francs, counted out the equivalent of

£96 and spread it out across a table, saying that I would be back in the morning to pack up the chairs.

The effect on the craftsmen was electric. They were speechless with astonishment. Such a thing as this had never before happened in the whole history of the country. Leaving them gaping with amazement I said good-night and went on my way.

I was spending that night in a mission station about fourteen kilometres up the Lindi. It was a pleasant drive, for the road runs for most of the way along the steep banks that drop away to the river. This was the time of day—when the air was still and the world was at peace—when the drums began to "talk", and as I drove I listened to their familiar sounds. Up and down the river their rhythmic beating echoed . . . te dum, te dum, te te dum, dum dum dum . . . one drum answering the other, relaying the message from village to village.

It took only twenty minutes to reach the mission station where I found none of the missionaries at home. A servant told me that the white men were out working in neighbouring villages and would be gone another hour yet. So whilst I waited I went for a stroll down to the river's edge. It was quiet and beautiful. The Lindi river, a little known tributary several times wider than the Thames, flowed swiftly by, eddying in whirlpools as it leapt over hidden rocks, rushing impatiently on to add its strength to the surging mother Congo. The bullfrogs were already beginning to croak in the undergrowth, and now and again a fish rose from the water with a lethargic plop sending concentric rings scurrying across the surface that were quickly distorted and lost in the surging flow. Suddenly a pale blue heron came gliding downstream low over the water, making idle swoops at shadowy forms beneath the water, and on the far bank a fish-eagle, changing its tree-top perch every few minutes, kept a watchful eye on its hunting grounds below.

The peace was broken by a sound of shouting, and the muffled splash of paddles. Several canoes, from upstream and down, emerged from the overhanging jungles and broke out across the current to the point where I was sitting. When I saw them first, I noticed nothing strange. But suddenly I was alarmed, for all the occupants were carrying spears, enormous spears, with blades two feet long and wider than a hand. Some also carried huge sickles, big as scythes—desperate-looking weapons—and they were heading towards me, shouting. Casually, not wanting to show my fear, I got up and began to stroll back up the path towards the mission. But there, ahead of me, and down the path along by the river my way was blocked by ten or twelve men, each with one of these enormous sickles or spears. I had never seen spears like these. One thrust would have opened a six-inch wound. One swipe of the sickle would have decapitated an ox. Surrounded by these frightening warriors, I stopped and awaited their approach. To my relief they were, all of them, smiling broadly, and their shouts were shouts of greeting, not of anger. They came straight up to me and spoke to me in Swahili. The Bwana wants to buy the native things? Would the Bwana like to buy our spears? Would the Bwana give me ten shillings for a sickle? How many does the Bwana want?

I looked at them incredulous. How on earth did they know I was buying this sort of thing? I had arrived only five minutes before and had not mentioned my business to the servant I had seen, or anyone else. But then it occurred to me. The drums that I had heard as I drove from Bengamisa had been spreading the word throughout the land—"... the white man ... spirit of the forest ... come to buy ... to buy the old old things."

Their spears were not spears of war, but an ancient form of money which, even today, are used for payment of bride-price. A man might give his daughter's hand in marriage for a dozen goats, some beer, a handful of cash and twenty spears. The sickles are used for bride-price, too; but in the olden days they were vicious and effective weapons of war. These things were in demand in the United States both for small museums, and for people who had visited Africa—and perhaps others who had not—to hang on their walls as trophies, and augment collections of weapons. So I bought spears to the value of two and a half wives, and half a wife in sickles.

The drums that had heralded my arrival in Bengamisa are remarkable instruments. Though they are usually referred to as drums, it would be more correct to call them "gongs" or idiophones, for they have no membrane. They are made in sizes varying from a few inches to ten or twelve feet long—sometimes in the form of stylised antelopes—from logs or tree trunks. Along the top of the tree trunk a small slit about two inches wide is cut, and through this the body of the trunk is hollowed out. When the work of hollowing is nearly done, the gong is then tuned to two tones. This is done by making one side of the cavity larger than the other, with a small ridge between them. The parts of the gong in the native language have

names. The ridge that divides the two cavities is the "backbone"; the small cavity is the "female" side, and the large cavity the "male" side. By beating the two lips on either side of the slit, the two tones are obtained.

In this part of Africa (though not everywhere) the method of sending a message is not, as one might expect, like morse code—high high low equalling dot dot dash—but is a language of its own. This language used on the gongs, which can also be spoken if required, is a totally different language to that used in normal conversation. Like most African languages it is "tonal", the voice rising and falling on different syllables—"nalibōgo" (a plantain) for instance is "low low high low"—and message sending is based on this principle. Obviously many words have the same tonal variation, for instance "mzungu" and "Bwana" would both be "high low". This makes the drum language very complicated, as practically everything has to be described and explained. As an example, a certain European nurse was given the drum name "Mama Elandu, ekekedi a koko, usungu lata kumbu, useka samalu, awetshi ambutshimba nyombo", meaning "Mama diseases, hen, white person tearing down fences [referring to the first colonisers who had torn down barriers and made peace among the tribes], she-goat, doctor shaking his gourd of charms." As any white nurse or woman doctor would sound the same, she also had other, more personal names that she was never told! Such names are usually abbreviated, but if the man at the receiving end is a dimwit, there is a full explanation at hand if necessary. Sometimes the meaning is obvious from the context. The words for "fiancée" and "rubbish pit" are the same: the phrase "alambaka boili" means both "he watched the river bank" and "he boiled his mother-in-law", but presumably it is fairly obvious which is intended.

The missionaries with whom I stayed in Bengamisa were an elderly English couple. Like the Womersleys with whom I had stayed in Kamina, they had been in the Congo for over forty years; and like the Womersleys, their house and their mode of life was more English than can be found in England. It seemed strangely incongruous to sit sipping cups of tea listening to the old man as he related stories from their early days in Africa. On their first two tours he and his wife had reached their mission by what was then the easiest route, up the Nile to Juba, and overland through Equatoria. The journey used to take them five months, and involved hazardous treks through country inhabited by cannibals. On one of these journeys the missionary had got to know a certain famous Azande chieftain who sounded a charming character. If any of his subjects sneezed in his presence, they were immediately put to death. There was the occasion, too, when the same chieftain held a great party which lasted several days, and to which chiefs of neighbouring tribes were invited. With a macabre sense of humour, at the climax of the party, the chief announced to his bloated visitors the names of their own tribesmen they had been eating. But the Azande chief was not all evil; he never harmed the missionaries.

The following day I returned to Bengamisa to pack the spears and chairs for shipment to the U.S.A. They were some of the bulkiest items I had had to deal with on this safari, and they presented some problems. Before leaving Stanleyville I had acquired several crates which now had to be broken down and rebuilt around the goods; but even so I eventually had to make two further journeys into the city as I neither had sufficient crates, nor could I transport all the chairs in one load. My routine here was the same as usual. I put the boxes in the hands of a shipping agent in Stanleyville who got them on their way, by devious methods of transport, to their ultimate destination. On items such as these I usually marked up about 100 per cent profit. I made additional charges for packing materials and, in this case, transport from Bengamisa to Stanleyville; but all other freight charges were paid by Al and Nat on arrival in New York. I never knew what the ultimate retail prices were in New York; but when duty had been paid, and allowing for a high retail profit margin my guess is that most goods sold for eight to ten times their original cost.

When I had despatched the spears and chairs there was one other journey I wanted to make while in the Bamanga area. When we had arrived at Stanleyville on the river steamer, John Carrington had taken me to a fishermen's village near the city where I had been fascinated by the canoes used by these Congo tribesmen, and I much wanted to see how they were constructed. When Stanley had passed this way on his famous journey of exploration, he too had been struck by the canoes in this area, and in particular, by their remarkable size. Some, belonging to the Mwana Ntaba, that he had measured, were over eighty-five feet long. But when he encountered the warriors of the middle Congo he noted that "their canoes were much larger than those of the Mwana Ntaba, above the Stanley Falls." He described a memorable river battle thus:

"A monster canoe leads the way, with two rows of upstanding paddlers, forty men on a side, their bodies bending and swaying in unison as with a swelling barbarous chorus they drive her down towards us. In the bow, standing on what appears to be a platform, are ten prime young warriors, their heads gay with feathers; at the stern eight men, with long paddles whose tops are decorated with ivory balls, guide the monster vessel; and dancing up and down from stem to stern are ten men, who appear to be chiefs."

A dugout canoe carrying a hundred and eight people! Even allowing for Stanley's tendency to exaggerate, these canoes were certainly vast, and so they are to this day.

There are two riverain tribes near Stanleyville famous for their canoes and canoemanship: the Baena fishermen who work up and down the rapids below the Stanley Falls; and the Lokele. Many of the Lokele tribesmen live on their canoes permanently, having no other home. They are traders who may be away from their homeland for months at a time, on expeditions that take them hundreds of miles downstream. Their huge canoes are built by the same tribe—the Bamanga—who make the Bengamisa chairs, and it was the canoe-builders whom I now set out to visit.

The canoe-makers' village lay about ten miles into the forest off the road between Bengamisa and Yangambi. Trekking through these giant Congo forests was a fascinating experience. Beneath the massive trees where the sun never penetrated, the air was cool and damp. The path underfoot, a carpet of rotting humus, was soft and easy going. Orchids hung from the trees, and a few large butterflies flitted through the undergrowth; apart from that nothing stirred. My guide and I moved fast along the forest paths, and after two or three hours could hear the distant muffled sounds of chopping, floating through the forest. Ahead of me the guide paused for a moment and told me he thought we ought to let them know we were coming. We were still a long way off, and I wondered how he would do this. If he called to them his words would be lost in the heavy, dank atmosphere, but so far as I could see there was no other way to tell them. Suddenly he broke into a startling song. In a high tenor voice he shouted as loud as he could, and I suddenly realised what he was doing. He was shouting the music of the gongs . . . ya oo, oo oo ya oo, ya oo . . . his voice echoed through the trees. And from the far distance, barely audible, came the reply. "White man . . . spirit of the forest . . . welcome, welcome . . . come to the big tree." We moved on, and guided by the sound of the axes, pushed our way through the undergrowth to where a canoe was being built.

The half-made canoe we saw, though not one of the largest, was big. It was about sixty feet long, and it lay in a jungle clearing where the huge tree had been felled.

Canoe-building is a family affair; the work being done by a man, his wife, and children. The lapse of time between "laying the keel" and launching is three years, and the sequence of events is this: far out in the depths of the forest, many miles from the nearest water, a tree is chosen and felled. There it is left to lie for two years to allow the sap-wood to rot away and the heart-wood to mature. At the beginning of the third year work begins. First the tree is cut to length, then it is levelled off along the top, and the external shape of the canoe is formed. This alone may take several months. When it begins to take shape the task of hollowing out the inside then begins. This is not as simple as one might think. Consider, for a moment, the conditions. The jungle is wet and rain is frequent. If one blindly hacks out the inside anyhow, the canoe will fill with water rapidly, and every morning before work can begin it will be necessary to bale out hundreds of gallons of water. It is therefore hewn out in sections about two feet long with watertight bulkheads between them. In this way the piece being worked on can be baled out in a matter of minutes. Work goes on slowly for several more months until the time comes to chop away the bulkheads, leaving a huge finished canoe lying many miles out in the forest.

While work is in progress, the father spends much of his time visiting Lokele traders, looking for a buyer. He may be lucky, and

find someone who wants a new canoe that year. If not, his canoe will lie in the forest until the next season, filled with water to prevent it cracking. A large canoe costs about seventy pounds, unlaunched. Potential buyers come to look at it whilst it is still being made, and the price is fixed before it is finished.

Now comes the business of launching it, and getting it to the "sea" (as the Bamanga call the Congo river). Before the canoe is finished a track has been cleared through the forest, across which, at intervals of six or seven feet, small lengths of timber have been laid to act as a slipway. These are put in position long before the launching to allow time for them to grow slimy and slippery with decay. At one end of the canoe, on the platform that forms the prow, a hole has been cut, through which the towing "rope" is fixed. The rope is a carefully chosen liana; this, so they say, being preferable to European rope as it does not cut their hands. There is an unwritten law amongst the Bamanga that they help each other at the launching, so sixty or seventy villagers are now called upon, and the monster canoe is hauled to the water. For two or three days the jungle echoes to the sounds of labour, as the builder urges his men on; "Balimatakalimatololo . . . HOO . . . Kimbumimbo . . . HOO . . . Kimbumimbo . . . HOO . . Kimbalamatalo . . . HOO . . . " At last the stream is reached, and the canoe is launched. It may take two more days for it to be floated down to the "sea", and only when it is safely on the Congo does the new owner take over. He has already paid half the price as a deposit; now he pays the rest, plus five or six goats for the villagers who have helped in the launching. And so begins the life of a new canoe that will proudly ply up and down the Congo for the next ten years.

Shortly before leaving East Africa I had had a letter from an American curio dealer with a very strange request—for "anything up to fifty thousand arrowheads". Just how or where he planned to sell these I have no idea; but those in the novelty market seem to be able to sell anything to someone, somehow. Though one can find arrowheads in almost any part of the African continent, to find them in the sort of quantities he required was extremely difficult. Most Africans buy perhaps six or a dozen at a time, use them over and over again, and when out hunting spend a long time looking for them. Whilst in Stanleyville, however, I learned that some of the forest people, who use small expendable arrows for hunting birds, produce them in very large quantities. One place where I was told I could buy them at least by the thousand was a small village called Wamba, not far from Paulis, about three hundred and fifty miles to the north east of Stanleyville. So when I returned from my journey to the canoe-makers I followed the arrows that led to Paulis.

Paulis was then a town of some importance, being the railhead for the whole north-eastern corner of the Congo where it borders

on Uganda and the Sudan. The tribes that live around Paulis consist largely of Bantu people traditionally ruled over by a remarkable group of Nilotic overlords called the Mangbetu. There were a number of things about the Mangbetu that made them, in Belgian times, a big tourist attraction. Their womenfolk, for instance, were famous far and wide as hair-stylists; and they were known also for their peculiar custom carried on until recently, of elongating their heads. This was done in early childhood, when the bone was soft, by binding the cranium tightly in strips of raffia. It was done primarily to enhance their beauty and appeared not to damage their brains in any way. Another interesting thing about the Mangbetu was their women's dress. This consisted of a little grass flap in the front, and a thing called a "negbe" behind. The "negbe" consisted of a flat oval of palm fronds sometimes woven in beautiful designs, so made that when the wearer sat down it automatically folded beneath her bottom providing her with a clean "mat" to sit on. The idea of the "negbe" is thousands of years old and, as can be seen on tomb reliefs, was once used in Egypt. Another thing for which the Mangbetu were well known was their house painting, which reached a far greater degree of sophistication than elsewhere in Africa. Many of the designs used were symbolic representations of the sun and the moon, shields, throwing-knives, and things of that nature; others of more recent origin were of animals and strangely rigid humans.

With the help of the Belgian Administrator of Paulis I had no difficulty in finding the local smiths, a subject people of the Mangbetu, who worked in several small hamlets near the main road to Wamba. Their task was a lowly one, and their products were rough. Their skill in no way compared to that of the Bushongo and Bamanga smiths of old who had produced the knives I had purchased earlier. To beat out a curved sickle blade a yard long, even in width and thickness, requires a degree of skill that even the best smiths in Europe would be proud of. These smiths of Paulis produced dozens of arrowheads an hour which they stored, like hundreds of thousands of coins poured into treasure chests, in old Belgian army ammunition boxes. In the course of the day, wandering from smith to smith. I purchased three thousand of these arrowheads, counted out laboriously one by one, at a cost of a penny each. I was not able to make more than two hundred per cent profit on these, but that covered the cost of my excursion to Paulis.

I was now slowly wending my way home towards East Africa. The road took me by way of the little hamlet of Mungbere to the town of Mambasa in the heart of the great Ituri forest, the home of the Pygmies. The last thirty-five miles of this road, once it crosses the river Dui, follows almost exactly the trail of Stanley's terrible journey from Ihuru to Fort Bodo (Mambasa) on his ridiculous expedition to relieve Emin Pasha in Equatoria. It was here, between the Dui and the Ituri rivers that Stanley came nearer to meeting his death than at any other time on his travels. Harried by bands of Pygmies unseen in the undergrowth; fever ridden, depressed and on quarter rations; it was here that he pitched the famous camp that he called Starvation Camp, where many of his men died.

"On my bed that night," he wrote, "the thought of the men sent to forage for food troubled me; but however distasteful was the idea that a terrible misfortune might befall them—such as being lost in the woods, or collapsing from hunger before they reached the groves—it was impossible not to regard the darkest view and expect the worst, in order, if possible, to save a remnant of the Expedition that the news might be carried to the Pasha and thence to civilisation some day. I pictured the entire column perished here in this camp, and the Pasha wondering month after month what had become of us, and we corrupting and decaying in this unknown corner in the great forest and every blaze on the trees healed up, and every trail obliterated within a year, and our burial place remaining unknown until the end of time.

"All they saw was the eternal myriads of trees with a dead black unknown environing the camp round about, shutting out all hope, and a viewless and stern prospect of rigid wood with a dark cope of leaves burying them out of sky and sunshine, as though they lived under a pall."

The journey took Stanley and his bedraggled, dwindling band of two hundred men twenty days to accomplish, a fact that I pondered deeply as I sped down the road through a rainstorm. Now, only a life-span after the explorer's epic struggle the same journey would take me little more than an hour. And as I pressed my foot on the accelerator I wondered what Stanley would have felt had he been able to cross this desperate forest as rapidly as I, with visions of a steaming hot bath, a whisky and soda, and a comfortable bed awaiting him in Mambasa. The "eternal myriads of trees", the "rigid wood", and the "dark cope of leaves" flashed by like majestic lines of unconcerned, unhindering spectators. I came to a bend—and suddenly, without warning, the Land Rover went into a skid on the slippery, fresh-laid, laterite surface. Slewing sideways, on and on it went, gathering speed towards a six-foot ditch by the side of the road. Vainly I struggled with the wheel and tried to break the skid; but it was no use. With a petrifying crump I hit the back of the ditch; and there I hung, tilted and bent, with the rain beating down upon me, and not a village, not a soul within miles.

I clambered out into the mud to look at the damage. The wing was smashed, the wheels had taken on an alarming squint, and I feared that the chassis might also be cracked. It was already dark and late, and the chances of anyone passing me now were remote. There was only one thing to do; to spend the night in extreme discomfort, curled up on the seat of the car, bruised and wet, and at an acutely painful angle. Damn that whisky and soda, I thought. Damn the jungle, and damn Stanley and his troubles too.

When dawn came no one had passed me. It was still raining, and I was shocked and depressed. This was a little-used road, and it was possible that no one would pass me for hours, or even the whole day and the next night. So I pulled myself together and set about the back-breaking task of trying to get the car back on the road by piling rocks beneath it and jacking it up inch by inch. But just then I heard a low moaning through the forest, an intermittent rumble and roar that grew louder, and suddenly a lorry came round the bend labouring through the mud. The driver stopped, and from the back of the lorry poured twenty hulking Africans who took one look at the car, surrounded it, and lifted it bodily on to the road as though it were a feather. The car could not be driven, so hitching it to the back of the lorry they towed me slowly the remainder of the way to Mambasa. There, to my relief, I discovered that the chassis was intact. The wheels were re-aligned and the wing beaten straight, and I was ready to continue the journey.

I saw a number of Pygmies while passing through the Ituri forest, but there seemed to be little point in spending any time among them. Apart from some of their knives and arrowheads which are wrought in attractive shapes, and their tiny bows which are sheathed with the skins of monkeys' tails, they produce very little of interest either to art dealers or to curio hunters. So leaving the Ituri I came out of the Congo forests for good, and up into the plains. From the business point of view my journey was more or less over, though I bought a few more bits and pieces by the road-side where I could.

Since leaving East Africa I had been able to pay my way from place to place, though the overall profit was small. I had found that some of the traditional arts and crafts were still being prac-tised, though many had died away completely. In many places, where old objects were falling into decay, they were not being replaced; and the quality of modern workmanship, where it existed, rarely matched that of the olden days. I do not know what has happened in the Congo since the Belgians left, but I can only con-jecture that such organisations as the Bushongo craftsmen's co-operative have crumbled. Without the spur of the Belgian Admini-stration I doubt whether the Africans have been able to keep them going. Very few African craftsmen have proved capable of running an export business on their own; language, lack of experience, inability to judge quality, bad packing, and a tendency to over-charge, being the main stumbling blocks. Tourism in the Congo has dropped right away; thus the main local market for commercial work has gone. Oppressed by so many economic, political and other problems it is doubtful whether the artists of the Congo will ever again receive sufficient official encouragement and backing to produce anything of value. The situation among artists and craftsmen was bad enough when the Belgians were there. Today it must be far worse.

And so my safari was done, and a few days later I arrived back in Mombasa. After nearly a year away the inevitable feeling of anti-climax which follows any exciting journey descended on me. But Mombasa was home, and it was good to be back. People in the streets greeted me; familiar faces smiled. It was good to see the sea again; to strip off and plunge into the waves; to hear the hushed wind singing in the casuarinas; and feel the sun-baked grains of sand between my toes. It was good to savour the smells of the Arab town once again, to flirt with laughing girls in purdah, and to see the lights of the big ships in the harbour and to hear their sirens wailing. I no longer had the shop now, but I still had the business. I rented a store-room and carried on as I had left off, buying salad servers by the score, feathered warriors by the thousand, heads and figurines and animals and bowls and stools and drums and more heads and figurines. But my horizons were larger now, and I had other ideas.

In the Congo, amongst many other things, I had been impressed by the art-schools and craftsmen's co-operatives. The Kenya government had once encouraged similar co-operatives among the Kamba carvers, and, indeed, had done much to establish this trade. But apart from that there was absolutely no official encouragement given to the arts in schools, or help for already established artists.

Admittedly, good artists and craftsmen were few and far between in Kenya, but there were some flagrant examples of government disinterest. One of my engineer friends working on the docks came to me one day and told me he had recently taken on an Arab carpenter to construct packing cases and crates. This man claimed to be a woodcarver by profession.

There used to be many Arab woodcarvers on the East African coast who carved the magnificent doorways for the palaces of Zanzibar and Lamu, and did other beautiful work in a similar style. So attractive did rich tourists find their work, in fact, that the export of Arab doors from Zanzibar had to be prohibited; the palaces were being denuded. But so imposing was this Arab workmanship, too, that the Kenya Government had seen fit to install a pair of doors in the new Legislative Council building in

Nairobi, just as the Tanganyika Government had installed Arab doors in the High Court building in Dar-es-Salaam. These had been recently carved in Mombasa at the Muslim Institute.

When I met this maker of packing cases and crates from the docks, I very soon discovered that he was one of the last remaining traditional Arab carvers. Abdulla Ali Skanda, in fact, had done much of the work on the Legislative Council doors and had made the set for Dar-es-Salaam. Since that time the Muslim Institute had had to close its workshop, and Ali, and one other carver, had been forced to find other work. Thus, the Arab craft that over the centuries had given so much to the character of East Africa was now dead; buried, in fact, in a cheap packing case.

This was typical of the general state of affairs of indigenous artists and craftsmen in Kenya. And it struck me that to combat it, two things were needed: first, more interest and opportunity for the arts in the schools, and secondly, an outlet through which indigenous artists and craftsmen could sell their work. Only with this encouragement would there be any hope of releasing any latent artistic talent among the Africans, or developing any appreciation of quality amongst existing artists and craftsmen.

So I launched forth on a one-man campaign. To arouse support for more "art in education" I felt that an exhibition of African child art might be useful. The man to help me here was obviously Laurent Moonens in Elisabethville. He was keen on the idea when I suggested it to him, and he sent me an excellent selection of work from his school. This I exhibited in Mombasa, Nairobi, Nakuru, Kitale, Kampala (and later, in the new art gallery in Salisbury, Southern Rhodesia), and the response was astonishing. Both Africans and Europeans were amazed that African children were capable of such work. We had excellent press notices; and through the exhibition, an entrée into government circles. The Department of Education was interested, and began to take notice of what could be done; though ultimately I fear that active changes in schools policy about art became bogged down in bureaucratic detail.

On the second front, developing an outlet for artists and craftsmen of quality, I had other ideas. My idea was to set up a centre where artists and craftsmen, if their work was good enough, could not only sell their products but also come to work. Abdulla Ali Skanda, and another young Arab carver named Ali Mohamed, were very keen on this idea, and would certainly have formed a good nucleus for the workshop. There were a number of Africans scattered throughout East Africa who would have come, in addition to several of the best Makonde carvers. The whole plan was worked out in detail, and circulated to business firms, farmers known to be interested, and organisations such as the East African High Commission. But government backing, I felt, was essential. The plans were therefore submitted to the Minister concerned, and discussions held. Letters went back and forth by the dozen.

It was quite amazing how much sympathy and encouragement the scheme received from all quarters, including the government. But when it came to the point, were the government prepared to back it? Finally it became clear that in their view support of the arts was not their concern. Though perfectly polite, they could not have cared less.

Had I had a workshop I might have employed Abdulla and Ali myself. But as it turned out, with the idea for the crafts centre rejected, my own plans were shortly to change. And so far as I know, Abdulla and Ali are still making packing cases and crates—unless by now they have joined the curio hucksters in the gutters of Mombasa.

CHAPTER FIVE

The "Big Big House"

For several months life continued in Mombasa as before, as I bought and packed East African curios for export to the United States. But as time went on I grew increasingly restless. My long journey across Africa had done more than provide me with an opportunity for some personal "exploration"—enjoyable though that was—for it had opened my eyes to many aspects of African culture about which I had previously known nothing. Above all, it had made me realise how lightly I was skimming the surface of the subject in which I was interested—African art and ethnography—by confining myself to the narrow bounds of the curio trade. And now an urge began to grow to study the subject on a more serious level—to go to a university, if I could, and take a course in anthropology.

Having no previous academic qualifications, finding a place in a university proved more difficult than I had expected; but after much correspondence I was finally able to sign on for a course in Social Anthropology at University College, London. So in due course, having made an arrangement with some Asian friends to take over my business, I put up my shutters in Mombasa and came back to live in England.

For anyone with an interest in ethnography—and African ethnography in particular—there is no better place to be than in London; for apart from the various private galleries and small museums in the home counties, there is that ever-present pile, the British Museum, where some of the finest collections in the world are housed. From University College it is only a few minutes' walk to the "B.M.", and there I spent many hours in the galleries and libraries. There, too, after a short while, I struck up a friendship with the museum ethnographers. The senior Africanist at the B.M. is a man named Bill Fagg, and through Bill I became acquainted with the work of his brother, Bernard Fagg, who was then the Director of Antiquities for the Nigerian Government.

Nigerians take immense pride in their artistic achievements, and their Government spends tens of thousands of pounds each year on the preservation of important historical and traditional work. This legitimate pride stems from a wealth of artistic tradition that has been developing for as long as maybe three thousand years. Most of the arts of Nigeria—the countless sculptures of the Yoruba and dozens of other tribes—are of relatively recent origin. But behind these lie the great traditions of places like Benin and Ife, whose masterful bronze workers had already achieved a high degree of technical skill as early as the thirteenth century; and the much earlier "Nok" culture whose fascinating pottery heads and figurines may date back to a period between 900 and 200 B.C. These antiquities and works of art are preserved in several museums scattered throughout Nigeria, the largest of which are in Lagos, and Jos—a small town on the high central Nigerian plateau where the Department of Antiquities has its headquarters.

One day I received a letter from Bernard Fagg suggesting that I might like to go out to Nigeria during the long vacation to set up a small museum in the Southern Cameroons. The Southern Cameroons, he told me, was an area rich in sculpture, much of which was in danger of being lost forever if no attempts were made to preserve it. Although I would not receive a salary for this job, all my expenses would be paid by the Nigerian Government, and I stood to gain a great experience that would cost me nothing. Obviously this was an opportunity not to be missed, so I accepted the invitation. And on the first day of the summer vacation I boarded a 'plane that took me across the Sahara to Kano, and on to Jos.

At Jos I was met at the airport by Bernard Fagg, a dark, good-looking chap, and a complete contrast to his learned brother Bill, who even in his appearance reflects the solidarity of the B.M. itself. In the course of the next few days I spent as much time as possible finding out about the area I was to visit, and receiving my instructions from Bernard. My headquarters in the Cameroons were to be in Bamenda, the main town in the high, cool grasslands. There was at the time no special museum building in Bamenda—a fact which presented a slight problem. However, from correspondence with the District Officer, it seemed that there was a building lying empty that might prove suitable, but this I would have to check. I would have plenty of money with which to make purchases, and both still and cine-cameras to make photographic records of dances, and of objects I was unable to buy. A junior assistant from the Jos Museum, named Osula, would accompany me to help with documentation and the technical problems of preservation. A Land Rover would meet us when we arrived in the Cameroons, and would be available for our use throughout our stay. Beyond that, as Bernard put it, I was on my own, and I would just have to do the best I could in the three months available.

"Oh, and one other thing," added Bernard, almost as an afterthought. "We are making you an unofficial agent of Interpol while you are there."

We had been sitting in his office in the Jos museum while he was briefing me, surrounded by sherds and beads and other esoteric archaeological and ethnographic objects, in an atmosphere scarcely appropriate to a remark of this sort, and for a moment I could hardly believe my ears. What on earth could this have to do with setting up a museum, I wondered, and I asked Bernard to explain.

"Well, I can tell you quite briefly," he said. "Recently a number of valuable pieces of sculpture have been missed from our museum at Oron—the sort of pieces that could fetch thousands of pounds on the world market. At first we thought they might have been taken by local people who wanted them as juju; but a short time ago one of them turned up in a gallery in New York, and it became obvious this was no local theft, but the work of an international organisation that really knew its stuff. So we got on to Interpol and asked them to make a check of all known African art dealers in Europe and the United States. One of their agents in Germany paid a call on a woman named Frau K., and reported that she had large collections of sculpture from Nigeria, which she said she had collected herself."

"What's wrong with that?" I said.

"Well, as you know, it's illegal to export works of art from this country without the consent of my department; and we have never heard of this Frau K. Although we've got no proof she was responsible for the Oron thefts, we became a bit suspicious when we heard she was planning another trip to Africa."

"You think she may have agents here, collecting for her?"

"We don't really know. Anyway, Interpol have been keeping their eyes on Frau K. She's in Africa now, and the last we heard was that she was in Brazzaville, about to come north to Nigeria. She's travelling with her son and daughter-in-law in a Volkswagen bus, apparently; and if she's planning to come overland, she must inevitably come through the Cameroons."

"And what do you want me to do?"

"Just keep your eyes and ears open. If you come across them try to find out what they are up to and where they are going. Send us a cable if you hear anything, or, if it seems urgent, cable the C.I.D. in Lagos. Incidentally the agent in Germany managed to get hold of a photograph of her. I've got a copy here." Bernard opened a file on his desk marked "Frau K . . . ", and from a bundle of correspondence took out a photograph and handed it to me. It was of a thick-set, dark-haired woman, who reminded me of a Bavarian hotelier's wife I had known on Kilimanjaro, whom I always pictured with an alpenstock and a rucksack on her back plodding through the high forests—tough as a root. There were probably lots of women like this in the Cameroons—Germans who had come back after the first war when the old colony of Kamerun had been handed over to Britain as a mandated territory—and I felt it was pretty unlikely that we would meet up with her unless we hung around the frontier post for days. But I pocketed the photo, and told Bernard we would do what we could.

Osula and I left Jos the next day, flying down to Lagos first, to buy film for my cine-camera, then straight on to Tiko in the Cameroons.

This was Osula's first experience of flying, and he was very nervous. He was a Bini tribesman from the city of Benin, a little chap in his early twenties, with round features and rather tired eyes. Later, when I came to know him better, I felt he was a nice person, though one of those who feel unduly sorry for themselves if things don't go quite their own way. At the museum in Jos he lived a tidy, comfortable existence, and I don't think he ever really wanted to come on this journey. He was not very adventurous, and longed for nothing more than to be pottering around in the warmth and safety of the museum workshop back home. Later, he was forever searching for excuses that would enable him to stay in Bamenda whilst I went on trek; and before we had left Jos, he had tried hard to persuade Bernard to let him travel to the Cameroons overland, as he didn't like the idea of flying.

It was therefore all the more unfortunate for Osula that the flight to Tiko was about as bad as it could have been. Tiko airport lies at the base of the 13,000-foot Mount Cameroon, the western slopes of which receive about 400 inches of rain a year, one of the highest rainfalls anywhere in the world. This incessant rain, and the clouds that forever hang over the mountain, make Tiko one of Africa's most hazardous airports, and as luck would have it, the day we flew in, it was shrouded in murky grey mist. For ten or fifteen minutes, when we should have landed, our Dakota droned through the clouds, endlessly circling. Inevitably, perhaps, with the huge volcano lurking unseen behind a wall of cloud, there was a feeling of nervous tension and expectancy amongst the passengers that was decidedly unpleasant.

"I hope this guy knows what he's doing," the man next to me said, as we droned through the clouds. "A 'plane flew straight into the mountain a couple of days ago."

Osula, who was sitting in front of me, looked round, his eyes nervously flicking from me to the man who had spoken, and a banana planter across the gangway added a reassuring comment.

"Christ, man, these chaps love the bloody mountain. We'll be the fourth to hit it this year."

I saw Osula fidgeting with his safety belt, tightening it a little bit more. The pilot's voice came over the intercom to say that we would have to land at Douala in the French Cameroons; but as he clicked off, the clouds below us parted. We could see Tiko airport down below, and we came in to land safely. Osula heaved a sigh of relief, but as we climbed down from the 'plane he told me that next time he would positively refuse to fly—and I couldn't help but sympathise with him.

As arranged before leaving Jos, a Land Rover met us at Tiko, and the same day we set off on the two-day journey up to the grasslands, and Bamenda. On our way we spent one night in Mamfe, a town in the low-lying forests of the coastal plains where, in my capacity as Interpol's "man in the Cameroons", I wanted to have a word with the police, as Mamfe lay on the route into Nigeria.

It was late on Saturday night when we arrived, and late the next morning before I was able to meet the police officer, who resolutely refused to have his Sunday morning lie-in disturbed. I told him about Frau K. and her entourage, and showed him the photograph Bernard had given me. His reaction was immediate. He had barely looked at the picture when he let out an excited oath.

"Well I'm damned!" he almost shouted. "I've seen this bitch recently! She was here only a couple of days ago with the other two. Had trouble with the car, and had to put up at the rest-house for the night. That's her all right. Said they were filming, or something, and making recordings for some T.V. outfit. Told me they were going straight from here to Lagos."

There seemed to be no doubt in his mind. But if they were going direct to Lagos it didn't sound as though they were planning to collect any "antiquities"* on the way, and I wondered if we were barking up the wrong tree. Neither of us wanted to chance it, however, so we roused the telegraphist and sent priority cables to C.I.D. Lagos, and to Bernard in Jos.

* An "antiquity" under the Nigerian Antiquities Ordinance covers anything made before 1918 (including many old German buildings), or any artistic or ethnographic object produced for traditional tribal purposes at any time. This means that a dance-mask carved yesterday might be considered an "antiquity".

My part as an Interpol man ended there, almost before it had begun. But brief though it may have been, it proved effective. C.I.D. Lagos contacted all shipping companies and found that Frau K. and Co. were booked out on a ship sailing on Tuesday, two days after our discovery at Mamfe. As no charge could be laid against Frau K. unless she was actually caught in the act of smuggling, the police planned to lie low and watch what went on in the Customs House. But unfortunately, before it ever came to that, things went wrong. When Frau K. went into the shipping office to collect her boat tickets, an over-zealous shipping clerk blithely informed her that the C.I.D. had been enquiring about her.

Realising what was afoot, Frau K. immediately declared everything she had. And what she had was quite astonishing. In three days, passing through Eastern Nigeria, she had somehow managed to pick up fifty crates of articles, the export of which were prohibited under the Antiquities Ordinance. How she had done it was a mystery; but her organisation must have been superb. She had nearly *eight hundred* Ibo and Ibibio masks—more than some experts thought existed in the entire region—and numerous other pieces worth £10,000 or more in the world markets, which must have been gathered for her by African agents in the bush over a period of many months. There was no doubt that she had intended to smuggle them out, as all the crates were carefully labelled "Personal Effects".

Later it transpired that on a previous journey she had taken out an even greater quantity, and that she had done so by bribing a customs official. Though no charge could be laid against her (because she had declared what she had purchased), the Department of Antiquities were determined to see that she didn't get away with this valuable haul, even though the only way they could do this was by purchasing the goods from her at a nominal price that they themselves were able to assess. This they did; and Frau K., to everyone's delight, left Nigeria in high dudgeon, vowing never to return.

I experienced a certain sense of pride that I had played a part in putting an end to this lucrative smuggling racket; but with memories of crossing from Moçambique to Tanganyika with a meagre haul of thirteen crates of masks when I myself was in business, I cursed myself for never having come to this more profitable hunting ground!

When early European travellers named the Guinea coast of Africa "The White Man's Grave", they did so with good reason, for much of West Africa consists of dank, low-lying forest that is oppressive, sombre, and not particularly healthy for Europeans even today. The forests cover the wide coastal plains that extend inland for many miles before gradually giving way to dry, sunburnt savannah, and finally the Sahara desert. Just occasionally, from this unattractive landscape, small areas rise like pimples, not to the great heights of the Ethiopian plateau or the Kenya highlands, but to sufficient altitude to break into the layer of cool air above the humid lowlands. Jos plateau is one such area, and the Cameroon grasslands another. As Osula and I drove up from Mamfe to Bamenda, we climbed gradually, out of the forests, to beautiful, rolling, open hills between three and five thousand feet above sea level, occasionally rising to peaks of seven and eight thousand feet.

Bamenda Station, the administrative centre for the Grasslands, sits on the edge of a cliff, with a glorious view across the rolling hills. Down below, at the foot of the Bamenda escarpment, lies Abakpa Township, the seething, colourful, commercial centre of the area. When we arrived, we went straight up to the Station where, for a few days, we installed ourselves in the rest-house.

As we expected to be almost incessantly on the move during the next few weeks, visiting every corner of the Grasslands, and others besides, I set about making some preliminary preparations as soon as I could. I needed large-scale maps of the area, a good interpreter, and a cook. I had to pay my respects to the District Officer; and also I wanted to meet a Baptist Missionary named Paul Gebauer. Paul was a ball of fire whose tremendous energy belied his age. He had served with the German navy against the British in the first world war but had since become an American citizen. He had been in the Cameroons for years, and knew as much, or more, about the art of the Grasslands as anyone else alive. He himself had an excellent collection and was able to advise me on many of the best hunting grounds, and he was also able to help in finding an interpreter and a cook.

John, the cook, was a cheerful character with a mop of black hair, who had had considerable experience as a cook "on tour". Having once had to look after a District Officer like a king, he meted out the same treatment to me. Everywhere we went, John carried with him a home-made oven, and never a morning passed without him preparing me a steaming hot camp-bath before he woke me up. As, later, I used to get very agitated at the casual way the porters treated my collections, John christened them my "children"; and I returned the compliment by making him chief "nanny" to see they were looked after properly.

My interpreter was one of the finest people I ever met in Africa. His name was Mr. Kisob, known affectionately throughout the Cameroons as Pa Kisob. For many years he had been the senior Government Interpreter, but was now retired. It amused and delighted me the way in which, on arrival at many Fon's palaces, Pa Kisob was given all the honours, and I was relegated to second place. But I think he deserved them. I had tremendous respect and admiration for him myself, and the ultimate success of the whole expedition was very largely due to his knowledge and sound judgement. An interpreter can make or break a job of this sort, and there was never any doubt as to which he did.

Another important question that had to be dealt with as soon as we reached Bamenda was that of the museum building. The District Officer had told us in a letter that there was a vacant building at our disposal. But what was this building? Was it suitable? Even when I asked the D.O. about this I thought I detected a fleeting look of doubt flash beneath his Irish smile.

"Ah, yes," he said, "I hope you will be happy with it. It's a little place up here on the escarpment that's been empty for some time now. It's very secluded and quiet, but it should be very good from the point of view of security. You see, it's the old mortuary."

Well, there are mortuaries and mortuaries. Possibly an old mortuary might make an excellent museum. I just didn't know. But as there seemed to be no alternative building, I felt I should have a look, at least. The D.O. gave me the key, and a messenger to show me the way.

We drove up the road, beyond a row of houses and into a plantation of gum trees. After about half a mile the messenger signalled me to stop by a small track that led off the road into the plantation. We got out of the car, and the messenger pointed into the trees. "In there", he seemed to be saying. "You'll find it if you go in there". I beckoned him to come with me; but he was reluctant, and preferred to stay by the car. So I went into the trees by myself. I had gone a few yards when I noticed over the track an archway of saplings tied together, from the centre of which hung a small brown bundle of rags. I had seen this sort of thing elsewhere in Africa, and wondered if it was what I thought it was, a juju, warning people to keep away. The gum trees were tall and closely packed; the plantation was gloomy and damp. Two or three hundred yards along the track I noticed the building. It was small, very small, with rusty iron on its roof and old grey whitewash flaking from its walls; tall leafy gum trees grew right up against it. I approached along a path overgrown with weeds and turned the key in a rusty lock. The door was swollen with damp, and it scraped with a chilling screech over the concrete floor as I pushed it open. No one had been there for months it seemed. The glass in the windows was broken, and cobwebs, matted and dusty, hung from the corners. There were two rooms; one was empty, and in the centre of the other stood the cold, stark, concrete slab—the resting place of countless bodies now rotting beneath the earth. I looked around. It was vacuous and silent like an empty skull, except for something that lay on a darkened ledge in the corner. I moved over to look, and my fingers closed round a broken rib, and a fragment of blackened cranium.

Secure from robbers I am sure it was; but what would be the use of a museum to which nobody would dare go? The mortuary was out of the question. I returned the key to the District Officer with thanks and wondered where to turn next.

Down in Abakpa there was a Community Hall, built co-operatively by all the tribes of the Grasslands. The hall was bright and large, and had, in addition to the main room, a small library with a few tables and chairs and a collection of educational books. When I visited the hall, it struck me that, although quite a few people used the library, the main room showed no signs of having been used for a long time. Furthermore, it seemed that at some time it may even have been intended as a museum of sorts, for in a corner stood several empty showcases.

I immediately felt that this would be a perfect museum in every respect. It was in the centre of the town and easily accessible to all the local Africans (for whom, after all, the museum was being set up). If security would be more problematical here than in the mortuary, the hall had every other advantage. So I spoke to the secretary and asked if we could call a committee meeting to discuss the possibility of making this into Bamenda's Folk Museum. He

himself thought it an excellent idea, and two or three days later the Committee gathered.

The population of the Grasslands is made up of a large number of small tribes, alike in many respects, but different in others. The tribes are ruled by Paramount Chiefs, or Fons, some of whom, like the Fons of Bafut, Bali and Nsaw, are very powerful, whilst others are little more than figureheads. The Committee consisted of seven Fons from tribes around Bamenda. The Fon of Bafut presided over the meeting, at which the Fons of Mankon, Bamessing, Bamunka, Balikumbat and Babanki were also present. The Fon of Bali sent a representative.

First, through Pa Kisob, I put my case to the assembled chiefs. As they knew, I said, the customs of their country were changing fast. Their children coming from schools were no longer interested in the fine things of the olden days. The juju of days gone by were losing their power; the new juju of the young generation were the books in the library, and the mammy-wagons on the roads.

The Fons nodded agreement.

It would be tragic, I went on, if, in the years to come, the old old things of beauty for which their country had become known across the seas and all round the world, were to be forgotten and lost. In my country—in England—and even in other places in Nigeria, there were many big big houses which we called "museums" in which all the fine old things of our ancestors were kept. In these big big houses they were safe and carefully looked after, and they were the pride and joy of the young people who were able to look at them, and say that these things were the wonderful things made by their forefathers.

Again the Fons nodded their understanding. I went on in similar vein, pointing out how easily the things of their country could be destroyed, how many in fact had already been destroyed by fires, and reminding them of the fact that in modern times the craftsmen among them were more interested in becoming mechanics than woodcarvers or metal casters.

When I had finished, I was asked to leave the room whilst the Fons went into a huddle to discuss it amongst themselves. And then after fifteen or twenty minutes, I was called in to hear the verdict. The Fon of Bafut spoke. They were pleased, he said, that the government were interested in preserving their old old things, and they first wished to express their thanks to the government and to me. They themselves were in agreement with what I had said, and had been worried by the way in which the fine things of their ancestors were disappearing. They were happy that these things could now be collected together and preserved, and they were in agreement that the Abakpa Hall should be the place where they were to be kept.

Thus we acquired the use of the Community Hall as our museum, and with one of the main problems now cleared up, we were free to set about the business of collecting.

The traditional art of the Cameroon Grasslands, like that of other tribal groups of Africa, is distinctive both in form and style. Most of the objects that I set out to collect were made of wood, and these included dance-masks, stools, beds, house-posts, and figurines. The style of this region is bold, though lacking in sophistication. The lines are generally curvaceous, and the effect is bulbous. The artists love to portray people, usually voluptuously; if a woman, heavily pregnant, and if a man, generously endowed with exaggerated sexual organs. Even more, they love animals of every description; "bush-cows" with large horns, elephants with smooth ears and lengthy trunks, leopards, spiders, bats, and monkeys—all executed in a simple, even crude, but powerful way with very little surface decoration.

Apart from woodcarvings I hoped to find many other things such as pipes, some of clay, and others smoked only by "big men"

and Fons, cast in bronze. In some areas the pottery is elaborate and beautiful; while other craftsmen are well known for making finely carved drinking horns.

Having studied the map of the Grasslands carefully, I found it hard to know where to begin. At the meeting at Abakpa I had met most of the Fons from the region around Bamenda with the exception of the Fon of Bali. So I decided, first, to visit him in his palace which lies about twelve miles to the west of Bamenda. I sent a message to the Fon the day before I planned to go, asking if my visit was in order, and he replied that he would look forward to meeting me. I had heard stories about this man, and he sounded an interesting character. He had the reputation of being the most powerful tribal ruler in the Grasslands—and one story I was told seemed to bear this out.

Not long before my arrival, the government had decided to build an airstrip near Bamenda. This was not particularly easy on account of the rolling nature of the land, and the choice of sites was limited But a flat-topped hill belonging to the Fon of Bali was finally chosen. The land was surveyed, and estimates for clearing the field drawn up. But to the horror of the Public Works Department who were to do the job, it was realised that their estimates far exceeded the budget that had been allotted. Furthermore, they calculated that the work would take at least six weeks, and that they would not be able to complete it, as they had hoped, before an impending visit from the Governor.

In desperation, the engineer in charge went to the Fon of Bali to see if he could help in any way, hoping that the Fon might be able to provide some cheap labour. Having heard the situation, the Fon, who was keen to have the airstrip on his land for prestige purposes, agreed to have his own tribesmen do the job, under the engineer's supervision. When asked how long he thought it would take his men, the Fon, after thinking about it for a bit, replied casually: "I should say about two days."

Early one morning the Fon's huge message gong was heard booming across the countryside, calling the tribesmen to work. From far and wide men, women and children streamed into Bali. The Fon's "police" shepherded them up to the hilltop, where they were organised in a long line across the field; and by eight a.m. a huge work-force was assembled and ready. Then the signal was given to begin. With one accord, like a mighty army of ants eating its way across the field, the long line of people moved slowly ahead, ripping out bushes and clumps of tufted grass and levelling earth as they went.

By half past ten that same morning the strip was cleared—the job complete. It was estimated that between five and six thousand of the Fon's subjects had answered his call to work.

The palace of the Fon of Bali is typical of many of those in the Grasslands. Rows of tall buildings with mudded walls and steeply pitched thatched roofs surround a series of courtyards used for different purposes. Old men, with long, coloured, toga-like cloaks and small knitted skull-caps hover around the doorways like vultures keeping a watchful eye on all that goes on; while the Fon's wives—the older ones naked but for a G-string and a coronet of cowrie shells, the younger ones more fully clad—wander in and out giving the palace an air of desultory activity.

When Pa Kisob and I arrived at Bali, we found the Fon seated in the main courtyard, giving audience to a group of vociferous tribesmen. There was obviously a bitter dispute in progress which it was hoped that the Fon might resolve, for two men were involved in a heated argument and looked as though they might at any

moment come to blows. The Fon seemed to be amused by the performance, and sat by, watching them with a broad grin, waiting for them to quieten down. In the meantime we waited at the entrance to the courtyard until he was ready to meet us.

As we stood waiting I noticed that around the verandah surrounding the courtyard were a number of beautifully carved pillars. Paul Gebauer had told me that such pillars were now rare in the Cameroons, and I therefore hoped to obtain several of them for the museum. Generally speaking this wasn't easy, for Fons were naturally reluctant to tear their palaces apart. But these pillars that I saw here were in fact serving no functional purpose. The verandah roof was held up by stout uncarved posts, to which the others had been tied with wire purely for decoration. Seeing this, I was determined somehow to persuade the Fon to let me have one or two.

When the argument in the courtyard was over, the Fon, having seen us waiting, motioned to the rest of the tribesmen to withdraw, and beckoned to us to go over and sit by him. Pa Kisob clapped his hands in obeisance before sitting down, and for a few minutes

he and the Fon chatted together. A servant brought a tall calabash of palm-wine, and as the others talked, I sat in silence sipping the "mimbo", revelling in the primitive splendour about me, allowing my imagination to cast me back to the days when the veil of mystery that enshrouded Africa was being folded back by the first European explorers. I saw myself as a Burton or a Cameron, come to pay my respects to a great and powerful chief who held in his grasp the power of life or death. In spite of my feeling of awe, however, I fear I had upon my face a supercilious smirk as I mentally compared the wonders of civilisation in my homeland to the simple grandeur of the palace about me—a feeling of inevitable superiority, of broader, worldly cognisance, by comparison with these people, whose horizons stretched no more than a few miles over the hills. Pa Kisob and the Fon fell quiet. The Fon motioned to his *chinda* to refill my horn of mimbo, then quietly turned on his throne towards me.

"Well," he said. "How is old London?" I looked up in surprise for I had no idea he spoke English. "London has many memories for me," he went on. "I liked to go to your Harrods—it is a most amazing shop. And your Rolls-Royces are so wonderful—so much better I think than the American Cadillacs. I had a Rolls-Royce in London . . . but no, I must not talk to you of these things. This is not what you have come to see me about. We must get down to business." The Fon had made his point. He was not a man to be trifled with.

With Pa Kisob's help I explained why I had come to see him, giving him much the same rigmarole as I had given the meeting in Abakpa. The Fon was interested, for he took great pride in his antiquities, and immediately he sent a servant into a back chamber to bring out some of his prize pieces to show me. There were several beaded calabashes, and royal stools supported by carved leopards, and by groups of squat men and women, and there was a beautifully cast bronze pipe-bowl in the form of an elephant's head.

I did not want everything—it was not my intention to rob the Fons of all they possessed, but only to acquire a representative collection of the best pieces—however, certain things caught my eye, a stool and the pipe-bowl in particular. Now, by slow and endless argument, I had to persuade the Fon to release them for the museum.

Though most of the works of art in the Cameroons are to be found in the palaces, they do not necessarily belong to the Fon himself. He is their custodian, on behalf of the tribe. Therefore, except on very rare occasions, the Fon himself could not make any decision regarding what should be done with them. Before any piece could be removed from his palace it was necessary to hold a meeting of the tribal counsellors to get their views. I knew what trouble could be caused if the Fon alone made the decision. One young Fon, the Fon of Bamessing, was at that very moment in dire trouble—to such an extent that a large section of his tribe was trying to have him deposed—for having broken his trust and sold certain tribal objects to an American anthropologist. Although in Bali, as elsewhere, the Fon was obliged to defer any decision until he had held a council meeting, it was first necessary to tell him which pieces I was interested in, and to get his personal approval. Though he liked the idea of the museum, he was, like many Fons, reluctant to let any of his own pieces out of his sight. So the business of persuasion was gradual, involving argument after argument as to why he should let me have them.

When we had discussed the pipe and the stool, I mentioned the pillars; and these turned out to be a subject of special interest to him. The pillars were made up of a series of male and female figures standing one above the other. Each figure was different, and each, according to the Fon, told a different story or represented a famous character from the tribe's past. Some of the figures were of men smoking, or riding horses, or climbing trees in search of honey. Another was a gruesome representation of a heavily pregnant woman; she had just been hanged, and a man stood above her clutching the rope that was knotted around her neck. This, I was told, was the wife of a past Fon who was paying the price of adultery with a commoner. But the favourite carving was of a girl named Daiga. Daiga was supposed to have been the beautiful daughter of a great Fon who had lived many years ago. She had married one of the noblemen of Bali, and in due course had delighted everyone by producing twins, and here she was, portrayed for posterity, feeding the twins with palm-wine. The Fon went into ecstasies, and told me many other stories about her; about her charm, her elegance, her ability, her wisdom and her beauty. I must confess that when I looked at the carving—although, to give it its due, it was of some age and weather-beaten—I found it slightly difficult to recognise Daiga's shining qualities. For one thing, for a girl with twins it struck me that Daiga had very small breasts. Admittedly she did hold one arm across her chest, and it was possible that the sculptor had found it difficult to make them any larger, and when I mentioned this to the Fon he dismissed it as being of no importance. Then, moving round to the side, and going down on to my knees to inspect the carving more closely, I suddenly realised to my horror what was wrong. Visible only from my undignified position, from which one could see beneath her skirts, was proof undeniable that Daiga was a man!

The poor Fon: nobody had ever had the courage to tell him. He was so shocked at this painful discovery that, there and then he promised me that, if nothing else, at least I would have Daiga. Eventually I got all the pieces I selected at Bali. On the guarantee that none of them would leave the country, the Fon and his counsellors allowed them to go to the Museum on the basis of a "permanent loan".

The next journey we made was to the country of the Widekum people, an area geographically beyond the limits of the Grassland people, but culturally linked to them. This was a journey to the village of Fontem—or that at least was our intention when we set out from Bamenda. Fontem lies deep in the forests in the rugged mountains near what was then the border of the French Cameroons. To reach it inevitably involved a considerable amount of trekking, and as there were a number of villages in that region that had not previously been explored from an ethnographic point of view, I decided to make this into a longish expedition. The plan was for vehicles to take us and our porters down to a little village called Assong, about forty miles from Bamenda, from where we would trek into the forests visiting whatever villages we found, finally landing up in Fontem. Ten days later the vehicles would meet us at the village of Tali, on the nearest road to Fontem, about a hundred and forty miles from Bamenda.

Pa Kisob did not accompany us on this journey. In the first place I felt it was unfair to ask an old man to come on what looked like being quite a tough trek, and secondly the District Officer had put me in touch with an ex-police sergeant who had spent a number of years in this region and was free to come. This interpreter's name was Martin Assongwet. Martin was only about forty, but he had recently been invalided out of the police and was now out of a job. He spoke English quite well, though nothing like so well as Pa Kisob.

It was easy to tell he had been a policeman by his bearing and general attitude, though frankly I felt then that he had an unpleasant streak in him. He was a bit loud-mouthed; he shouted at people, and hit them if they didn't do as he told them. But, however unlikeable he may have been at times, there is no doubt that he was extremely useful. He was there to interpret for me, and to help me collect; and if only to please me, he pursued his job ruthlessly.

When we arrived at Assong there were thirteen of us; Osula,

John, Martin, myself and nine porters. I was travelling in comfort compared with the rest, with everything including John's kitchen stove. We had with us several crates of beer with which to soften up the village chiefs, and about two hundred pounds worth of silver shillings, weighing nearly half a hundredweight. These and the cameras were carried by myself, Martin and Osula, while John carried the kitchen equipment. The rest of the baggage, which included several tin boxes and rolls of cotton wool in which to pack the more delicate collections such as clay pipes, were carried by the porters.

We set out from Assong in a long line, travelling for the first few hours along narrow paths across the open Grasslands. Soon we came to the top of a hill, and there, stretching away below us and into the distance, we looked out over ridge upon ridge of precipitously steep forest-covered hills, lurking like giant primeval monsters beneath a sinister grey sky.

We descended, and no sooner had we entered the forest than it began to rain. At first it was a light shower, spattering on to the leaves above us, and dripping into the undergrowth beneath. But soon from over the hills an angry rumble of thunder closed in on us; the spattering gave way to a dull drumming, and the heavy dripping became an incessant stream, churning the muddy paths into treacherous slime and obliterating all but the grey forms of the nearest trees. For the rest of that day the rain stayed with us as we slipped and slid up the steep hill paths, wading to our waists through swollen streams that plunged across our path and down into the gloomy valleys below.

In the later afternoon we came to a small hamlet called Bamenji, which consisted of no more than two dozen rather derelict huts. We had not intended to stop there; but all of us were soaked to the skin and tired, so we decided to stay the night. We were greeted by the headman, named Kweti, who was welcoming and hospitable. With a few words of explanation from Martin, two huts were cleared out and put at my disposal, one for my personal use, and one for John and Osula. Martin lodged with Kweti, and the porters found themselves a roof elsewhere.

These forest-dwellers live a poor life in comparison to the people of the Grasslands. Their huts are small and dirty, and the people themselves lack the impressive bearing that gives an air of nobility to the people around Bamenda. Being such a small and derelict

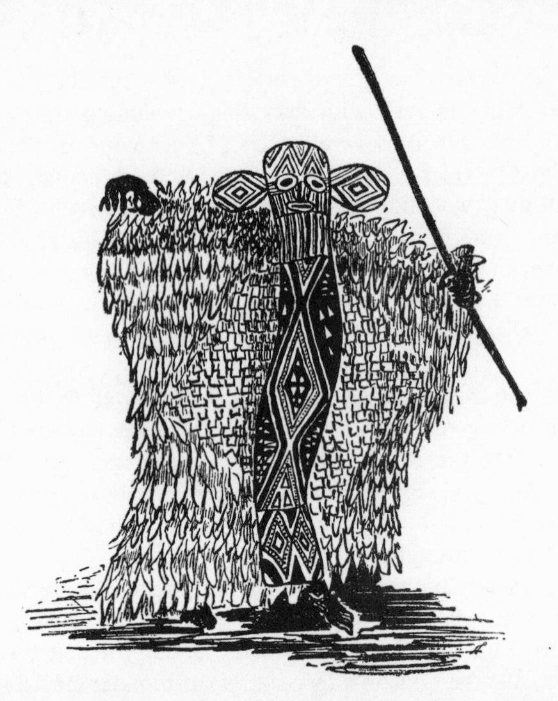

little village, I didn't expect to find many "old old things" in Bamenji. Nevertheless, I thought it was worth getting Martin to make a few enquiries, and it transpired that this insignificant place had one of the largest collections of dance-masks in the district.

These were the masks of the Akambum society, which dances at funerals and other important functions. There are many different societies among the Cameroon tribes, each of which has its own types of masks, and those of the Akambum, made of cloth covered with multi-coloured beads, are perhaps the most dramatic of all the masks in the Cameroons. They represent an elephant, having large ears, and long flaps hanging to the ground fore and aft, the front flap being the trunk. They are worn with magnificent cloaks made of orange, brown and white feathers that completely envelop the dancers. To the people of Bamenji, the "Akambum" masks are a source of income. A short time before my visit—at the inauguration of the Fon of Pinyin, a village several miles away—twenty-four members of the society had been paid seven pounds in cash and given four days of feasting and drinking, in return for dancing at the inaugural ceremony. Generally they were paid in kind, rather than cash—at an average funeral they might receive a fully grown sow, which in the long run might well be worth more than seven pounds.

I wanted to buy a complete Akambum outfit. Kweti, and the other village elders, were quite agreeable, but asked me for the staggering sum of forty-five pounds. My first reaction was to tell them in no mean terms what they could do with it, but when Martin saw me getting indignant he called me to one side. He knew about Akambum, he said, and knew their masks would be expensive. Apparently they were not made at Bamenji, but in a Bamileke* village some miles away in the French Cameroons. He agreed that forty-five pounds was too much, but said we would not be able to get one for much less. We finally agreed on thirty-two pounds for one outfit which was, I discovered later, only about two pounds more than they themselves had paid the maker.

That night we fed off avocado pears, bought at the usual Cameroons price of four for a penny, and a chicken given me by Kweti that John roasted in his portable oven. Kweti had given me the chicken following an episode shortly after our arrival. While our rooms were being cleared out, and our fires being lit, we sat with Kweti in his hut drinking mimbo and drying out by his fire. We had been sitting for some time, not talking much, when Kweti got up from his stool and reached up for a soot-covered bundle that hung from the rafters. I wasn't paying much attention, and thought he was getting a bag of tobacco; but when he had cut the string around the bundle, he unfolded the wings of two large, half-rotted bats.

"I go cook 'um for chop," he said grinning. "You like go chop 'um?"

I said I wouldn't dream of robbing him of his dinner; whereupon he went out and brought me the hen instead.

It was pouring with rain when we went to bed, and still at it when we woke up the next morning. Rivulets of rain ran across the village square as I sat in the entrance to my hut despondently eating my breakfast. Kweti and Martin saw me and came over to talk to me.

"Is the rain going to stop today?" I asked them.

Kweti looked around knowingly before replying. "You watch the chickens," he said eventually. "If the chickens are dancing, then

* An important cultural area of the Grasslands.

the rain will not stop. If they lie under shelter, then it will stop soon."

I looked around for some chickens. There were several bedraggled specimens lying under a pile of wood by Kweti's hut.

"They are lying there," I said. "That's good".

The others didn't reply. They didn't seem to believe the chickens; and sure enough a little while later several of them left their shelter and started to hop about in the rain, pecking at grit and pebbles. The principle, I was told, was that if the chickens thought it was going to stop, they would wait and look for their food in comfort; but if they thought it wasn't going to stop, then they had to scratch for what they could find, regardless of the weather.

The chickens seemed to be right. It rained solidly the whole day. But if the chickens had to eat regardless, so we had to move on regardless if we were going to reach Tali on time. The whole day long, slithering and sloshing through the mud, we plodded on towards a village called Mbechaw.

Mbechaw lay at the foot of a long, very steep escarpment which gave the porters considerable trouble, and as I only had a light load of money-bags and a camera, I went on ahead. Near the bottom I noticed a silent gathering of old men, standing about in the rain in their Sunday best. Not thinking their presence was in any way connected with me, I greeted them, and walked straight on towards the village. But suddenly I realised that they were all following along behind me, so I stopped, and asked one of them what was going on. The old men obviously didn't understand me; but a small schoolboy in their midst spoke for them, slowly and deliberately.

"Father—we—have—come—to—greet—you."

Indeed they had, and it was very moving. The old man whom I had addressed was the village chief, and the others were his counsellors. I was filthy with mud and soaked to the skin, but the circumstances now suddenly called for an assumption of gravity and pomp for which I was scarcely prepared. Doing my best to appear suitably dignified, I went the rest of the way to the village accompanied by this silent band. Apparently they had heard we were coming from some villagers who had passed us earlier. Martin must have told them to warn the chief, but obviously he didn't tell them who I was or what I was doing. The small boy had addressed me as "Father"—I thought simply because I was old enough to be his

father—but now suddenly everyone who spoke to me addressed me as "Father". Realising that I was nothing to do with the Administration, they had concluded that I must be a missionary.

As I have mentioned already, most of the best works of art in the Cameroons are to be found in the palaces of the Fons and chiefs, but here in Mbechaw, by a lucky accident, I was to find one of the most interesting pieces in my entire collection in the house of a commoner.

That night in Mbechaw, accommodation having been arranged for everyone in advance, Martin went to stay with an old man named Bayembi, head of a family of the same name. During the evening, when they were alone in Bayembi's hut, the two of them got talking about our job. Bayembi listened attentively as Martin explained what we were doing, and when he had finished the old man let slip that he had a very fine "old old t'ing" that had been in his family for many years. Martin asked him if he could see it, and the old man, clambering up into the rafters of his house, brought down a beautiful pipe. In all the years he had spent in the Widekum region, Martin had never seen a pipe like this, and he knew immediately that it was something I should see. It was about two feet long with a carved clay bowl, and a wooden stem delicately worked in geometric designs and overlaid with zinc or tin foil, in a way that I have never seen before or since. The bowl itself was geometric, and the whole thing was beautifully proportioned. Martin told Bayembi that he must show me the pipe; but the old

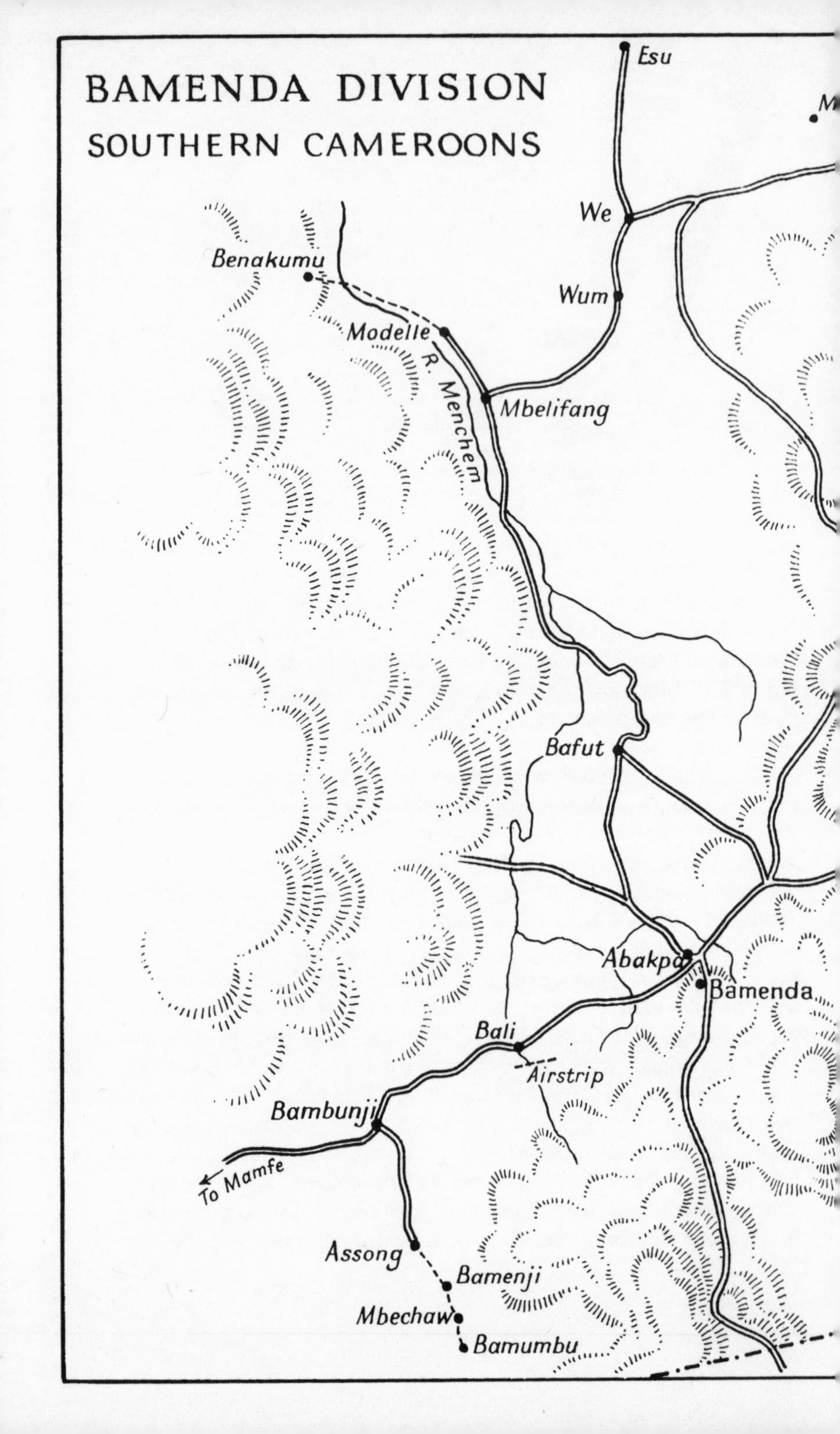

BAMENDA DIVISION
SOUTHERN CAMEROONS
Esu
We
Wum
Benakumu
Modelle
R. Menchem
Mbelifang
Bafut
Abakpa
Bamenda
Bali
Airstrip
Bambunji
To Mamfe
Assong
Bamenji
Mbechaw
Bamumbu

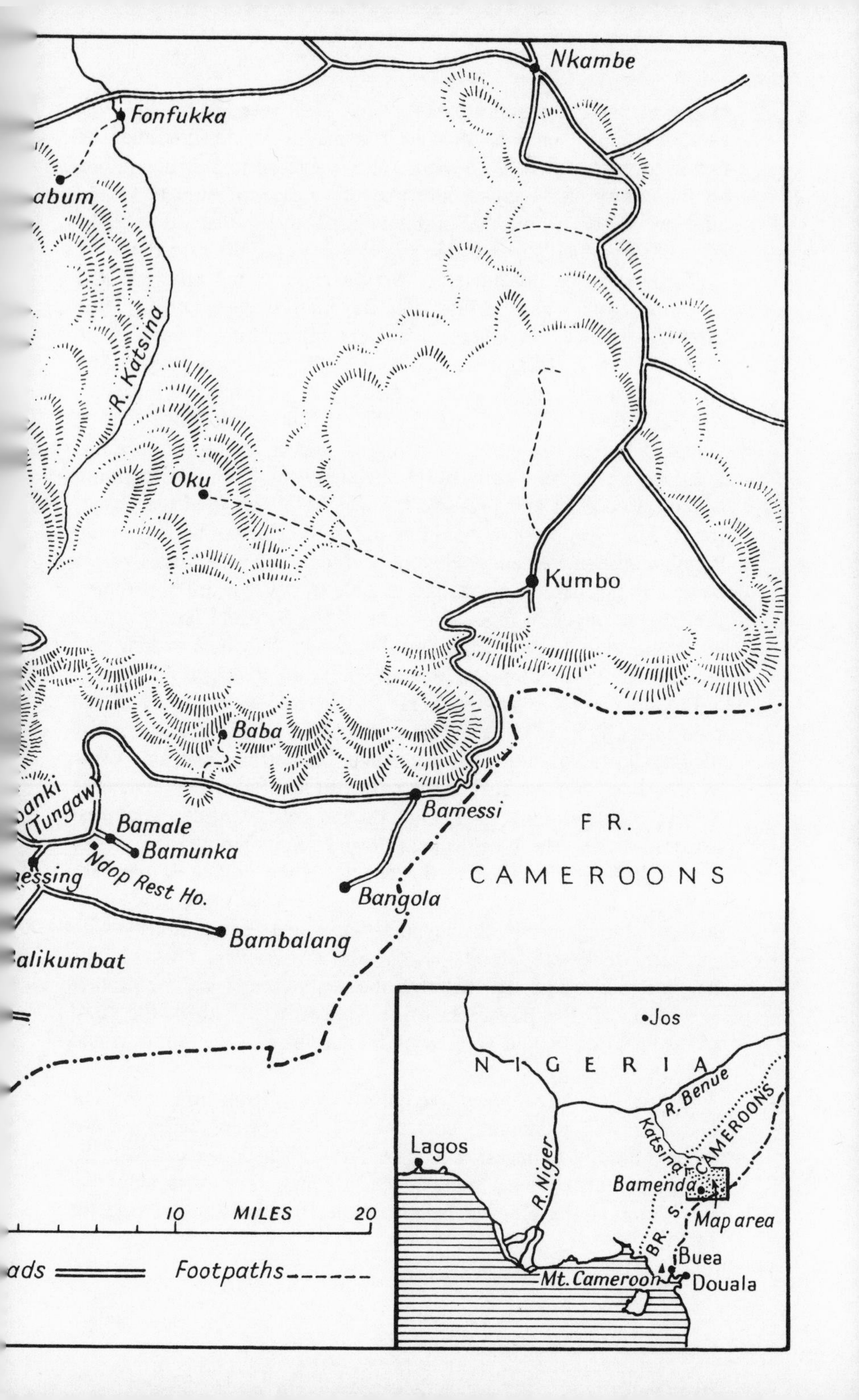
Nkambe
Fonfukka
abum
R. Katsina
Oku
Kumbo
Baba
Bamessi
banki
(Tungaw
Bamale
Bamunka
Ndop Rest Ho.
essing
Bangola
Bambalang
alikumbat
FR.
CAMEROONS
10 MILES 20
ads
Footpaths
Jos
NIGERIA
R. Benue
Katsina
CAMEROONS
BR. S.
Lagos
R. Niger
Bamenda
Map area
Buea
Mt. Cameroon
Douala

man's instinctive reaction was "No!" He seemed to feel immediately that if once he showed it to me, he would ultimately be forced to part with it. So Martin got to work on him, bringing out all the arguments, assuring him that, if he did not want to sell it, all I would do would be to photograph it, and late that night Bayembi was finally persuaded to bring it to me the next day.

Martin came to my hut early, very excited, to tell me what had transpired, and a short while later Bayembi arrived with his pipe carefully wrapped in layers of ancient raffia cloth. I confess, as soon as I saw it, I knew we had to have it, and I was prepared to go to almost any lengths short of robbery to get it into the museum. All that morning we sat discussing the pipe surrounded by absorbed villagers. Martin brought out his biggest and most outrageous guns. I had been sent personally by Her Majesty the Queen of England, he said, to collect and preserve the wonderful things of the Cameroons. The pipe, he said, would be put in the place of honour in the big big house in Bamenda. He and his family for generations would be able to go there to see it, and be able to say that this was theirs, the famous Bayembi pipe. The name of the Bayembi family would go far, not only in the Cameroons, but across the whole wide world. On and on and on he went, mentally battering the poor old man.

But Bayembi was adamant. He in turn told us the story of the pipe, and why he refused to part with it. It was, he said, acquired by his grandfather about ninety years ago, before the white man came to Mbechaw. In payment for the pipe his grandfather had given one of his daughters in marriage. Only on great occasions and at annual celebrations was the pipe brought down from its hiding place, when it was proudly displayed to the people of the village as the very symbol of Bayembi unity. In all its long life it had never once been smoked, though when displayed it was filled ceremoniously with tobacco which was later taken out and given away. This was the tangible and visible link between the old man and his grandfather —between all the Bayembis. If he were to part with it, the spirit of his ancestors would be angry, and the unity of the family would risk destruction.

Martin and I redoubled our efforts. We offered him cash. The old man was indignant; how could he dream of selling it for money. Finally I suggested that he part with it on a basis whereby the government would publicly declare that they were acting as custodians of the pipe on behalf of the Bayembi family; that the pipe still belonged to the family, and in case of dire necessity could be taken out of the museum. Furthermore the government would donate to Bayembi the sum of £15 for the express purpose of purchasing another pipe or similar heirloom. We had been at it for over four hours, and finally we literally wore the old man down physically, and to this last suggestion he agreed, on condition that the money was paid in public so that all the village knew that he was accepting it on behalf of his family, not for himself.

Even at that time I felt that we had been thoroughly brutal to old Bayembi, and that the pressure we had brought to bear on him was more than he might reasonably have been expected to withstand. I often felt the same when making purchases from people obviously reluctant to sell, but, though from a personal point of view I felt sorry for them, I had no compunction about doing everything within my power to get them to change their minds. My justification for this slightly ruthless attitude was borne out later when I visited the palace of the Fon of Nsaw, one of the three great Fons of the Grasslands. Happily, after lengthy discussions and meetings, the Fon finally allowed me to dismantle some rare and valuable door-posts for the museum. Several weeks later his entire palace was destroyed by fire.

Fire has been the main cause of the destruction of the African artistic heritage throughout the centuries. African houses, built of timber, thatched with dry grass, and with open hearth fires inside them, are about the most impermanent type of buildings conceivable. Sooner or later, maybe next year, maybe in fifty years' time, a family's compound or a Fon's palace is almost inevitably going to burn; and unless a miracle happens, many or all the works of art within it are going to be destroyed. Unhappily the favourite medium of artistic expression in Africa has always been wood, with the result that very little of Africa's artistic past has survived.

The oldest piece that I collected in the Cameroons was at the outside limit two hundred years old, probably less. The "throne"-stool of Bangola was such a piece, which according to tradition had been used by seven Fons, each of whom had reigned for twenty-five to thirty years. It was in excellent condition, having been well looked after by a special servant, or "chinda", whose first responsibility was to save it in case of fire. But the "throne" of Bangola was the only antiquity the Fon possessed. Everything else had been destroyed by fire.

Almost everywhere I went there was evidence of this hazard. The palace of the Fon of Bammessing had been burnt down shortly before I arrived, and though many things had been saved, many others not to be replaced were lost. One of the largest and most impressive objects I collected—a seventeen-foot house-post—I had only managed to acquire because it was lying outside the palace of the Fon of Babungo waiting to be rebuilt into a building that had been recently partially destroyed by fire.

Many people believe that termites have been responsible for the destruction of wooden objects, and in some cases this may be true. I collected many pieces that were half eaten by termites, but in each case the object had at some time or other been left out in the bush for several months or more. Termites can be, and usually have been, defeated by the constant care of the "chinda"; but when fire sweeps through the compound at dead of night, nothing can defeat it. It was for this reason, and this reason alone, that I was at times brutally avaricious in my attempts to get certain pieces by almost any means. But the fear and the threat of fire was at the same time their greatest enemy, and my greatest ally in persuading people to part with antiquities.

When we left Mbechaw we set out across some of the wildest forest country I had ever seen to visit the village of Bamumbu. Except for a few breaks during which I had had a chance to film some dances at Mbechaw, the rain had not let up, and as we struggled up the hills to Bamumbu it kept coming steadily down. Osula was morose and complained of a headache; everyone's spirits were low. During the night I began to develop a cough; and in the morning it was still raining.

I was in a dilemma, and did not know quite what to do. If we waited for the rain to stop we might wait for days, yet the prospect of a long trek across the hills to Fontem in this weather was uninviting. Eventually, as it seemed that Bamumbu might be a good collecting ground, I decided to stay there for at least two days, and then see how things went.

In Bamumbu, one of the most interesting things I found was a complete "orchestra" of double iron gongs belonging to a society called "Kwifon". The Kwifon society, found in all the tribes of the Grasslands, is by far the most powerful of all societies, being the Fon's special society to maintain law and order throughout the land.

In several places I visited I was "introduced" to Kwifon's executioner who, though only playing a symbolic role today, still cannot leave the Fon's palace without wearing the terrifying uniform of his profession—a closely woven net cloak that entirely envelops his head and body—and carrying with him the vicious gnarled wooden club that denotes his profession. The symbol of Kwifon everywhere is the double iron gong; but nowhere else did I ever see such an orchestra as the one I found in Bamumbu.

The gongs ranged in size from about ten inches to three feet tall. The complete orchestra consisted of ten gongs of different sizes with, in addition, two tall drums, two grass rattles, and a raucous iron rattle made up of six single gongs that achieved their effect by being banged together with a deafening clatter. The sound of the orchestra was one of the most fantastic I have ever heard, and rhythmically one of the most complex. The rhythm beaten out on each instrument was different; yet the overall effect was one of unity. When playing, the fourteen members of the orchestra stood in a semi-circle so that they could see each other. At the beginning one gong—no. 5—set the pace. With a rhythm that interwove with no. 5's, no. 4 gong then came in, and so on down the line, each player taking his rhythm from the gong next to him, until all ten gongs were playing. Then, each in turn, the two drums came in, adding a deep-throated throb to the hollow boom of the gongs. The drums were countered by the harsh scraping sounds of the wicker rattles; and finally the bundle of single gongs punctuated the whole din with a series of resounding clangs like a thousand blacksmiths at work.

The noise was phenomenal; but this was no wildcat jazz, for each player conformed strictly to well-defined and practised rhythms. The sound of the Kwifon gongs echoing along the forest-clad valley of Bamumbu in the olden days must have been at once the most stirring and the most disturbing that the Fon's subjects could hear, sufficient to instil fear and respect into all but the most black-hearted rogues.

The Kwifon society very rarely plays, and I was lucky to persuade them to do so for me. But when it came to trying to obtain some of the gongs for the museum, it was a different matter. Understandably, as the gongs made up a complete set, and as they were no longer being made, the society were unwilling to part with any. However, by the kindness of the Fon of Bamumbu, we managed to obtain one small gong that was not part of the orchestra.

Our presence in the Widekum forests must have upset the rain gods in no mean way, for after two days at Bamumbu torrential rain was still churning the mountain slopes into torrents of mud. Although we had been away from Assong only five days, we were already two days behind schedule, and none of us relished the idea of the long slimy trek to Fontem, a tough journey even in fine weather. I discussed the situation with Martin, and although he felt that we would be able to reach Tali and rendezvous with our vehicles in five days' time as arranged, we agreed that there was little point in slogging out the journey, as we would have scarcely any time for collecting, and it would therefore be pointless. So we decided, whatever the weather the next day, to head back over our tracks to Assong, and from there get a lift back to Bamenda.

If the outward journey had been uncomfortable, the return journey was thoroughly unpleasant. Osula, who had been complaining of a headache while we were at Bamumbu, now developed a fever, and for most of the journey was on the point of collapse. I, too, began to feel ill and exhausted, and every step became an effort, The wretched porters could hardly keep on their feet in the mire, and, as we had not been able to pack all my "children" in the tin boxes, I was worried about the condition of the rest, which were wrapped, and only partially protected, in coverings of banana leaves.

After two long days we came eventually to Assong, where we tottered into a beer hall, and collapsed exhausted and soaking on rows of grimy wooden benches around the walls. We had been there, I think, about half an hour, when someone at the door said they could hear a vehicle approaching. I went out and stood in the road, and a minute later a Land Rover came round the bend and stopped. Never in my life have I been more thankful to see a familiar face. It was Paul Gebauer. He knew we had gone on the trek to Fontem, and hardly expected to see us here; but he wasted no time in conversation. Taking one look at Osula and me, and telling the others that he would send a lorry from Bamenda to collect them, he bundled us into the car and drove off. The only conversation I remember was when Paul asked if either of us was allergic to penicillin. I said I was, and I remember him muttering an unmissionary-like oath under his breath, adding that we would have to go to Belo. I had no idea what he meant, and didn't care. I was beyond feeling anything.

The next day Osula and I awoke in Belo leper colony sixty miles from Assong to be told that we had bronchial pneumonia. Belo was the only place in the Cameroons where there was any aureomycin, and had we not met Paul we would have been in serious trouble.

CHAPTER SIX

The Alphabet in Bronze

As soon as Osula and I were on our feet again, we made plans for a less strenuous expedition to a part of the Grasslands called the Ndop Plains. Pa Kisob now took over again from Martin Assongwet; and as we expected to make sizeable collections, I hired a second Land Rover and arranged for a three-ton lorry to stand by if necessary, to transport larger pieces. Then we left Bamenda to set up our headquarters in the Ndop rest-house from which we were within easy reach of all parts of the district.

The Ndop plains are inhabited by numerous small tribes, all of whom are closely related, but each of which has its own Fon or chief. Arrangements had to be made, therefore, to visit each one in turn—Babanki, Bamessing, Bamali, Bamunka, Bambalang, Babungo, Bangola, Bamessi, Baba and several others with similar names, some of which were so similar as to become, at times, confusing. In addition to making these arrangements we saw to it that word spread around the country that we were in Ndop, and willing to consider purchasing anything that any commoners might care to bring to the rest-house. This last move was rewarding, and every morning before the cold mist had risen from the valley, we held a market outside the rest-house haggling over a vast assortment of odds and ends which, in the eyes of the business-like people of Ndop were invariably amazingly rare and valuable. (The only truly rare pieces I bought in these markets were a pair of foot-high richly patinated ancestral figures which must have been stolen from a juju house at some time or other. So powerful a juju were they that neither Pa Kisob, John, nor any other Cameroonians apart from the man who sold them would dare touch them. This was the only occasion on which I ever saw a juju fill the Cameroonians with such fear.)

Each village had something different to offer. In Bambalang, for instance, I was fascinated by the enormous main building of the

Fon's palace, the roofs of which drained into a small opening in the middle of the building. Beneath the opening was a grotto-like court with a pebble floor, where the Fon's wives could collect rain-water without having to venture outside. Bamessi was famous for its delicate pottery; Babanki was the supposed home of woodcarving—though when I visited it I found only one old woodcarver. At Babungo it was the Fon himself who was of greater interest—a jolly young fellow of twenty-one who already had thirteen wives and twenty-two children.

The Fons differed greatly in age, power, personality, political status, and wealth, and each one had to be approached in a different way. It was here that Pa Kisob was absolutely invaluable, for after years of interpreting for the Administration he had come to know the quirks of the Fons like the back of his hand. He knew their various jealousies and secret rivalries, and exactly how to play one off against the other. Success with one frequently led to greater success with the next, who refused to be outdone by someone whom he looked upon as being an inferior Fon.

When we came to visit the Fon of Baba, however, Pa Kisob warned me that we might have difficulties. The Fon of Baba, a middle-aged man, was well known as an avaricious and selfish character. He was disliked by most of his neighbours—by some because he had shown himself to be too successful as a businessman, and by others because he was inclined to shun tradition. He

had a very lucrative coffee plantation from which most of his wealth came; and he had built himself a "smart" new house with wooden window frames, a corrugated iron roof, and linoleum on the floor. Probably because he was so unpopular—or was it one of the reasons why no one liked him?—he distrusted everyone, and I was no exception. It was as much as I could do even to arrange a meeting with him, and when we did get together he was at first totally uninterested in the whole museum project.

I would have left Baba without even bothering to argue with the Fon, had it not been for the fact that he possessed one "antique" that I badly wanted. This was an old carved bed that had been used by the Fons of Baba for generations. Such beds as these were at one time quite common in the Cameroons, but today they are extremely rare; and I particularly wanted the one from Baba to complete a collection of "palace" furniture for the museum. At the time I knew of only one other such bed—a beautiful piece belonging to the Fon of Bafut—but this I had already tried, and failed, to obtain.

No amount of explanation or argument seemed to change the Fon's unhelpful attitude, and ultimately only one thing aroused his interest—money. Once it had occurred to him that the bed, together with one or two other pieces I was after, might be worth a considerable amount of money, he changed his tune. And though he suspected his counsellors might well be against him selling anything, he said he would be prepared to let us have the bed without even consulting them—if the price was right. This, as he realised himself, was a risky thing to do. He knew perfectly well that his people might easily accuse him of betraying his trust. And he knew, too, that in their superstitious minds they might look upon such an act as a direct insult to their ancestors. And once the wrath of the ancients was invoked, who could guess what disastrous form of retribution might befall the people of Baba? But to the Fon this was "old hat"; and for the money he was prepared to risk their disapproval.

With most Fons I would have been reluctant to make any agreement on this basis as, with the wretched Fon of Bamessing in mind who had been disowned by half his tribe for having sold ancestral objects and had his palace burnt down in anger, I knew just how much trouble it could cause. But after discussing it with Pa Kisob, we both agreed that we could let this cocksure Fon worry about this problem himself. At least he knew what he was doing, and was aware of the possible complications. So far as I was concerned, it was the bed I wanted to see preserved, not the Fon. So we finally sat down to the prolonged business of bargaining.

The price he initially asked was ridiculous; but finally we beat him down to a round figure of £75 for the bed and several other valuable pieces, and having counted out this sum in shillings, with the miserly chieftain checking every one to see if it was good, we went our way.

I had an engagement in the museum at Abakpa the next day, so, as it was already getting late when we left Baba, Pa Kisob and I drove direct to Bamenda, leaving John and Osula at the Ndop rest-house for the night. In the back of the Land Rover we had the Baba collection, and as we drove through the fading light Pa Kisob and I discussed the Fon, hoping that for our sakes as well as his, his underhand sale of the bed would not lead to any tribal rift or other cataclysmic disaster.

We were approaching the village of Babanki, having gone only about fifteen miles, when we were confronted with a roadside scene that had by now become familiar in the Cameroons—a lorry, slewed across the road, up-ended in the ditch. The accident could only just have happened, for apart from one rather dazed man wandering about the road, and another lying groaning on the grass verge, there was no one else around. We jumped out, and ran over to the man on the ground. He was conscious, but he was obviously in considerable pain; and it looked to me as though he might have broken his leg. Whatever was wrong, he clearly needed hospital treatment, so we cleared the "great bed of Baba" in the back of the Land Rover, and carefully lifted him on to it to take him into Bamenda. His dazed companion came with us, and as we bounced and jolted down the rough road, he sat in the back with the injured man keeping him as comfortable as possible on the hard wooden bed until we reached the hospital.

As one does on these occasions, we felt a certain responsibility for the man, having picked him up, and though the hospital staff now took over, we went inside to have a word with the doctor in case there was any other way in which we could help. The only things the doctor asked us were who he was, and where he came from. But as these were things we hadn't bothered to find out by the roadside, he was now asked.

There had, until that moment, been no possible connection between the lorry and Baba; but as he told us his name, I saw Pa Kisob cock his head in disbelief, and let out a surprised "EH!"

"What's wrong?" I asked him. But Pa Kisob was obviously shaken, and for a moment he didn't reply.

"Well? Who is it?" He turned to me with an ironic but rather frightened grin on his face.

"It's the Fon of Baba's brother!"

"Oh Lord," I thought. "The ancestors are taking their retribution! *Now* what's going to happen?"

But fortunately I think the wretched prince of Baba was far too preoccupied with pain to realise that he was the last of the Babas ever to rest his head upon the family bed. Had he done so, God knows what troubles might have stirred.

We spent ten days in the rest-house at Ndop making a profitable haul; but we had still barely scratched the surface of the Grasslands. Several people in Bamenda told me that I must at some time visit the Fon of Bum, who was said to live in the most beautiful surroundings a few hours' walk from the village of Fonfukka, about seventy miles north of Bamenda. According to Paul Gebauer, the Fon at one time had a fine collection of woodcarvings; but his palace had been burnt down a year or so earlier, and no one in Bamenda knew what had become of the Bum sculpture.

When we left Ndop, therefore, we planned an extensive tour of villages to the north of Bamenda that would bring us finally to Lagabum, the palace of the Fon of Bum. En route we would visit villages with fascinating names like We, Esu, Kuk, Za and Bu; but of all those intermediate stops, those in which we ultimately made the most interesting collections were Isimbi and Wum.

Isimbi was not, strictly speaking, on my beat. It lies in dense forest country similar to that we had visited on our journew to Bamenji, and its people are in no way related to the Grasslanders. But Bernard had asked me to go there if I found a chance, as no one from the Department of Antiquities had hitherto been, and nothing was therefore known of the Isimbi art (if any existed). The people of Isimbi are by far the most primitive of any in the Southern Cameroons, and they had remained unadministered by the colonial government long after any other people in this region. Pa Kisob had been up there only once before, when he had accompanied the first administrative expedition as interpreter; and now he was none too sure what sort of reception we would have. For, on that previous visit many years earlier the Isimbi had proved thoroughly hostile and had, in fact, only agreed to accept British rule under the threat of the rifle.

To reach Isimbi we drove up the dusty road to Bafut, and north to Mbelifang, where we branched off up a Land Rover track to a small village called Modelle about forty miles from Bamenda. Here we spent the night, and the following morning embarked on a half-day trek along the fringes of the Grasslands and into the dank, rain-sodden forests of Benakumu, the main centre of Isimbi. For most of the way the trek was without excitement, and the scenery uninspiring. It had been pouring with rain the day before, and very soon we were soaked with moisture from the waist-high grass that bent over the narrow, muddy, tracks. Then after about three hours we came to a broad river, beyond which the jungle-clad hills of Isimbi rose above us, their tops lost in a blanket of grey clouds.

The river we had arrived at was the Menchem, one of the larger rivers of the Southern Cameroons that drains much of the western part of the Grasslands. We had been following it north the whole way from Bamenda, catching glimpses of it from the road as it poured down deep gorges on its journey to the Katsina and thence into the Benue and the Niger; and often, as I had looked at it, I had wondered how we would get across it to reach Benakumu. It was twenty or thirty yards wide, and after the previous day's rain it was a swollen torrent that hurtled down its course swirling and leaping alarmingly over hidden boulders. Any thought of wading it was absolutely out of the question—one foot in it, and a man would have been whisked away to certain death. But now, as we approached it, I saw that there was a precarious liana suspension bridge stretching between two trees high above the water.

The bridge was a rickety-looking affair with a four-inch wide causeway, and "handrails" on either side. But though it looked a bit primitive I felt sure it was safe, and I had no fears as I swung myself up on to the tree to which it was attached, and jauntily started across. But I had never crossed a bridge of this sort before, and therefore did not know the hazards that are involved. The further I got out into the middle, the more the bridge began to swing from side to side, until when I was about half way across, it was swaying like a giant hammock in a gale.

Then, suddenly, I made a dreadful mistake. I looked down. It happens that I am one of those wretched people who suffer abominably from sea-sickness, vertigo, and any other malady that results from one's sense of balance being disturbed. And to look down in the present circumstances was absolutely catastrophic. To the sensation of swinging was suddenly added the indescribably sick-making sight of the foaming brown water, gurgling and swirling fifteen feet below. Nothing was still; and everything was moving in the wrong direction—except me, who froze solid. But worse than that. Apart from being unable to move, I suddenly began to vomit violently, no doubt gravely polluting the drinking water for miles downstream. I was there for at least five minutes, before being able to take another step; but having to move one way or the other, I eventually forced myself to creep slowly across to the far side.

I thought that such ridiculous effects would probably be experienced only by mollycoddled Europeans such as myself. But when we were all across, we witnessed a very peculiar spectacle. Five or six Isimbi women, naked as the day they were born but for flimsy grass G-strings, had gathered on the far bank, with huge baskets of bananas on their backs that they were taking across to the market at Modelle. Amongst these was a girl of about nineteen or twenty, who must surely have had to cross the Menchem many times before in her life. But now, suddenly—perhaps having watched me in difficulties—she positively refused to go. Despite all efforts of older women to get her on to the bridge, she just stood at the end screaming her head off in terror. This extraordinary spectacle went on for some time, until eventually one of the other women had to carry her across pick-a-back. This looked far more frightening than going across alone; and the screaming did not stop until she was safely landed the other side.

Having crossed the Menchem we trekked through the forests towards Benakumu, passing straggling groups of people on their way down to Modelle. Most of these were women, such as we had seen at the bridge, but amongst them was a young man who caught my eye on account of the strange load slung over his shoulders. This was a bundle consisting of a dozen ancient-looking iron machete blades, which, to judge from their appearance, had never been intended for normal use. It turned out that they were, in fact, money to be used for the same purpose as the heavy-bladed spears that I had collected in the Congo—for payment of bride-price. Pa Kisob and I tried for some time to buy the bundle from the boy. But the acquisition of a buxom little Isimbi sweetheart obviously surpassed any interest in silver shillings, and our efforts were in vain.

Though Benekumu featured in heavy black letters on my map of the Cameroons, it turned out to be a tiny village of dilapidated grass huts—one of the most primitive of any I had seen. Nevertheless, the Isimbi chief was a "shorts and shirt" man who, unlike most of his fellow tribesmen, had been to Bamenda several times, and who had, indeed, recently received a decoration of some sort from the British Government. Just what he had done to warrant Government praise I did not discover; but it meant that he was at that time particularly well disposed towards the British, and I was welcomed into his hut for a horn of filthy beer.

By no stretch of the imagination could the Isimbi people be called artistic, and though we did not go away empty-handed, I could see from the start that Benakumu was no treasure-house of antiquities. Being so close to Bamenda and the Grassland tribes, this total lack of artistry was surprising. But frequently in Africa I am astonished at the illogicality and unpredictability of the patterns of culture contact and the spread of ideas from one tribe to the next. Mostly one finds that ideas (and art styles) have spread to some extent across tribal barriers. At Bamenji we saw how the Widekum people use Bamileke artwork; and all along the western fringe of the Grasslands the art styles mingle with those of the Cross river tribes in the forests to the west. Influence and borrowing has sometimes travelled further still—possibly along with movement of peoples. One can, for instance, detect striking similarities in certain art objects of the Bushongo, a thousand miles to the south-east, to those of the Grasslands. Sometimes, indeed, one can trace influence even further. Iron gongs of the Kwifon type have been found in Southern Rhodesia, nearly two thousand five hundred miles away. Yet in this corner of the Cameroons, it might appear that the primitive people of Isimbi had never heard of their

neighbours in the Grasslands. Such is the strength of African tradition, and the cohesion of small social and religious units, that despite proximity, and the passage of time, people have sometimes been able to live side by side without borrowing a single idea from their neighbours.

Those objects that we collected from the Isimbi chief numbered only two; an ingenious chair made from the forked branches of a tree, undecorated; and an example of the one and only type of juju mask in use by the Isimbi. This consisted of fibre netting that covered most of the body, with a skirt of rustling strips of raffia. Both these pieces were of only ethnographic, rather than artistic interest; all the same, it was possible to feel how awe-inspiring the mask must have been, as the dancer whirled through the trees to the rhythm of the drums.

We spent only an hour or two at Benakumu, returning to Modelle over that terrible bridge the same day. And from Modelle we drove about fifteen miles to Wum where we spent the night. The Chief of Wum was a young man named Chief Ngah, who

dressed in the traditional embroidered robes of the Grassland Fons. He had a number of "old old t'ings" to show us, including several very fine carved wooden face masks. Two of these were of considerable antiquity; but what interested me about them was that they were carved in a style so similar to others I had seen from Fumban, over a hundred miles away in the French Cameroons, for there to be no doubt that they had been made by the same craftsmen. Sponsored, no doubt, by tribal leaders anxious to increase their prestige in remote villages, the manufacturers of juju in times gone by seem to have distributed their wares over wide areas.

I purchased the two masks from Chief Ngah and also a little wooden stool; but one or two other objects he refused to part with. So, for the records, I obtained his permission to photograph these. All my still photography was done with a Retina camera, and Ilford FP3 Film, tropically packed in screw-top canisters. It so happened that I needed to change my film at Wum, and having unwrapped it I threw the empty canister into a corner of the Chief's compound, where I saw a small pile of debris.

The Chief had been watching me change the film, absorbed. But when he saw me throw the canister away he gave a little gasp of disgust and went chasing after it like an excited small boy. Gathering it up, he came running back, and asked Pa Kisob if he could have it. Pa Kisob relayed the question to me, and naturally I said yes. Judging from the Chief's effusive thanks, I might have given him a present worth a small fortune.

Weeks later when I had returned to London I received the following letter written by the Chief's Secretary:

Chief Ngah of Magha,
Aghem-Wum Division
Bamenda Province,
Southern British Cameroons.

Mr. Robert Dick Read,
29 Montpelier Place,
London, S.W.7.

(Written by Chief's Secretary)

My friend,

I refer to your letter which was received here and all the contents were quite understood and the enclosure was also seen. I was very glad to see that you reached your home and still remember me.

I thanked you very much for the picture you sent to me and I hope to visit Bamenda as you mentioned in your above mentioned letter, to see what you have done for Bamenda and the Cameroons.

I should be grateful if you would kindly send to me an empty tin of Ilford F.P. Film just as the empty one you gave me in my Palace. I should wish to have two or three. Your kind action would be appreciated. I trust I shall be happy of your meeting again when you next visit Wum.

May God be with you—and families
Yours very sincerely,
Chief Ngah of Magha.

From Wum we went on to We, and from We to Esu without incident. Then cutting back from Esu to We we joined the main road that took us past Kumfulu and Fungom to Fonfukka. Here we left the car, and Pa Kisob, Osula, John and I, with a local boy to guide us, set off into the hills by foot for Lagabum, the seat of the Fon of Bum.

The walk was delightful, paths leading us through patches of fresh, rain-washed woodland with lichens and mosses hanging from the trees, and out over rolling down-like hills spread with a vivid green carpet of thick tufted grass. On the hill-tops an occasional outcrop of rock broke through like a miniature Dartmoor Tor, and in the valleys the ground underfoot squelched and sprang like a

Connemara bog. The shape of the land, and the vegetation, differed radically from the highlands that I had known in Eastern and Southern Africa, and it was hard to believe we were within a few miles of the steaming Guinea coast jungles, and the fever-ridden swamps of the Niger Delta. As we climbed higher, the view across the seemingly endless Grasslands became more and more impressive. Finally we reached Lagabum, and, unannounced, we wandered into the courtyard of the Fon's palace, which stood alone in splendid isolation high in the hills.

The Fon of Bum was a rotund, jovial character, who appeared delighted to see us. Like the Fon of Bali, he had once been in England, and spoke English well, but unlike him he did not stand on ceremony, and in his presence we immediately felt that we could relax. When we were all seated comfortably on the verandah of the "palace", the Fon called one of his wives, and sent her off to brew a pot of tea. This was brought in on a cheap tin tray, with a plateful of Dad's Cookies—an unexpected luxury so far from home. Now, as we sat round sipping our tea in a terribly English manner, other servants were sent off on different errands. One came back with an enormous bowl of maize meal, enough food for Osula, John, and the guide to live on for a week. Another came back with a ram, a chicken and a dozen eggs for me, which, having been presented, were handed over to John for him to deal with. (We slaughtered the ram for dinner; and the chicken we took home.) After tea I was shown to my room, which, to my amazement, was well decorated with deep indigo blue patterned cloths round the walls, and rush matting on the floor and ceiling. It was furnished with an iron bedstead on which was a mattress, and blankets from Fortnum and Mason; and in the corner was a full-length zinc bath, and a Victorian washstand with a bowl and jug of water.

Lagabum, a thatched paradise high in the cool dew-laden hills, lent itself to the sort of idyllic existence that the Fon obviously enjoyed. He himself was a strange character, something of a mystic and a poet at heart, contented with his isolation, but frustrated by his responsibilities. The gentler things in life held more appeal for him than the problems of power and authority. Generosity and hospitality came naturally to him, and though during our short stay he gave us much, he asked for nothing in return—except that, when we left, I should take his radio back to Bamenda to be repaired, and that when I returned to London I should buy him an inexpensive telescope.

Regrettably—and the Fon regretted it more than anyone else—when his old palace had been burned down, not a single piece from among his woodcarvings had been saved. Now the only ancestral relics with which he was left were a few beaded gourds, and a fine bronze pipe made up of a composite design of frogs, a cow's head, and a human face. But among the Fon's worldly possessions there was one thing of which he was inordinately proud. This was his herd of dwarf cattle. These curious little creatures, *Bos brachyceros*, came originally from Egypt to West Africa thousands of years ago, and have long been highly valued by the noblemen and kings of the Cameroons. In appearance they are not unlike miniature Friesians, three feet high at the shoulders, and they are valued more for their horns than for their creamy milk.

Horns of every shape and size are used in the Cameroons for drinking. Anyone going on a journey will carry with him his horn for a draught of palm-wine in a roadside hamlet when he is thirsty. But horns have more than practical value; for they are, indeed, one of the greatest status symbols of the country. When, later, I visited the people of Nsaw, I was invited to become a member of their Mandjong society, in the old days a society of warriors, but today little more than a hunting and drinking club. However, it was forbidden for me to enter the Mandjong house until first I had acquired a sword and scabbard to wear round my waist, and a horn from which to drink.

In my experience, though there were many horns around, they were among the most difficult things to buy. Frequently they had been handed down from father to son for generations, and people would rather have gone naked than part with their horns. The most commonly used horns are those of ordinary domestic cattle,

often finely carved; but in my collection in the museum I had others made from buffalo, water-buck and kudu. Some were not even made of "horn". I had several made of pottery; one carved in wood; another cast in bronze; yet another made from the horn-shaped tip of a calabash; and one of the best I collected was entirely encased in an elaborate covering of beads. But the finest and most prized of all drinking horns are those of the dwarf cattle. In the olden days, these were considered of such great value that one such horn might change hands for two slaves; and even today, if anyone is willing to part with one, their value is over £10.

The Fon's dwarf herd consisted of six cows and a bull—or thirteen living horns, for one was broken—and these creatures were more dear to him than anything else he possessed. I asked him if I might see them, and no request could have pleased him more. He immediately gave instructions for the herd to be rounded up and brought into the palace yard. We waited almost half an hour, but still there was no sign of them. The Fon asked what was happening and was told that the cows had run into some thick undergrowth in a copse and refused to come out. Several servants were sent to help the herd-boys and we could hear them all shouting and beating the bushes, but the cows defied all efforts to round them up—until finally the Fon himself went out. This rotund, Farmer Giles-like figure, in his long embroidered robes made a comic sight as he stood at the edge of the copse calling to each of his cows by name like a small child calling a litter of reluctant puppies. I was sceptical that he could achieve anything after eight stick-wielding servants had failed to drive them out; but suddenly, one by one, the cows came straggling through the trees, and followed the Fon obediently back to the palace. Here, with evident pride and pleasure, he fed each of them a Dad's Cookie, and allowed them to lick him to their hearts' content. The Fon, it seemed, was the only person of whom the cows took any notice at any time.

Before we left Bum the next day, the Fon presented us with one rare mini-horn to add to our collection. I tried also to persuade him to let us take care of his bronze pipe for him, but as this was almost his last ancestral piece, and as it was bronze and therefore not easily destroyed, I did not press him too hard, and he preferred to keep it.

I have mentioned several bronze pieces that we found in the

Cameroons. The art of bronze casting in West Africa is usually associated with the famous city of Benin, and the more ancient city of Ife in Western Nigeria. Bronze casting, however, was practised throughout the Guinea coast at one time, from the Côte d'Ivoire in the west, to the Gabon just north of the Congo river. The method of casting used in West Africa is called "cire perdue" or "lost wax", and is the same as that practised in the European Bronze Age, and in ancient Egypt, India, China and Peru. Some of the casters in West Africa achieved an astonishing degree of technical skill, especially in Nigeria where some old castings of human figures nearly three feet tall and others made long before Europeans came to Africa are only about a millimetre in thickness throughout.

The Cameroons was never particularly famous for its bronze work, although the art was doubtless practised there for a good many years, until modern times. So far as I could discover there was only one small group of craftsmen (who worked in brass rather than bronze) still in existence; and they were living and working just outside Bamenda. So, soon after I returned from Bum, I went to watch them at work.

They worked as a team, and their products were extremely rough, being produced these days essentially for tourists. When I arrived they were making pipes. In one corner of the workshop two young boys were making models in clay, roughly the shape of the pipe-bowls ultimately to be produced. Over each "core", as the rough model is called, the master-craftsman moulded a thin layer of beeswax, in which, with a variety of small knives, he sculpted the final image of the pipe—in this case, an elephant's head. When this was done the core with its wax overlay was moved on to the next stage. Here, another craftsman painted it with several layers of liquid clay—liquid so as to run into every cranny—thus making a precise cast of the wax image. Now, one or two nails were driven right through the wax into the central core, to hold it firmly in place when the wax was later melted out. Before the "slip" was completely dry more clay was applied, until the whole piece was entirely encased in a large ball of clay, except for two holes at the bottom from which two rods of beeswax protruded from the wax pipe inside. Now the whole thing was fired, and as it grew hot the wax melted and ran out, leaving a cavity inside, the shape of the pipe; and into this cavity was poured molten brass heated to a temperature of about 1150 degrees centigrade. When the casting had cooled off and solidified, the clay was broken away, and the interior core scraped out, leaving the finished brass pipe identical to the wax model.

In the olden days the craftsmen would have had to do no more than file away the "rods" that had formed the channels through which the metal was poured, such was their skill. But today, with castings being turned out cheaply and quickly with little heed to the finer details, they were more often than not rough and in need of a considerable amount of work with a file before being put on sale.

In parts of West Africa (Ashanti in Ghana) there was an amusing variation on the "lost wax" theme, which has become known as the "lost beetle" process. In this, a dead beetle, or any other natural combustible object, was used instead of the wax image. Having been encased in clay, the beetle was then burnt out at a very high temperature leaving a beetle-shaped cavity into which the metal was poured just as in the lost wax casting.

Perhaps the most extraordinary of all feats of bronze-casting in Africa, at any time, was the manufacture of a complete set of type for a printing press to print an indigenous African form of writing. The criticism often heard, that Africans never had a written language of their own, is by no means true. Had it not been that Europeans colonised Africa when they did, written African languages might well be in widespread use by now. But sadly for Africa, those that did exist before Europeans arrived with the presses and more advanced form of writing were nipped in the bud hardly before they had had a chance to become established. Two such written languages existed before the beginning of the colonial era; that of the Vai tribe in Liberia; and that of one of the greatest of the Grassland tribes, the Bamum, who at the time of my visit lived in what was then the French Cameroons.

Though the Bamum themselves freely admit that the original idea of writing came from the Arab world—several Muslim books having been brought to their country by Hausa traders—their script bore no relation whatsoever to Arabic or any other type of writing. The man responsible for the Bamum script was their extraordinary young King, Njoya, who is said to have received the initial inspiration in a dream. This was in 1895, six years before the first Europeans came to Bamum. In his dream he was told to call together all his noblemen and courtiers and get each of them to design a series of symbols to represent different words and ideas. From the symbols thus amassed he then himself devised the first Bamum "alphabet", known to his people as "the Book".

The "Book" consisted of 510 symbols (including ten numerals), many of which had fairly obvious meanings, being pictographic or ideographic. A few examples are shown in the illustration.

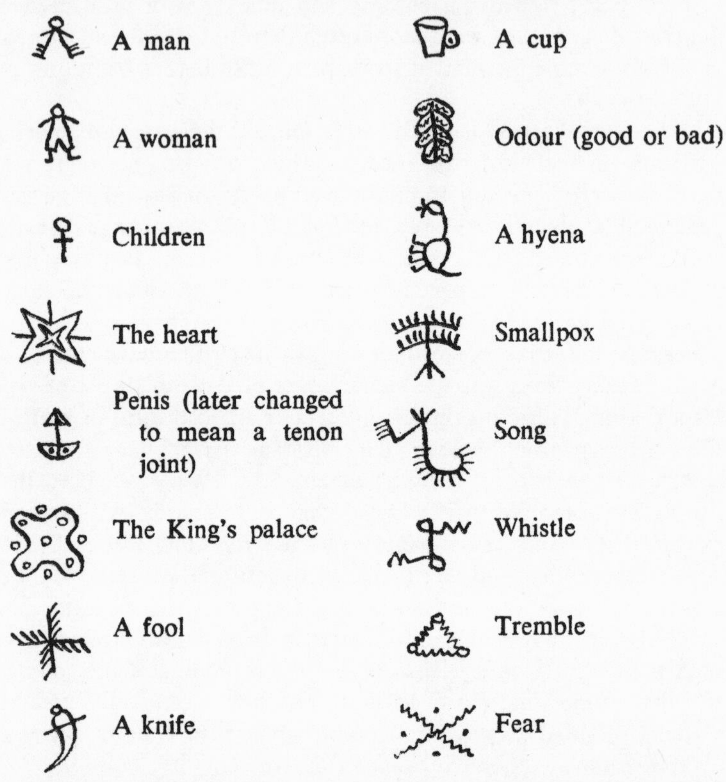

Over the next twenty years Njoya set out to simplify "the Book", producing altogether seven versions; the one that finally came into general use being known as the "New Alphabet". In this, the pictographic and ideographic aspects of "the Book" had been replaced by a system in which each symbol represented a sound. This from every point of view, was a far more advanced type of script, though strictly speaking it was a syllabary rather than an alphabet. It consisted of over eighty characters and is shown in the illustration.

King Njoya himself taught the writing in schools set up specially for the purpose. The materials used originally consisted of wooden boards or specially prepared bark on which the characters were written in charcoal or ink made from a liana. In the early days it was used mainly for recording court cases, or sending messages; but at about the time that the Germans occupied Bamum the first of several major works made its appearance. This was the *Complete History and Customs of the Bamum,* written on cheap lined paper purchased from the first German trader in the area, which ran to 1190 pages in the Royal edition. The "History" was followed by a book on Bamum religion, and a highly popular best-seller on tribal medicine and pharmacopoeia. There is also a "map" of Bamum territory, in which the Palace seems to cover about one-tenth of the whole area!

In 1913 Njoya had an idea that might have had resounding consequences; he decided to set up a Bamum printing press of his own. Calling in his master bronze-caster, a poor man named Monliper Njimonjap, experiments were made until perfect type could be cast in the cire perdue method. And Monliper got to work on a project that was to take him seven long years to complete.

In 1920 all was ready for the production of the first Bamum printed book, in their own language, with their own type, and on a press designed by themselves. But alas, at that time, Njoya, a temperamental genius, was in the throes of dreadful arguments with the post-war French administration. These troubles had put Njoya into a mood of deep depression. And one day, suddenly bursting into a fit of uncontrollable anger, the King descended upon poor Monliper's workshop and callously destroyed the press, the type, and seven years of Monliper's life. So ended, tragically, a feat of invention unequalled in the history of the African continent; one that, had it come a hundred years earlier, might well have flowered and spread far and wide. The Bamum script, handwritten, remained in use for many years, until after the second world war. But today, if it has not died completely, it is nearly forgotten, having been superseded by the roman alphabet.

For ten weeks, with Osula, John, and one or other of the interpreters, I roamed the Cameroons, sometimes driving to villages, sometimes trekking for hours or even days over the open rolling hills to visit a distant palace or hamlet. Wherever we went we were greeted as equals and treated accordingly by the refreshingly easy-going country people. "Hallo Whiteman!" the children would call with unselfconscious recognition of our differences; and giggle with delight when I called back to them "Hallo Blackboys!"—words which would cause a riot in the befuddled lands of Kenya or Rhodesia. We were everywhere looked after well, given food, and sometimes massive celebrations with dancing and drinking, presided over by the Fon. Only rarely were there difficulties, as at Baba, though sometimes we had to pay heavily for objects of special value. On the other hand Fons, either naturally generous or valuing the prestige to be gained from such a move, sometimes gave or lent things to the museum with no financial inducement.

At the end of this period we had over four hundred pieces large and small, piled up in the Community Hall at Abakpa. And now began the tedious business of documenting, numbering, and photographing each piece, and finally setting up the display. Bearing in mind that we were making this museum for the people of the Cameroons—a Folk Museum—I wanted to display as large and representative a selection of pieces as possible. But obviously it was not possible to show everything, and boxes had to be specially constructed in which to store the remainder.

Often while I was setting the museum up I found myself marvelling at the astonishing variety of things we had found. Though in any single village or palace this variety was not always apparent, when everything was collected together it was clear that the material culture of these African people had, in the past, been quite as complex as that of rural Europe in the nineteenth century and a good deal more grandiose.

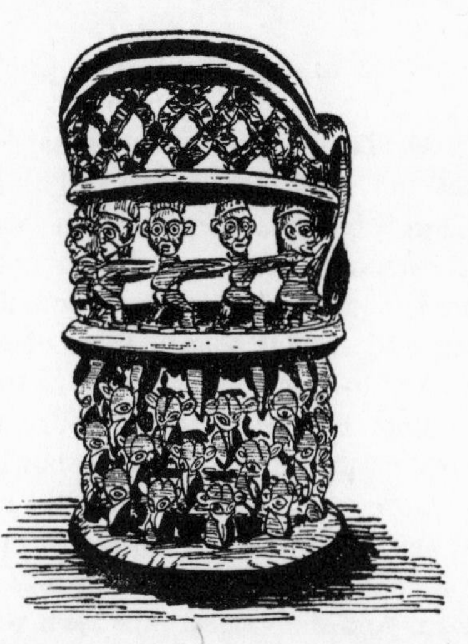

I tried, where possible, to give the museum the feeling of a single richly furnished house. In the centre of the room, as though holding up the roof of the house, we erected the massive seventeen-foot carved house-post we had collected at Babungo. Around this, on low stands, was arrayed a collection of palace furniture—the Baba bed; numerous stools ranging in size from a foot to three feet high; a high-backed, elaborately carved chair purchased from Baba together with the bed; and the reclining wooden chair from Isimbi. In the corners of the room, on simple wooden dummies, were examples of the voluminous embroidered robes worn by different Fons; and near them were displayed blankets, and ornate "batik" drapes such as had decorated the walls of Lagabum.

As with most African art, the finest pieces in the Cameroons were those associated with male societies, and men in general. It was hard, for example, to display examples of women's clothing, for in the olden days the wives of the Fon, who may have numbered two or three hundred, went around naked but for a few coils of leather or bark-cloth, reddened with powdered camm-wood, slung around their bellies. Just occasionally on special occasions they might have worn small beaded "cache-sexe" fore and aft that swung provocatively from side to side as they walked through the palace yard; and a few of these were given a place of prominence in the museum. Other things that entered into the lives of the women were kitchen utensils. These included many elaborate and beautiful pots from Bamessi in the Ndop plains that would have done justice to any *avant-garde* Chelsea kitchen. They varied in size, design, and purpose, being used for storing, cooking and serving food. Then there were spoons, ladles, and knives of various shapes and sizes—though no forks—as elsewhere in Africa, so in the Cameroons, the Fons eat with their fingers.

Of personal articles we had a good selection. There was, for instance, a small leather bag containing six Y-shaped iron razor blades, and several combs, some of which were attractively decorated. And the pipe rack was a thing to marvel at. All the pipes were larger than European pipes, though their design and size was of limitless variety. Some had twin bowls that could only be used by men whose wives had presented them with twins. The largest and finest pipe-bowl was a superbly cast bronze fish that curled upwards with its huge mouth open and ready to receive a vast quantity of tobacco. And the longest pipe stem was well over six feet in length —which conjured up delightful pictures of a proud nobleman seated upon his stool with a young wife squatting before him, tending to the pipe. For tobacco there was a selection of ornamented wooden bowls, some supported by stumpy caryatids, one with a rather stupid looking duck for a handle on the lid. The tobacco would normally have been lit with an ember from the kitchen fire; but failing this there was a small leather pouch with compartments containing several flints, a couple of iron strikers, and some tinder, from which a flame could be obtained in a matter of seconds.

There were liquid containers of every conceivable sort. From

Mandjong houses where the men gather to drink, we had collected several enormous beer bins, each holding ten or twenty gallons. Three of these were carved from wood; but the largest, which stood about four feet high on its decorated wooden stand was of pottery, from We. From the forest areas we had other beer bins woven in grass, waterproofed with resin, and decorated with cowrie shells; and yet others made from bark. Apart from all the drinking horns, there were also pottery mugs with handles for drinking beer. And there were colourful bead-covered gourds for palm-wine, one of which we displayed—as it might be seen in a Fon's palace—being held by a stiff wooden "chinda", or servant, who stood about three feet high.

Then there were ancient weapons of war—spears, shields, cutlasses, and bows and arrows. These were displayed high up on the

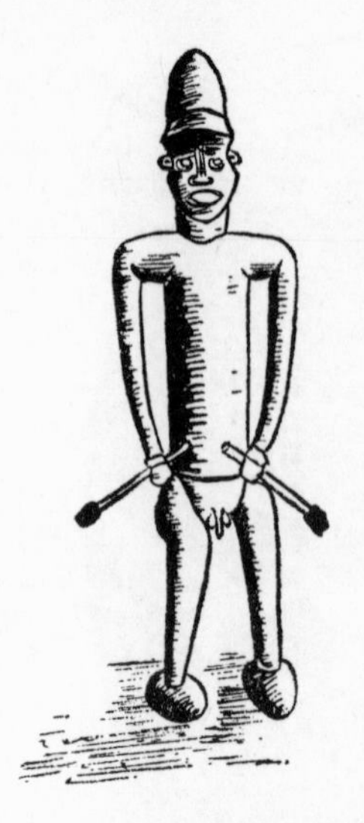

walls. And there was a large selection of musical instruments—a xylophone, several "finger-pianos", iron gongs, grass rattles, various pipes to blow, two-stringed harps to twang, big drums to bang, and several strange "friction" drums played by rubbing the fingers up and down a bamboo protruding through the membrane, which produced a rude, low-pitched, "BfhlBfhlBfhlBfhl". More unusual was a wooden message-gong carved in the form of a man who, himself, held the sticks with which he would be beaten.

Most prolific of all were the jujus. These included figurines from ancestor houses—richly patinated after years of being sprinkled with palm-wine, oil and salt in tribute to the ancestors. And there was a rich assortment of masks.

Wherever I looked in the "Big Big House" I was astonished by the number of animals portrayed in all these works of art. It was as though I had suddenly stepped into a vast, but stunted zoo. There were chimpanzees, monkeys, cockerels, guinea-fowl, frogs, horses, spiders, bats, snakes, leopards, hippopotami, elephants—more than two dozen recognisable varieties in all. This absorption with the animal kingdom seemed to reflect a deep-seated preoccupation among Cameroonians with the unity of living creatures, and the continuum of life, which it is hard for us Europeans to understand fully. We can dissect their life sociologically in almost every detail; we can discover the patterns of change and evolution that might be expected; but as Europeans we cannot enter into their life as we might wish. To the Cameroonians, however, the traditions of their past are a very real part of their present-day existence and one for which, more and more, as I drew back the shrouds from their elaborate material culture, I developed deep respect.

After three days the "Big Big House" was furnished. My time was already running out, but before I could depart there were still a few problems to be taken care of. Most important was that of finding a suitable caretaker for the museum. As I had had neither time nor money with which to set up elaborate showcases, the risk of theft was great, and I therefore needed someone reliable who could exercise a certain amount of authority. Though I had found Martin Assongwet difficult to get on with at first, he had proved a valuable assistant in the end; and being remembered in Abakpa as having been a tough policeman in his day, he seemed a suitable person. Martin readily agreed to the proposal; so, subject to Bernard Fagg's approval, he was appointed. Letters of recommendation had to be written for John, who had proved to be an excellent cook. And all my assistants, including Pa Kisob, who now returned to a life of retirement on his farm, had to be paid. Finally, arrangements had to be made to get Osula back to Jos. He was still insistent that he would never set foot on an aeroplane again, after our alarming flight to Tiko, and we eventually managed to get him on to a bus to take him overland to Nigeria.

As for myself, having said good-bye to all my friends in Bamenda I loaded my baggage into the Land Rover and set out on the two-day drive, via Mamfe, to the coast. In Buea, after returning the car to its owners, I then hired a taxi to take me to the frontier of the French Cameroons. Having crossed the frontier river by canoe with all my baggage, I took another taxi to Douala, on the French side, from which I planned to fly to London. Though I had a day to spare before I caught my 'plane I never expected to return to the British Cameroons quite as soon as I did. But in Douala I visited friends who within minutes of my arrival had recruited me to play rugger against the British Cameroons that very same afternoon in Buea; so back across the river I went. A reception committee of Englishmen was there to meet us, and with a specially lubricated accent I managed to pass myself off as a Frenchman to the first fourteen people who thrust out their hands to greet me. But the fifteenth was a friend of mine, and thus I could not escape being branded a traitor to the British Cameroons. The game over,

I accepted some English hospitality before rushing back to Douala to catch my 'plane; and so returned at last to London.

In London during the next few weeks besides Chief Ngaw's request I also received several other delightful letters from the Cameroons including one from Martin Assongwet:

"Martin A. Asangwed
Bamenda Museum.

Dear Mr. Robert Dick Read,
Sir,

I have the honour to thanking you for the letter you send me with my picture. I am very please for that I am in the museum doing my work as you left me only you know that this are the hart time you will be the only Master to recommand me to the Director at Jos you know that I have children.

(*Martin's appointment had not yet been confirmed by Bernard*)

Please Sir, the Rev. Paul Gibuare presented Museum with one Record Book then I opening on 9/11/59 at ending I got 386 Visitor on December 886 Visitor.

I am waiting to here from you

May God be with you and families
I am yours faithful

Martin Asangwed."

For Abakpa, nearly thirty visitors a day was a large number, and some evidence of the enthusiasm shown in the Grasslands for the idea of collecting together all the "old old t'ings" in one "Big Big House". But further to this was a touching postscript to Martin's letter, as follows:

"Please Sir, I think you will write application for the Cameroon Government to come back. Many Chief wanted you to come back and work here in the Cameroon and so many come to asking you for me—I told them I did not know if you will be back to the Cameroon again.

Thank Sir,
I am your faithfully

MA. Asongwed."

But after a while these letters inevitably stopped coming. The French Cameroons gained their independence; and after a short time the British Cameroons elected to join them in the one great nation of Cameroun. I have met people who have visited the museum since I was there, and the last I heard was that all was well. But Bamenda is a far-flung corner of a large land; and one can only hope that the "old old t'ings" of the Grasslands will be treated with the respect they deserve, and grow yet older and more revered as time goes on.

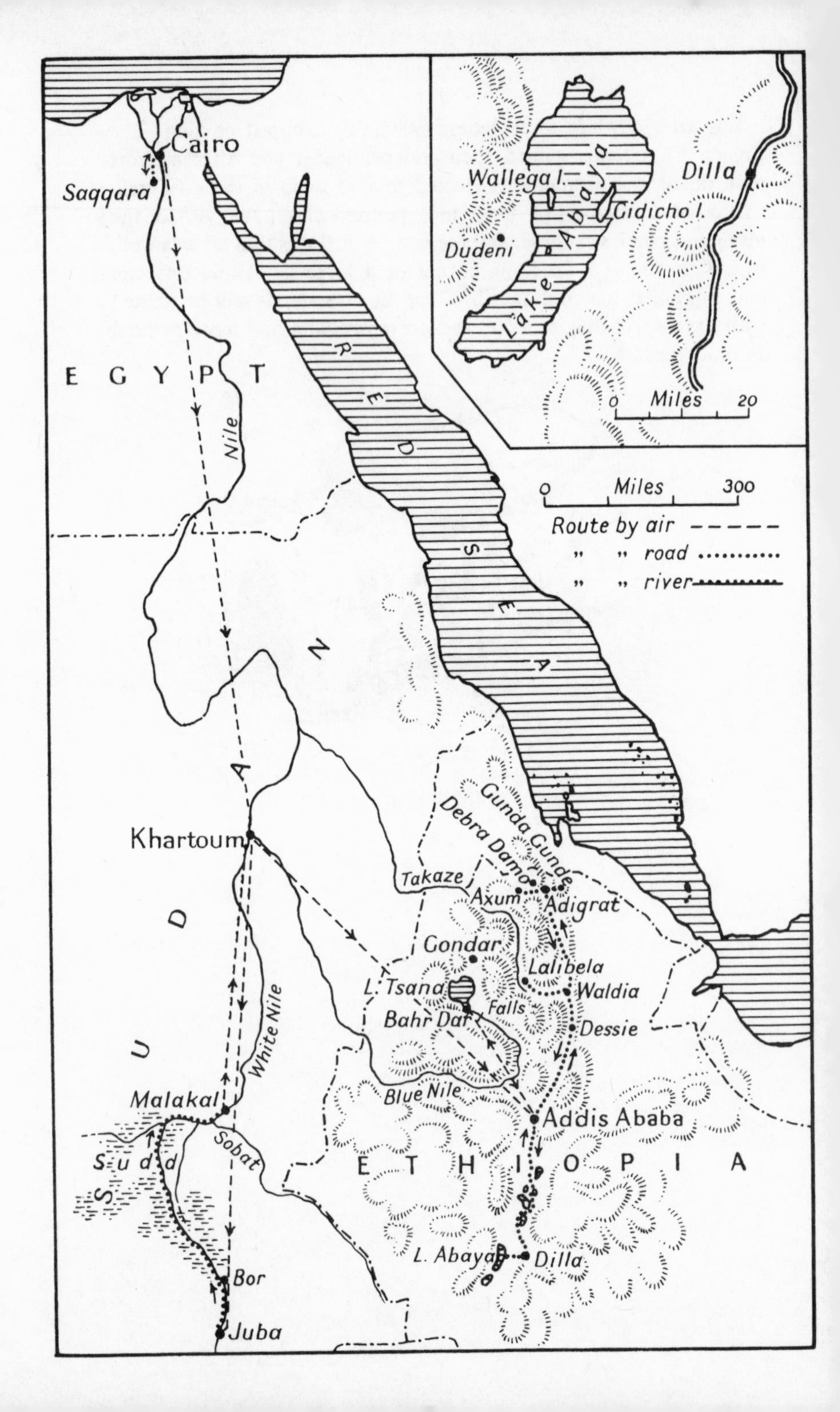

Cairo
Saqqara
EGYPT
Nile
RED SEA
SUDAN
Khartoum
White Nile
Malakal
Sobat
Sudd
Bor
Juba
Takaze
Debra Damo
Gunda Gunde
Axum
Adigrat
Gondar
Lalibela
L. Tsana
Waldia
Falls
Bahr Dar
Dessie
Blue Nile
Addis Ababa
ETHIOPIA
L. Abaya
Dilla
Wallega I.
Gidicho I.
Dudeni
Lake Abaya
0 Miles 20
0 Miles 300
Route by air
" " road
" " river

CHAPTER SEVEN

Reed-boats of the Nile

In a number of villages in the Cameroons I had had the chance to shoot several reels of 16 mm. film. Mostly this was of ritual dancing, showing different types of masks and other tribal paraphernalia, and it was shot primarily for the Department of Antiquities for record purposes. Soon after returning to London, however, I felt it might be worth trying to see whether I could get some of it on television, and accordingly approached the B.B.C. At the Television Centre I was put in touch with David Attenborough who at that time was producing the B.B.C.'s "Adventure" series down at Ealing Studios. In due course arrangements were made to "screen the rushes", and, though David politely regretted that the footage was insufficient for his programme*, this contact later proved extremely valuable. The "Adventure" series was at that time in the throes of expanding to a programme each week, and David was anxiously searching for new material. If I could organise another expedition to Africa, he told me, he would certainly arrange a contract for at least two films.

The idea of filming professionally was completely new to me; but now it suddenly opened up a fresh horizon. For I saw in it an opportunity to fulfil two old ambitions, neither of which had I previously believed I would ever be able to afford. Both of these involved expeditions to the north-east corner of Africa. One was to explore the Christian highlands of Ethiopia, in search of ancient churches and Ethiopian art. The other, a rather more unusual ethnographic quest, was to look for certain strange and ancient types of boats.

Since man first started exploring the world, the development of satisfactory methods of transport has been fundamental to his progress. And of all the means of transport he has ever made, none has taxed his ingenuity and inventiveness over a greater period of

* The film was later shown on another B.B.C. Programme.

time than boats. The people of Kon-Tiki were dependent upon their quaint rafts for the successful exploration of the Pacific; Indonesians relied on their out-riggers to traverse the Indian Ocean when they came to inhabit Madagascar; and Columbus—or the Vikings—in their turn, would never have been able to weather the stormy Atlantic seas had it not been for the ingenuity of the men who had designed and built their vessels.

But as with so many other aspects of civilisation the home of some of the most ancient types of boats known to mankind was in the Nile Valley of Egypt. And it was in this area that my search was centred.

The great age of boat-building on the Nile began with the rise of dynastic Egypt nearly four thousand years before Christ. Even at that time many of the Nile boats were remarkable examples of inventiveness and craftsmanship, and some of the Pharaonic ships reached colossal size. For instance, the boat used to transport Queen Hatshepsut's mammoth stone obelisks to Karnak—each of which weighed three hundred tons—was at least two hundred and seventy feet long. But though the Egyptian shipwrights must have reached a high degree of technical achievement, the Nile boats of the Pharaohs, like other ancient vessels, ultimately gave way to newer and better designs, and most of them eventually disappeared from the scene altogether.

One type of boat used in ancient Egypt, however, somehow managed to side-step the obliterating influence of progress. This was a vessel that was already ancient even when the pyramids were being built, and was probably one of the earliest forms of water transport ever devised by man—the mean little papyrus canoes once used by fishermen and hunters in the swamps along the Nile. These boats were tiny when compared with their big brothers made of timber, being no larger than Eskimo kayaks or Irish coracles; and there was nothing complicated about their construction. The truly remarkable thing about them is that they outlasted all the others—indeed all boats in any part of the word—and that for five thousand years, and probably a good deal longer, they have continued to be constructed in parts of the Nile Valley right up to modern times. What I now wanted to discover was just how much, or how little, their design and construction had altered over the thousands of years they are known to have been in use.

From researches I made while still at London University, it

seemed that there were several areas where I might find boats similar, or related, to the ancient papyrus canoes of Egypt. And on the basis of this research I was able to make my plans for the journey. First, I planned to visit Egypt where I wanted to study relief carvings on the walls of Old Kingdom tombs that depicted papyrus canoes both in use and being constructed. These I knew to exist, though I was unable to find photographs of all of them in England. Having discovered all I could about the methods employed five thousand years ago, I would then fly up the Nile to the swamplands of the Southern Sudan, where I hoped to find the first group of contemporary boats similar in design. Then I would travel on to Ethiopia where I planned to visit two areas far removed from one another. The first of these was a lake in southern Ethiopia, roughly on the same parallel as the swamps in the Sudan, called Lake Abaya. The second and last area to be visited was Lake Tsana, further north near the source of the Blue Nile, where I had heard that the papyrus canoes had the closest resemblance to those of ancient Egypt.

I arranged to meet a friend, Chris Konarski, in Addis Ababa, and having finished the film on boats, he and I would then embark on several journeys into the heart of the Christian highlands, to make our second film—on Ethiopian art.

Early in 1959, I left England by air—for Egypt. I did not know Egypt at the time, and though I had no doubt it would be a fascinating place in which to dally for several weeks, I could not then afford to spend any more time there than was necessary. On arrival in Cairo I went straight to the Cairo Museum where I hoped that Dr. Shukri, the Director, would be able to give me advice on where to go to find the best, most illustrative relief carvings. But he did more than that, and arranged for a guide from the Antiquities Department to accompany me on a short journey to visit several tombs at Saqqara. The following day we drove up the Nile, through fields of cotton and beans, towards the sandy hills of Saqqara, where the great step-pyramid of Djoser dominates the valley. Soon we left the green fields, and drove up a winding road to the deserts; and parking the car near the step-pyramid, we began a day of trekking from tomb to tomb.

It was in the tomb of the Vizier Mereruka that I found the first relief carvings of papyrus boats—a splendid scene of boatmen standing on a slender craft (that surely would have buckled under their weight in reality), poling their way through a dense mass of papyrus. Around them were represented all the animals and birds of the papyrus jungle; catfish, crocodiles and hippopotami beneath the water; lizards and frogs in the reeds; and herons and ibises above them. This showed the boats well, and gave a wonderful impression of how thick the papyrus swamps must have been at one time along this part of the Nile. It was fantastic to reflect that today, apart from a few scrawny roots in a postage-stamp sized pond outside the museum in Cairo, there is not a single blade of papyrus growing in all Egypt. Over the millennia, as the population has grown and grown, skilful irrigation experts have gradually drained the swamps and turned every available inch of swamp-land into productive farms.

I moved on, and elsewhere I saw other reliefs. In one, a swamp scene like the first I had looked at, three men in a boat were fishing. One man, sitting upon a bundle of papyrus to keep clear of the water that flowed through the uncaulked boat, used a line with multiple hooks. Another used a net that was dragged through the water on a wooden rack. The third man knelt in the stern, punting the boat through a subaqueous zoo using a slender pole with a forked end. Another relief showed boatmen taking their herd of cattle across the river. A man kneeling in the stern, wearing what looked like a papyrus life-jacket, was holding a calf close to the boat as a lure for its anxious mother who followed, and who in turn became the leader of the whole herd. They were in deep water here, obviously, for the boatmen were using paddles—and underneath were ever-present crocodiles and fish.

Now I came to the tomb of Ptahhotep, son of Akhtihotep, Grand Vizier of the fifth dynasty king, Asosi, who lived and reigned nearly four thousand five hundred years ago. This period, from the beginning of the fifth to the sixth dynasties of the Old Kingdom, was, so I had been told, one in which some of the finest of the tomb reliefs were carved. They were in very low relief, yet somehow the craftsmen had managed to give them an amazing sense of life and dimension. Muscles and bones of the limbs seemed to stand out; and the skin fell in life-like folds on their bodies. There were hundreds of superb carvings here; but those that caught my attention showed a series of papyrus boats under construction.

In anticipation of what I might find later on on my journey, I

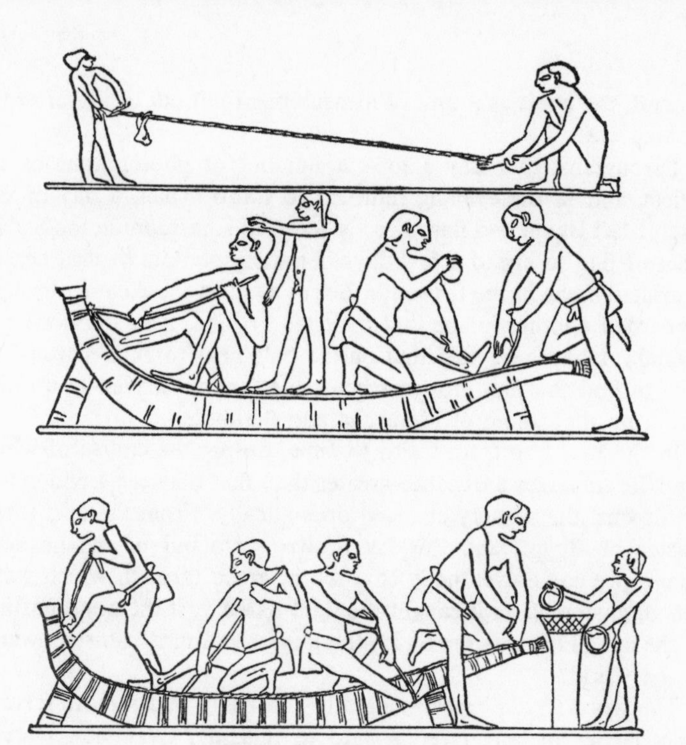

took careful note of what was going on. Most of them were simply tying the bundle of papyrus, knotting it tightly together with cord, at the same time pressing the boat into shape with their feet to get the correct curve at the stern and in the bow. Near one craftsman stood a boy holding what appeared to be two rings, which at the time were quite inexplicable. On another squatted a man holding up what looked like a jug—another point I did not then understand. Above this boat a boy and a man were making rope, presumably to be used by the craftsmen below. One final thing that I noted was the approximate size of the boats. This seemed to vary; but most of those that I saw (taking the scale from the figures) were about ten or twelve feet long. In Egyptian terms this would have been about six or eight "cubits", a "cubit" being approximately the distance between the elbow and the tip of the longest finger. The word actually comes from Latin; but in pre-Roman times the same measurement was commonly used. The Hebrew cubit was about 22 inches; the Roman cubit measured 17.4 inches; and the Egyptian cubit, which was employed in the design and building of the Pyramids, measured 20.64 inches. In general, the cubit as a unit of measurement fell out of use after the Roman era.

Throughout that day I took a number of photographs of the reliefs, and in the evening returned to Cairo. Then, a day or two later, I left Egypt and flew directly south to Khartoum in the Sudan. There I had to spend a few days obtaining permits to visit certain restricted areas in the far south. But as soon as these came through, I boarded another 'plane that took me to Juba, near the border of Uganda. I had been told that on the Nile near to Juba I would be able to find the first group of boats that are descended in a direct line from the canoes of Mereruka and Ptahhotep.

In the vast hop from Cairo to Juba, during the course of which the Nile traverses a distance greater than that between London and Damascus, the scenery changed dramatically. From the arid sandy wastes of Egypt, and the dry brown scrubland of the northern Sudan, we came eventually to a sea of green through which water shone, glistening as it caught the light like a vast diamond flashing in the sun. This was the Sudd; the largest and most sinister swamp in the world.

The word "Sudd" means literally "barrier"; and a more formidable barrier on any river is hard to imagine. Even now, certain Nile tributaries that flow through the Sudd are closed to river traffic each year when, in the dry season, matted reeds converge and obliterate the channel from sight. Each year before traffic can resume, a fresh channel has to be forged through the swamps, the reeds being so thick in places that they can only be moved with dynamite. In the ancient world a few explorers must have managed to trace the Nile's course beyond the Sudd, for on the Ptolemaic map of the second century A.D. the Great Lakes of East Africa and the Mountains of the Moon (the snow-clad Ruwenzori range) were clearly, if inaccurately, shown. But as a barrier to the progress of civilisation and any large-scale interchange of cultures, the Sudd proved insurmountable to Egyptians, Greeks and Romans alike. Only after the middle of the nineteenth century, when Samuel Baker and his wife forged their way through the swamps tracing the main stream of the Nile, was it possible to open up a permanent channel through these swamps.

Later on I made the three-day journey through the Sudd by steamer. It was a remarkable experience. Hour after hour, with our stern paddles churning the shallow water behind us, we wound our way down-stream between twelve-foot walls of papyrus reeds. It seemed that the river itself was bewildered by the swamps, never from one moment to the next knowing where to go, twisting and turning on its northward journey like an angry serpent. Often when we came to bends too sharp for our unwieldy boat to negotiate, our Sudanese-Arab captain, giving a blast on his hooter to warn on-coming shipping, merely let it choose its own course, allowing it to drift uncontrolled into the springy wall of greenery. As we slithered and scraped into the jungle of slender papyrus stems, the first of the barges that we pushed ahead of us lurched and bumped on the soft muddy bottom, which held its bows for a moment so that the ship swung broadside into mid-stream, tearing itself away from the swamp, and after turning a full circle continued on to the next bend.

Nothing seemed more natural than that people should use this papyrus for boat-building. Indeed, apart from the manufacture of paper (which is only just now beginning to get under way in the Sudan), there seemed to be absolutely no other use for the thousands of square miles of reeds.

Having reached Juba, I planned to take the weekly mail-boat to a small riverain village called Bor on the edge of the Sudd, where I had been told by people in Khartoum that I would find all the reed-boats I wanted. I would stay there a week until leaving, in the only possible way, on the next boat north, through the swamps of Malakal, a town about four hundred miles downstream from Juba.

Everything went according to plan until I arrived in Bor. But there, having unloaded my baggage and bid farewell to the stern-wheeler, I discovered to my horror that all the information that had led me to go there in the first place was absolutely without foundation. Not only were there no reed-boats in Bor, but no one there had ever heard of them. And there I was stuck for a week.

After a long and expensive journey this was a shattering blow. But I had discovered by then that this sort of thing can easily happen in Africa, where communications and sources of information are often notoriously inaccurate. It was not the first time that I had been stuck in a place against my will, unable to move, and as it turned out, it was no burden at all; for Bor was one of the most fascinating places in Africa that I visited. It is one of the District Headquarters of a huge Nilotic tribe called the Dinka who are well known for their tall slender physique; and amongst the Dinka I was able to find plenty of interesting activities to film.

The District Commissioner of Bor was a young Muslim Sudanese-Arab from Khartoum. Despite political and religious differences between the ruling Arabs of Khartoum and the pagan people of the southern Sudan that had given rise to bloody conflicts a few years earlier, the D.C. seemed to be popular locally, and in complete command of affairs. Like many native African administrators who have taken over from their colonial masters, he had inherited also many of their habits and customs. He wore a large bush-jacket, and baggy shorts of the type that the British Administration used to wear. And in his antiquated office, behind walls of mosquito netting, he sat beneath a richly cobwebbed brocade "punka"—a true relic of the old raj that must surely have been there since the earliest days of the Empire. The punka was worked, as in the days of old, by an aged servant who sat outside the office wall, sucking lazily at a pipe as he flapped the elephantine fan slowly to and fro, to keep his master cool. The D.C. went out of his way to make life comfortable for me. He provided me with a Dinka interpreter, and put at my disposal a truck to take me wherever I pleased.

Though miles from anywhere, on the edge of the swamps, Bor town was not unpleasant. In the centre of the town were several rows of typical African shops, cheaply put up with corrugated-iron roofs and narrow verandahs. Trade in this wild region was not exactly brisk; but most of the merchants made as much from buying and exporting cowhides and coils of locally made fibre rope as they did from selling pots and pans and cotton piece-goods to the villagers. But the selection of food in the shops was limited to maize meal and sardines, and I was glad I had brought enough food with me to last the week. Around the periphery of the shopping centre were several broad "streets" of thatched dwellings laid out in rectangular blocks on the New York pattern, with a few mango trees and palms providing shade.

One of the more unusual things about the people of this region is their dress—or in most cases, their lack of it. The Dinka girls have a variety of clothing depending on their status. Young virgins, for instance, wear a fantastic collar of beads braced with bones in such a way that they can barely turn their heads, and all women after puberty cover the lower parts of their body. The men, however, plaster their hair in cow-dung and go around stark naked except for brightly coloured beaded "corsets" that cover their diaphragms but nothing else.

Soon after I arrived in Bor my interpreter took me to a Dinka dance being held in a clearing a short distance from the centre of the town. Officially these days, all Dinka men are supposed to wear trousers when they come into the town; but on this occasion very few were wearing them. The reason, so I was blandly informed, was that Dinka girls prefer their men naked. Watching a Dinka dance—in which men and women prance round in circles jumping up and down—I took it that the girls' preference for nakedness was for obvious reasons. But apparently this was not the case. Women all over the world are inclined to be more conservative and conscious of tradition than men, and it was simply that Dinka women have more respect for men who "undress" in the traditional tribal way than those who feign an education by wearing trousers.

The Dinka have amusing ideas on modesty. These were made clear to me one evening when I was taking a stroll down the waterfront in Bor town. As was the case every evening, men, women and children were down in the river having their daily bath. No one seemed to care who was who; women strolled down to the water's edge—perhaps carrying a water pot which they would later fill—take off their clothes and go into the water side by side with a bunch of naked men. And no one was the slightest bit self-conscious—until I came along. Then suddenly all the women let out a little shriek of horror, and plunged under the water giggling with embarrassment. Some, who happened to be standing in only about four inches of water, simply fell flat on their faces and squirmed their way into the mud in an effort to hide their bodies from view. To see and be seen naked by Dinka men meant absolutely nothing to them. But to be seen naked by a European (who was dressed) was evidently more than they could stand.

Most of the Dinka are cattle owners who live with their huge herds in the plains beyond the river. But many of the Dinka around Bor belong to a sub-tribe called the Dinka "Montaigne", who are fishermen and live by the river. Even if they had no papyrus boats, I felt it would be interesting to see how these riverain Dinka lived, and in particular, how they fished; and it was with them that I decided to spend as much of my week as possible.

The various methods of catching fish in different parts of the world are about as multifarious as the contents of a woman's handbag. Nets and hooks and gadgets of every conceivable variety have been used by different people at some time in the world's history;

but the Dinka people use traps and spears. One morning, when the interpreter and I arrived in a riverside village, the fishermen were just going out on a fish-spearing expedition, and we were able to go with them. From their village we set off in several wooden dugouts to a large area of swamp-land some distance downstream.

Travelling into the Sudd in a canoe was of great interest and showed vividly what an extraordinary effect these huge swamps have upon the flow of the Nile. Where the White Nile passes Bor it is already a thousand miles from its source in East Africa; and being the watershed for the whole of Uganda, parts of Kenya and Tanganyika, and the high rainfall area of the eastern Congo, by the time it reaches the Sudan it is no small river. Yet between Bor and Malakal, three hundred and fifty miles further north, as it passes through sponge-like Sudd, the Nile loses fifty per cent of its total water from evaporation beneath the burning tropical sun. So rapid is the evaporation that the level of the water in the swamps is for much of the year below the level of the river itself. At first I found it hard to believe that the difference in the levels could be so marked; but when, in our canoes, we turned off the river through a wall of reeds, it was almost as though we were going down a series of shallow rapids as the river drained away into the vast sea of papyrus.

The hunting party was made up of twelve slender naked men with long thin spears. When we approached a clearing in the swamps we left the canoes, and waded through the knee-deep water. Two men moved slowly round to the far side of the clearing to a narrow channel through the reeds. Whilst we remained behind, still and quiet, the two who had gone ahead built a rough stockade of reed stems across the mouth of the channel. When all was ready the signal was given for the remainder of the fishermen to begin beating through the open water. As they moved forward, shouting like a gang of happy children, they hurled their spears into the weed-strewn water ahead of them in the hope of piercing an unseen and unsuspecting fish, and beat the surface of the water with their hands. Slowly we converged on the stockade where the other spear-men waited to join in the final fray. Suddenly, not two yards ahead of me, a fish jumped out of the water and plopped back with a splash. An excited yell went up from the fishermen as they began to beat the water more violently. As we neared the stockade more fish began to jump. Suddenly one of the hunters, seeing a fish escaping almost between his legs, broke away and went off on a futile chase. The others, furious, called him back to close the gap. Now, shouting fierce hunting cries, they were ready for the final assault. On a signal they went wild, plunging towards the trapped fish, jabbing and thrusting like men possessed, yelling as they impaled a fish, lifting it into the air, and shaking it in triumph. Flailing limbs and leaping fish churned the water into a turbulent, frothing pool. But as suddenly as it had begun, the climax was past; and in an instant all was quiet. Many fish had escaped; but five cat-fish of five and six pounds amongst them, were being carried triumphantly back to the canoes.

One of the biggest difficulties when filming scenes such as the fish hunt was to avoid filling the screen with too much genitalia. In some countries where I hoped to sell the film no nakedness, even among primitive people, is allowed to be shown on the screen. Often the difficulties were enhanced by the legitimate pride of the Dinka people who would stand squarely facing the camera, and on more than one occasion I found myself having to tell them to turn about so that only their bottoms might be presented to the audience. Though they were very willing photographic subjects they could never quite understand my reason for this; indeed I believe they thought I was rather strange. Nevertheless I was very content with the material I had gathered before the week in Bor came to an end.

Having taken leave of my friends, I boarded the stern-wheeler going north through the Sudd to Malakal, from where I planned to take a 'plane back to Khartoum. Among the passengers on the boat was a Sudanese veterinary officer travelling to Malakal on leave. In the course of conversation I happened to mention why I had visited Bor in the first place, and how I had been disappointed in my search for reed-boats. He was highly amused, but not in the least surprised. Of course there are no reed-boats to the south of the Sudd, he said; but there are plenty near Malakal. And he promised to show me some.

We docked in Malakal late at night; and hiring a taxi early the next morning, drove for several miles down a dusty track by the river back towards the swamps. Soon we came to a small village of Nuer tribesmen, whose grass huts nestled on a ridge above the river. I saw immediately that we were in luck; for there, leaning up against a tree, were several boats that looked to all intents and purposes like those I had seen in Egyptian tombs. But taking a

closer look I was surprised. For after all that, and though there was enough papyrus in view to build a fleet for all the angels in heaven, they were not made of reeds. Instead, they were made from slender branches of a tree called an "ambatch" tree, which grows in the water along the edge of the river. Furthermore, on close inspection, I saw that the design was different to those of ancient Egypt—the stern of the boats seemed to have been cut off square so that they lacked the graceful curves of their predecessors.

I was beginning to feel slightly disappointed when I noticed something going on that quickly changed my mood. At the far end of the village some herdsmen were having great difficulty with a small herd of cows. It seemed that they were trying to get them into the river, to take them across to the pastures of swamp-grass on the other side which, at this time of year, were beginning to dry out sufficiently for grazing. Nothing could induce the cattle into the water; until eventually, getting an ambatch canoe, the herdsmen tied one of the calves to it and paddled out into the mid-stream. The calf's mother, frantic with worry, followed; and as soon as she went into the water, the rest of the herd wallowed down and began to swim across too. Though the boats might have been slightly different, it was as though the scene in Mereruka's tomb had suddenly come to life. And doubtless such a method of taking cattle across the Nile will be used for centuries to come.

The first leg of the journey was now over. It was unfortunate

that the boats I had found were not reed-boats at all. It would certainly have been more exciting had I been able to bridge the past five thousand years in one clean span. But still there were two other places to visit where this might possibly be the case. Whatever its outcome, my journey to the Sudan had been rewarding if only for the fact that the Sudanese are such delightful people, lacking the complexes that so often mar relations further south. But now I had to leave the Sudan and fly directly to Addis Ababa, high up in the Ethiopian mountains.

Before leaving England I had been told that I might find it difficult or even impossible to obtain permission to film in Ethiopia. Since the war, no one had been able to wander across the country filming what they pleased; but this potential difficulty only added to the challenge. Though I grew to like the Ethiopians quite quickly, they are, as a race, extremely suspicious of foreigners, and especially foreigners with cameras. This suspicion probably stems from the fact that they have always lived a secluded life up in their mountain homeland being badgered for years by Muslim neighbours, and more recently by the Italians. Also, they are touchy about the impression they create abroad, and feel, usually without foundation, that foreign press-men are apt only to present a picture of the poverty and backwardness that is still to be found in parts of their country. Having been warned about this suspicion I went to great lengths to convince the authorities that my intentions were not impolite; but on the contrary, beneficial to the Ethiopian image abroad.

One of the first people I had to meet in Addis Ababa was the late Ato Amde Mikael, then Vice-Minister for Information (the Emperor himself being Minister). I quickly became acquainted with Ethiopian custom, having to wait in an outer office of the Ministry for two hours beyond the scheduled time of my appointment. But ultimately the Vice-Minister's secretary ushered me into his office. Amde Mikael, who spoke good English, was a powerfully built man, though running slightly to fat. He had the reputation of being a yes-man to His Majesty, and of having reached his position only by marrying into the right family. There was that glassy look in his eyes that one associates with people who like to live well, and would sacrifice much for it, and when I first saw him I felt that his appearance lived up to his reputation. Summing him up, I felt also that he was probably a terrible coward. But later I found out how wrong a first impression can be.

Amde Mikael was somewhat peeved that I had given the government no warning that I was coming. He implied, too, that had I done so permission for a filming expedition would not have been granted as the government was at that moment involved in a bitter dispute with the British authorities over two Englishmen who had come out a short time before on a similar quest. They had received permission to film in certain areas; but only two weeks after their arrival they had been shot by their interpreter, though not killed, and this had involved the Ethiopians in a protracted dispute over damages. Now that I was in the country he could not easily turn me away; but he made it clear that he could still make my job difficult, or even impossible, if he wished. This antagonism had to be overcome somehow; but I did not immediately realise that I had the means of overcoming it in my coat pocket.

Suspecting that there might be difficulties, I had prepared a lengthy typescript outlining with great precision exactly what I planned to do whilst in Ethiopia, listing every small item that I wished to film. This, in fact, bore little relation to what I eventually did; because in a country like Ethiopia it is almost impossible to plan anything in advance. All that I had done was to go through half a dozen books, isolating many of the most obscure objects of ethnographic interest, and building these into an imaginary film outline.

We had still not progressed far with our discussion, when I pulled out this document and handed it to him rather huffily, saying "This is exactly what I want to do while I'm here. If you can't

17. Gidicho islander with his gopashi

18. Sundown on Gidicho

19. Filming the Tis 'Abbai falls

20. Paddling my own canoe—a Tankwa on Lake Tsana

21. The monastery buildings of Debra Damo on top of the massive cliffs of the plateau

22. The monastery of Gunda Gunde

23. *Far left:* An illustration from an early manuscript at Gunda Gunde

24. *Left:* The stool of the Four Evangelists, Bieta Stefanos

25. *Below left:* A young deacon rings the phonoliths

26. *Below:* The Memhir Amsala looks down from his "eyrie" in Lalibela

27. Bieta Gheorghis–Lalibela

28. Monks studying the ancient gospels

29. Two minstrels of Abuna Aaron

30. A beam of sunlight illuminates the lectern in the monastery of Abuna Aaron

31. The twelfth-century cave church of Imrahana Kristos

32. The cave church of Mechena Medhanie Alem

give permission, well, I'll have to go; if you can, please let me get on with it!"

For twenty minutes I sat quiet while he read through the document. Then I was aware that he had stopped reading, and was sitting quite still, staring at me. I waited for him to say something; but for two minutes he remained, gazing at me blankly. Then suddenly he spoke, softly, incredulously.

"Mr. Read, this is unbelievable! You have been in Ethiopia one day only, yet you write about things in my own country of which I have never heard even myself! I do not understand! It is amazing!"

He seemed to be unaware that many books had been written about Ethiopia. But this touch of magic so impressed him that from that moment onwards I had his fullest co-operation in everything I wanted to do.

Nevertheless nearly three weeks passed before any move could be made towards the next port of call, Lake Abaya. My "outline" had to be translated into Amharinya to be shown to His Majesty; and the Emperor's approval had to be obtained. As the Emperor takes an interest in even the smallest things going on in his country, he is a very busy man, and generally speaking it takes a long time to obtain the Royal stamp. This delay did not worry me unduly, however, as Chris Konarski was due to arrive at any time, and I was relying on him coming with me to Lake Abaya.

Several years earlier I had lived with Chris in Mombasa. He is an engineer by profession; but also an excellent amateur photographer. He was working on a civil engineering job in the Persian Gulf when I was planning this expedition; but his contract was coming to an end, and as he enjoys roaming around the world when on leave, he readily agreed to join me in Ethiopia. Polish by birth, naturalised English, he speaks Arabic, French and Italian apart from his native languages. In appearance, Chris is small and dapper and he is extremely dark skinned. Dressed in a sarong and an old pair of sandals, many people used to mistake him for an Indian, or an Arab, in Mombasa; but this was probably due as much to the sort of places that he frequented as to his appearance.

Chris arrived when I had been in Ethiopia two weeks. In the meantime, apart from obtaining a sheaf of necessary permits from Amde Mikael, I had purchased a very old Volkswagen bus, and borrowed a boat from a missionary to use on the lake. So, within a few days of Chris's arrival, with the dinghy lashed to the roof of the bus, we set off on the journey south to Lake Abaya.

Lake Abaya is one of several lakes in Southern Ethiopia that lie along the bed of the Great Rift Valley where it extends northward towards the Red Sea from Lake Rudolf in Kenya. Though it is on the same latitude as Bor in the Southern Sudan, being over five thousand feet above sea level and surrounded by mountains, its climate and vegetation are very different. Apart from Lake Tsana, four hundred miles to the north, it is Ethiopia's largest lake—over forty miles long by eighteen miles across at the widest point. The people around the lake are mostly of the Wallamo and Sidamo tribes who grow coffee in the surrounding hills, and Galla who herd cattle around its shores. But in the middle of the lake, on a small island called Gidicho, there is another tribe about whom very little is known. There are probably no more than seven hundred and fifty of these Gidicho tribesmen whose island home is about four and a half miles long and a mile and a half wide; and they live in three villages, called Bysore, Shigima and Harura.

The people of Gidicho are the masters of Lake Abaya. They alone have boats upon its waters, and they alone hunt the animals in the marshes around its edge. Linguistically and culturally they differ from all their neighbours, and to anthropologists they are something of an enigma. But it has been suggested that they came originally from the west, from the Nile valley, perhaps travelling up the Sobat river that flows down from the Ethiopian hills to a point five hundred miles away near Malakal. The boats of Gidicho had, so far as I knew, never been fully described. I had read early reports of them and they sounded extraordinarily interesting. Could they, I wondered, find a place in our pattern of ancient Nilotic boats?

In our somewhat battered old bus it took us a day and a half to drive from Addis Ababa to a town named Dilla in Sidamo district, where we spent the night in a Mission station. From the Mission we could just see the lake—a sliver of silver that might have been mistaken for a morning mist, nestling at the foot of the high mountains of Gamu Gofa, forty miles to the west. The following day we set off on a rough drive down to the lake along a muddy track that now and again disappeared from sight as it crossed wide expanses of sparse bush and grass.

Until a year or two before, it had been impossible to reach the lake by car, merchants who traded with the island people having had to travel by mule. But a wealthy Ethiopian who owned land along the lake shore had recently established a small factory by the lake to extract fibre from the wild *sansevieria*, a sisal-like plant that grows there in abundance; and a rough track to the factory had been cleared. Not only was this the only road to the lake, but we hoped that the Italian manager of the factory would be able to supply us with an interpreter who could speak Italian as well as a local language.

The factory was a ramshackle place, and we found the manager —who lived there with a woolly-haired Ethiopian mistress—in a bad state of nerves. His employer had sent him no money for several weeks, and his labourers were on the point of becoming violent. Most of them had long since refused to work with no pay; and as they were sitting around idle we had no difficulty in finding an interpreter (of sorts) from among them. This was an Amhara named Walda who spoke a smattering of several languages including Italian and Gallinya.

We could see Gidicho clearly from the factory—a low, hump-back island about two miles off-shore. None of the lake-boats was over on the mainland that day so, as soon as we had arrived and launched our dinghy, we began to ferry ourselves and our baggage across to the island. With camping equipment (this had been sent out to Ethiopia by sea while I was in the Sudan) and all the other paraphernalia, several journeys were necessary; so I went across with Walda and the camping gear on the first trip, leaving Chris to look after the remainder of the baggage.

The island was surrounded by reeds, and when we reached it we at first experienced some difficulty in finding a way through them. But eventually, being directed by shouts from the shore, we found a channel, and nosed our way through. Beyond the reeds we came into a small lagoon, only a few yards across, which was by now fringed with inquisitive men and women who had heard our outboard as we chugged up and down outside. The women were wearing hide skirts, but were naked about the breasts, while the men wore shorts and off-white cotton "sammas", an Ethiopian garment that is draped toga-like from the shoulders. And in the lagoon were fourteen of the most interesting boats I had ever seen —the extraordinary "hobolos" of Gidicho.

The hobolos are best imagined if one first tries to picture a

Venetian gondola, or a Maltese *dghajsa*, with one end cut away diagonally from the high prow to a point in the stern just beneath the waterline. All were exactly twenty-four feet long, four feet in beam, with a stem-post that swept up from the keel in a graceful curve to a height of seven feet from the ground. They were made of the same ambatch wood as the canoes of the Sudd, though the hobolos being many times the size, their timbers were much thicker. And like the Sudan canoes they were uncaulked so that water flowed freely through them. Although at first sight they seemed to bear no relation either to the canoes of ancient Egypt or to those of the Sudanese, the more I looked at them the more I became convinced that the designs of all three were related. This, I felt, might be an interesting case in which a change of environment to an area better endowed with boat-building materials had led to a natural evolution of an age-old design. The canoes of ancient Egypt, as we have seen, were made of papyrus, the only suitable material at hand. In the southern Sudan, where papyrus was available in vast quantities, they were nevertheless made of slender ambatch stems, as this was doubtless more durable and more buoyant. Owing to the problems of manipulating ambatch, however, the canoe makers of the south had gradually done away with the unnecessary upward-curving stern. Here on Lake Abaya, the development had gone several stages further. At this altitude and in this climate, the ambatch trees grew to far greater size, providing an ample supply of straight baulks five and six inches in diameter. With timbers of such size, it was possible, by cunningly notching them in such a way that they lost little strength, to bend them in gentle curves. This had been done with the stem post; but the stern remained cut away like the canoes of the Nuer. I felt it was possible, even, that the very method of construction might itself have been a relic of the early Egyptian era, for the hobolos are not bound with cord like the smaller canoes, but carefully jointed with wooden pegs like the larger wooden ships of the ancient Nile.

If these strange boats—of which there are perhaps no more than fifty in existence—are unusual in appearance and construction, the method of propulsion is even more extraordinary. The boatmen—there may be up to four of them—stand in the low platform at the stern which is most likely submerged if the hobolo is fully laden. In shallow water they punt the boat in the normal fashion with a long pole. But when in deep water they use a curious implement called a "gopashi".

If one tries to force an inflated rubber ring, or anything buoyant for that matter, under the water, it naturally exerts considerable counter-pressure. If it is pushed into the water at an angle from a boat, the force is sufficient to propel the boat in the opposite direction. And this is the principle on which the "gopashi" works. It consists of a large block of ambatch wood shaped like a bent howitzer shell about two feet long, with two slender wooden "tusks" bound to either side of it. The block is attached to a long curved pole which the boatman manipulates with a punting action. In appearance the gopashi is a thoroughly unwieldy implement; but in use it is both efficient and remarkably ingenious.

Later I was able to try the gopashi for myself; but I never managed to master it. I found a natural tendency to use it as a paddle; but when I did this it bobbed to the surface and twisted in every direction nearly landing me in the lake as I leant on it with all my weight. The secret, I believe, is to push it downwards. In this way the curve of the pole ensures that the block enters the water at the correct angle, and the two tusks act as stabilisers, stopping it from twisting. I believe this form of propulsion is unique to Gidicho.

On arriving at Gidicho I left Walda and the camping gear surrounded by a large crowd of people, and returned to the factory. There we loaded up again, and with Chris returned to the island. As we were nosing our way along the reeds, trying once again to find the entrance to the "hobolo" harbour, we had a very alarming experience. I was sitting on the side of the dinghy at the time, controlling the outboard, when suddenly the boat gave a horrible lurch. I looked down just in time to catch a glimpse of the top jaw of a crocodile crunching into the boat about three inches from me, as its bottom jaw came up with a "wham" underneath. The whole thing happened so quickly that for a moment I didn't quite gather what was going on. The crocodile must have mistaken our churning propeller for the flailing limbs of a cow or a man, and attacked on impulse. Thank God our boat was aluminium for, beyond denting it badly, it did no damage. Had it been wood it would certainly have crushed it, and the chances are that I would not be here to tell the tale.

During our stay on Gidicho the same thing happened on two other occasions, but fortunately with no more damage than on the first occasion. The lake, we discovered, was riddled with crocodiles which went up to an enormous size. Some local hunters killed a fifteen-foot beast one day, in the belly of which were the horns of several goats, and the shell of a tortoise. On another occasion we were actually chased by a large crocodile out in the middle of the lake. It came after us rather like a porpoise on the surface of the water, moving at an astonishing speed, but not, fortunately, fast enough to catch our boat.

When all the equipment was across, we pitched our tent near the harbour. The island had only seen a handful of Europeans in its history (in fact Chris and I probably came to know it better than anyone else) and our tent created a considerable stir. Throughout our stay we were never without a crowd of admirers. Young and old, male and female, they would come down to the tent quietly and politely, and just sit in a circle watching every move we made. These observers rarely spoke to one another unless we did something exceptionally strange, like lighting the primus; then they would draw one another's attention to what we were doing, jabbering excitedly. Occasionally we would give them a concert with our tape recorder. I had several tapes on which were recorded some European music. But we soon discovered that Fauré's Nocturnes, and even "An American in Paris" bored them to distraction. What really gripped them, however, was the sound of their own voices and their own discordant songs. These sent them into the wildest laughter. They took remarkably little interest in the machine itself. Presumably they felt they would never be able to understand it, and therefore did not try.

The Chief of Gidicho, or Balabat as he was called, was a very tall lean man who was always recognisable from afar off on account of his solar topee that came down over his eyes. He lived in a huge beehive-shaped hut, thatched down to the ground with rushes, in the largest of the villages, Bysore. The inside of the house was divided into several rooms in which the family lived with their goats and hens. Outside his house was a compound partially fenced with old hobolos.

Gidicho had once been extensively cultivated, as could be seen from the terraced fields on the gentle slopes. Now only a few small fields near the villages were tilled and planted with weedy crops of maize, the rest having been badly eroded by generations of grazing goats. In recent years the islands have acquired land from the people of Gamu Gofa, on the mainland to the west, on which they grow astonishingly rich crops of maize and millet fifteen feet high, and herd most of their cattle. On the island a few wild monkeys chatter in the trees, and Chris observed a snake; but the most prolific of all Gidicho's animals are its tortoises, eighteen inches to two feet long, that mingle, well camouflaged, with the rock-strewn earth of the hills.

Once we went across to the mainland of Gamu Gofa, to a little village called Dudeni, where there was a market, and on this journey we saw some remarkable performances by local musicians and dancers. We encountered the musicians, of the Wallamo tribe, in a small hamlet where an old lady had just died. There were five or six of them playing a funeral dirge on the most enormous horns I have ever seen. These were made out of long hollow reeds, to the end of each of which was fixed the horn of a cow. They were over fifteen feet long, some of them, and emitted a series of rude burps that hardly deserved to be called music at all. The dancers were of the Dorze tribe, great weavers in Ethiopia, and famous for their acrobatics. During their dance many of them, without any other spring-board than the brown earth, turned double somersaults in the air with apparent ease.

The greatest sport of Gidicho island is strangely confined to the people of only one village—Harura. This is hippopotamus hunting. Though there is a good market for hippo skin from which mule whips are made, they hunt them primarily for their flesh, which they allow to rot in the sun for several days before eating it raw. Harura village, as one might imagine, is a nightmare of stench and filth. Scores of vultures hover above the roof-tops and in thorn trees that surround the village, waiting for hunters to come home with cargoes of hippo meat in their hobolos. The fields around the village are an open graveyard of hippo bones, picked clean by the vultures and bleached by the sun.

We went on a hunting expedition with six of the Harura villagers in hobolos to the swamps at the northern end of the lake. There was a wind up that day and the lake was rough—far too rough for us to venture out in our eleven-foot dinghy—but the hobolos rode through the waves without fear of overturning, and even had they done so they could not have sunk. The leader of the expedition was a young man named Dama who had at first been reluctant to take us, telling us that we would never be able to keep quiet enough. He had acquired his leadership, I believe, by owning a rifle, an ancient Italian weapon, with cartridges that cost him seven shillings each on the black market (for he had no licence). Apart from this rifle, our only other weapon was a ten-foot harpoon spear, attached to which was a long line with an ambatch float. We "gopashied" for most of the day round the edge of the lake, watching and listening for any signs of hippos.

As we were likely to be away only two days, Chris and I had taken no food of our own with us, and were reliant upon our hosts for our meals. In the bottom of the boat had been thrown several large flat slabs of "ensat", a cake made from the pounded roots of a tree that looks like a banana-tree, but produces no bananas. This was the staple food of these people, and though wholesome, was sour and not all that palatable. We would have liked to do some fishing, but although Lake Abaya is teeming with fish of many varieties, including Nile perch that weigh half a hundredweight and more, the Gidicho islanders never eat fish. They say, for some strange reason, that it makes their teeth fall out. We had several gourds of sour milk with us that we had purchased from some Galla girls we saw on the mainland, and every now and then, as we entered the swamps, we would stop to pull up young reeds, the shoots of which, called "arafu", make a good nutty-flavoured salad. As soon as we had got out of sight of the island, away from the embarrassing gaze of the women-folk, the hunters had taken their clothes off, preferring the freedom of nakedness to the cheap shorts bought in the local market. Chris and I kept our clothes on for protection from the sun, if nothing else; but once, when we were collecting arafu, I stripped off to go wading chest high through a patch of swamp. The hunters grew unexpectedly curious at the sight of a naked white man, and thereafter I kept at least some of my clothes on.

In the evening we sighted a hippo puffing and blowing, out in the lake, and as it would almost certainly come in to the shore during the night, we lay in wait for it in the reeds preparing to attack it as soon as it lumbered into shallow water, or out on to the dry land. As the sun set the hippo moved slowly towards us; but it was a wary beast, and seemed to sense that all was not well. Three of the hunters went ashore with the rifle to lie in ambush for it there; the rest of us stayed in the hobolos with the harpoon spear. But the hippo never went on land that night, hiding instead in the thick reeds. In the fading light we followed it, slowly and as quietly as possible pulling the boat through the swamps. One moment it seemed to be just ahead of us puffing and snorting; and then, as we approached, it was away to one side. Never was it far away; but nor did it ever come within sight.

We slept that night on the hobolo beneath the stars, with a cake of "ensat" as a pillow. During the night it began to rain, and soon our blankets were wet through. Then suddenly I realised that water was seeping up from below, and before long we were soaked. We had learned one disadvantage of the hobolo; for though, when dry, the ambatch wood is as light and buoyant as cork, it is spongy, and quickly becomes waterlogged. After only two days without being allowed to dry out, these elegant craft begin to settle in the water, becoming not merely uncomfortable but heavy to propel.

The rain stopped in the early hours, and the clouds parted to reveal a full moon that flooded down on the lake and swamps around us adding an eerie sense of isolation to the already remote scene. Suddenly above the lapping of the water in the hobolo, one of the hunters thought he heard the hippo grunting again in the reeds. Gingerly, as silently as possible, we began once more to pull through the marshes towards it. But just at that moment the still night air was shattered by the crack of the rifle on land, followed by a fiendish bellowing and shouts from the men. The agonised bellowing continued for what seemed like an eternity as the rest of us struggled ashore; but as we came near to the scene of the horrible slaughter, the noise had already died, and three men, blooded from head to foot, were embroiled in an indescribably gruesome piece of butchery. The vast two-and-a-half-ton carcass was by now barely recognisable.

For several hours that morning the hunters flayed the wretched hippo, cutting the skin and the flesh into strips on the spot. The meat and the legs and the strips of skin were then loaded into the hobolos, and the tail hung in triumph from the prow. Then, when all was ready, we laboriously pushed our way back to Gidicho.

Before we left Lake Abaya the Balabat came down to our tent to say farewell. He brought with him a small white kid which was presented with a brief ceremony in which he self-consciously invited us to become "Brothers of Gidicho", and to return whenever we pleased. He then produced several bottles of "araqui", a locally brewed white spirit guaranteed to produce a terrible internal storm, which we drank until we could drink no more. And not very early the following morning we left the island for the last time with a small fleet of hobolos bringing our baggage along behind.

The search for hobolos had been a great success. We had seen more than we had expected of these, the least known and most beautiful boats on the African continent. But still their link with the ancient boats of the Nile was tenuous and far removed. But now, as we drove north to the village of Bahr Dar on the southern end of Lake Tsana, I fully expected that we would find boats far more closely linked than any that I had yet seen.

Lake Tsana lies on the western edge of the Ethiopian Highlands, four thousand feet above sea level. It is the largest of Ethiopia's lakes, being over forty miles across in almost any direction. Though the scenery around the lake is not impressive—the hills rising neither high nor precipitously—it is in most respects more pleasant and congenial than Lake Abaya. The water is clearer, and the area is less subject to the violent storms and winds that on occasions nearly blew our tent away on the island of Gidicho. And as it is cool and temperate there are no crocodiles, though these abound in the Nile only a short distance from the lake.

In keeping with its less savage appearance and milder climate, the people of Lake Tsana live far less primitive lives than those we had visited in the south. Some of Ethiopia's oldest and most famous monasteries are to be found around the lake shores, and on various of its islands; and in these have been buried many of Ethiopia's greatest Emperors. Not twenty miles to the north, in the hills overlooking the lake, lies the seventeenth-century city of Gondar with its many imposing castles. For a long period the capital of Ethiopia, Gondar also became famous, as it still is to some extent, as the most cultured city in the land. On the lake shore near Gondar stands the impressive ruin of an ancient palace built for an Ethiopian king by a Portuguese Jesuit priest. It is not difficult, when wandering in the scrub beneath the walls of Old Gorgora, to imagine elegant and noble picnics taking place upon the palace lawn, with royalties and guests resplendent in fine imported silks and the best of Gondarine embroideries.

Apart from its historical and cultural associations, Lake Tsana is of considerable geographic and economic importance; for it is, to all intents and purposes, the source of the Blue Nile upon which the livelihood of the vast territories of the Sudan and Egypt depends. Though the White Nile, meandering north from the Mountains of the Moon, flows steadily throughout winter and summer alike, it is the Blue Nile, thundering down from the Ethiopian mountains for a few months each year that provides the arid land of Egypt with seventy per cent of its water. The valley of the Blue Nile, or the Abbai as it is called in Ethiopia, provides some of the most spectacular scenery on the continent of Africa. Later we had occasion to fly over the Nile gorge, and no sight could have induced a deeper sense of the passage of time than that an apparently diminutive stream should, through the ages, have eaten its way doggedly through the earth's crust.

Yet it is far from being a diminutive stream, as we saw when we visited the Tis'Abbai Falls ("where the Nile smokes") soon after we arrived. These falls lie about a day's mule ride to the south of Lake Tsana. Here the Nile, in one tumultous leap, plunges over a cliff all of two hundred feet high and three-quarters of a mile wide. I have seen most of the superlative falls in Africa; Victoria, the most commercialised; the thousand-foot Chutes Lofoi, the highest; and Kiubo, supposedly the most beautiful. But none have filled me with such awe as the wild and inaccessible falls of Tis'Abbai. From all angles one can see them—from the hills opposite; from islands in their midst; from the tropical chasm into which they plunge; and from natural caves that slice into the cliff face behind them. For hours one can wander back and forth, seeing the clean stream slide into space in a gracious arc, shattering into a raging torrent of spume below; and hearing it as it rushes on with a deep roar that vibrates through the earth as though all the devils in hell were beating upon an infernal orchestra of gongs. Having taken its leap it turns sharply to the right, and within three hundred yards, in defiance of all the laws of nature, the gigantic stream converges and gathers its strength to pour through a gap in the rocks barely twelve feet wide. And from there on, for the next five hundred miles, despite all its grandeur and importance to mankind, the Nile is one of the least known rivers in the entire world.

Though the Blue Nile gorge is all but impassable (no one so far as I know has ever followed its course every inch of the way) the river itself has always been the main life-stream of the Egyptians; and at some time in the distant past there can be no doubt that riverain peoples from the lower Nile valley have traced it to its source. For when we arrived on Lake Tsana, we found living proof of a connection between modern Ethiopia and ancient Egypt.

On arrival in Bahr Dar we paid the normal courtesy visit on the Governor, Ato Bahranu, a well-spoken, forward-looking Ethiopian of the younger generation, who kindly supplied us with a guide to take us to a village where the lake-boats are constructed. Our guide was a little incredulous that we should want to visit the boat-builders, for being of a lowly tribe they are looked down upon by other people of the lake. Their homes are mean hovels, and they are dirty, so he told us; and besides, most of them are Muslims. They are all members of the Waito tribe; and the Waito, together with the Agau, are thought to be the earliest inhabitants of this region. When I came to know them later I could not but wonder whether they had come originally from the lower Nile, where perhaps they were once fishermen who withdrew to the Ethiopian highlands as the papyrus swamps of Egypt gradually disappeared forever.

At the Waito village we immediately saw plenty of the boats for which we were searching. Here they are called "tankwas"; but in appearance, this time, we could see that they are virtually identical in every respect with those depicted in the Egyptian tombs. But this was not enough. Having some knowledge of Egyptian building methods, I was determined to watch in detail how the tankwas were constructed. For this purpose we agreed to buy a tankwa (for

3*s.* 6*d.*), providing that the Waito would allow us to film it being built.

First we went down to the swamps to cut the reeds. This was done by two people; one, with a sickle, deftly chose and cut the stems and threw them into the chest-deep water behind for his mate to collect and stack on a tankwa. When they had cut a sufficient quantity they pulled their load ashore and carried it up to their village, where it was left leaning against a hut for several days to dry out.

When the papyrus was ready, a team of builders gathered and set to work. Most of the work was done by one man, the "master-builder", who started by laying a spine of papyrus like a keel. This was done by binding bunches of three or four stems to one another, each bunch overlapping the other by about eighteen inches until the "keel" was of the required length. Our tankwa was about twelve feet long, but sometimes they make them much larger, capable of carrying eight or ten people.

As the master-builder worked, two men squatted to one side rolling cord from fibre stripped from the bark of a nearby tree—the first of many scenes portrayed also in Ptahhotep's tomb. The cord was made in lengths of about fifteen feet which were then coiled and stacked; and standing by was a young boy cutting the coils into lengths ready to hand to the master-builder.

Then something caught my eye that made me tremendously excited. A man was standing by the pile of papyrus measuring it and breaking it into lengths, and he was measuring the stems in *cubits*—from his elbow to his fingertips—each piece five cubits long. This is a measurement that I never saw or heard of being used in Ethiopia at any other time. Suddenly, in front of my eyes, it made ancient Egypt come alive. One could see those semi-naked builders twenty-five centuries before Christ, as they began the boats that were portrayed in Ptahhotep's tomb, doing precisely and exactly the same thing. For century after century, long after it had fallen into disuse elsewhere, here in Ethiopia it had lived on.

Now, by binding bunch upon bunch, the tankwa rapidly took shape. The method differed in one respect from that of the tombs; beneath the prow and the stern the Waito placed no blocks to give the boat an up-sweeping curve. They raised the stem and the stern nevertheless by lifting it and bending it bodily into shape. As they did so a boy stood by with a calabash of water to splash over the dry reeds and make them supple—surely what the man in the ancient relief was doing with a precisely similar gourd. (So the boy I had seen cutting the coils corresponded with the boy with the rings on the relief.) The internal shape of the boat was made by treading it out, pushing and pulling it into shape; and when it came to making the tapering ends this was done by carefully thinning the stems and paring down those that remained until the curling stern and protruding prow were no more than the width of a forearm.

When the boat was finished, a bundle of papyrus reeds was fitted into it as a seat, and a paddle was cut. Apart from the curvature—the tankwa being rather flatter than its ancient counterpart—the finished product was precisely similar. The whole job took less than four hours.

One other small thing that differed between the tankwas, ancient and modern, was the paddle. Whereas the Egyptian paddles were single-ended, and broad, we were supplied with a simple hollow "bamboo" cane to be used as a double paddle though it had no flat plates on either end. With such a stick I thought it would have been difficult to get much motive power; but when we took the tankwa down to the lake to try it out, we found it was so light that it sped through the water with ease.

On the Nile in ancient Egypt, these boats were doubtless used—as for the most part they were portrayed—in the shallow water of the swamps; or at very most to cross the river. For such work they seemed best suited, for they appeared to lack stability, and several times as we paddled about the lake we lost our balance and turned ours over. I was sitting with my feet in front of me, as do the Ethiopians, not with them tucked underneath me as seemed to be done in Egypt. I presumed that the position in which one sat was a matter of personal preference and comfort; but a day or two later I noticed one very good reason why the Ethiopians sit this way. We were crossing the lake in a large motor launch. It was quite a stormy day, and the lake was choppy; but suddenly, right out in the middle, we saw a tankwa with two men in it. Apparently the Waito frequently cross the lake; it takes them about twelve hours, and they can only just do it before their tankwa becomes waterlogged and sinks.

What caught my attention about this Tankwa was that it was fitted with a pair of very interesting "outriggers". These must have

been an indigenous invention designed to overcome the problems of crossing a large stretch of water in a highly unstable craft, for they were unlike any other outriggers I had ever seen. Though they looked simple, they were actually extremely ingenious, and seemed typical of the lively inventiveness that one finds every now and again in Africa. They were fixed to the middle of the boat, and they stuck out behind like the tail of a kite, or a swallowtail butterfly. They had been so placed that the rear paddler sat with his feet on them, and thus was able to vary their pitch, for the same reasons that modern scientists are struggling to invent variable-pitch wings for supersonic jets. The wider the angle the more stability they gave, but the more resistance to movement; the narrower the angle, the greater the speed. This was a technique that I believe had not previously been observed, and it is probably unique to Lake Tsana. Certainly the Egyptians used nothing of the sort, but on the narrow Nile they had no need.

Crude though these tankwas have seemed to many travellers, after observing them closely our impression was that they are far more sophisticated than they appear at first. Like most other products of primitive people, they have been designed to fulfil a special function; and over many centuries they have done this admirably. Perhaps in a way this is not surprising; for if they were good enough to have survived in the land of the pyramid-builders, they cannot have been too bad.

So the first of our films was now finished. We made a gift of our tankwa to the people who had built it, and having packed up our belongings and said good-bye to the Governor, we made our way back to Addis Ababa.

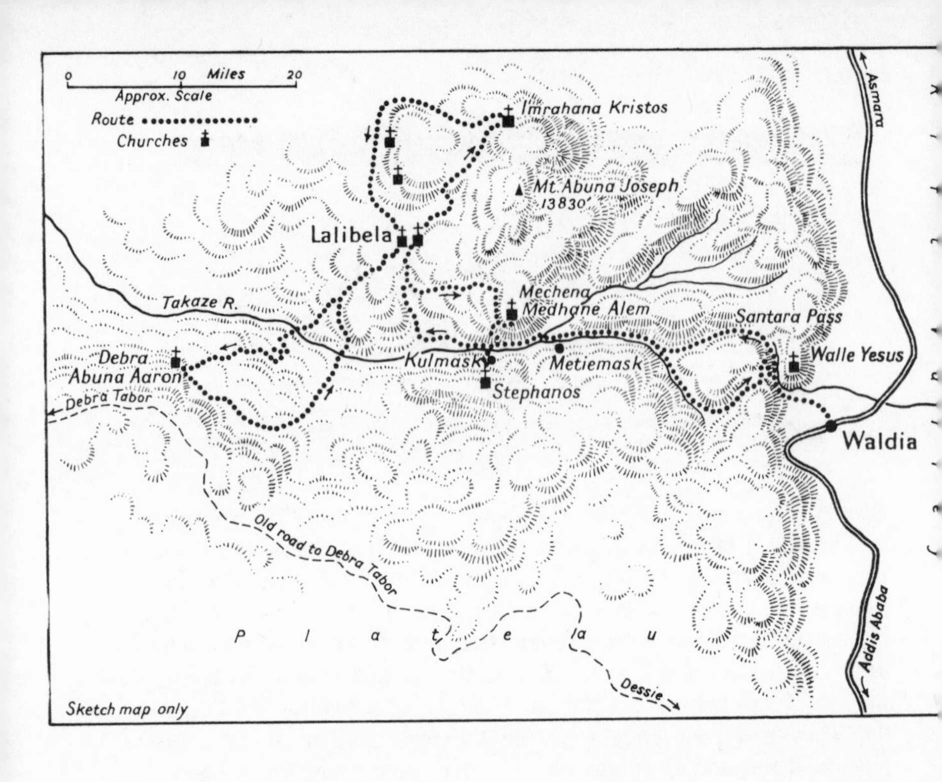
0 10 Miles 20
Approx. Scale
Route
Churches
Imrahana Kristos
Mt. Abuna Joseph
13830'
Lalibela
Takaze R.
Mechena
Medhane Alem
Santara Pass
Walle Yesus
Debra
Abuna Aaron
Kulmask
Metiemask
Stephanos
Debra Tabor
Waldia
Asmara
Old road to Debra Tabor
P l a t e a u
Addis Ababa
Dessie
Sketch map only

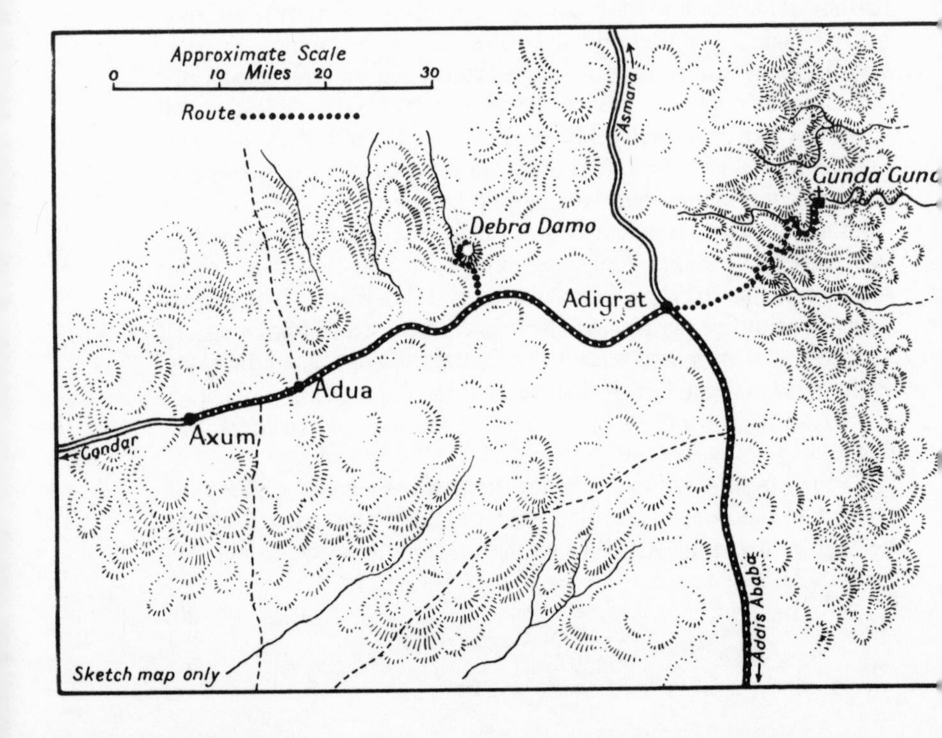
Approximate Scale
0 10 Miles 20 30
Route
Asmara
Gunda Gunc
Debra Damo
Adigrat
Adua
Axum
Gondar
Addis Ababa
Sketch map only

CHAPTER EIGHT

Monasteries and Manuscripts

Geographically, the continent of Africa, like the fabled Jack-in-the-Bag, can be divided into two main parts: the vast desert areas north of a line from Somalia, through Timbuctoo to the Atlantic Ocean; and the more vibrant jungle and bush of "black" Africa to the south of that line. But rising as it does, rather like a hawk in an aviary of thrushes, Ethiopia fits neatly into neither of these divisions. It is a sort of equatorial Tibet; a "Shangri-La" perched high in the mountains, inbred, inward looking, inward thinking. Very little of what has gone on around Ethiopia in the course of history has affected it, and equally little of what has happened within it has touched the outside world. Cut off in its mountain fastness—and doubly isolated from its neighbours by surrounding deserts—it is a country that is without equal.

The Ethiopia to which I refer is not the modern State that extends into Muslim and pagan areas such as those we had been visiting around Lake Abaya, but the Ethiopia of the Christian highlands of Tigré and Shoa. This, in a sense, is the true Ethiopia—the source of the nation's power, culture, and special atmosphere.

When Chris and I had finished our film on the boats, it was to the heart of the Christian highlands that we next headed. We were now embarking on the second half of our project, to make a film about Ethiopian Christian art. We planned this film to cover a wide range of subjects which included different types of architecture, manuscript paintings, frescoes in ancient churches, and anything else of artistic interest connected with church life.

As a starting point we chose to go to Tigré, a large and important province of Ethiopia in the far north. We had several reasons for this choice. We had by then discovered just how ignorant we were about the country in general, and before we embarked on our quest for Christian art we felt it would be both valuable and interesting to get acquainted with that part of Ethiopia in which

Christianity first took root. And the capital of Tigré, Axum, apart from being to this day the most important religious centre in Ethiopia, is in a sense also the nation's birthplace.

Very little is known about the early history of Ethiopia. The people of the highlands are mostly of Hamitic stock, though the languages they speak are of Semitic origin. Before the days of Christ the country was undoubtedly greatly influenced by the Sabaean civilisation of Southern Arabia. Indeed, northern Ethiopia was once a Sabaean "colony", and to this day one can see relics of that civilisation, as, for instance, the remarkable stone temple of Yeha, a short distance from Axum. We visited this temple while we were in the north and came away with the strong impression that the early Ethiopians' prowess at building was in all probability derived from the architectural genius of Sabaea.

Axum is the earliest Ethiopian city that can be looked upon as being a truly indigenous creation—and in its day it may well have been one of the greatest cities that the continent of Africa has ever known. When Axum was founded is not known. The first historical reference to it is in the famous "Periplus of the Erythraean Sea", a journal written by a Greek navigator in the first century A.D. The writer of the Periplus mentions it as being a city eight days' journey into the mountains from the Red Sea port of Adulis—or Berenice Panchrusos, as the Greeks would have known it—whose king, Zoscales, was sufficiently worldly to be acquainted with Greek literature. But even at the time of this first historical mention, Axum had already "arrived". It was by then a great city and an important entrepôt through which came ivory and gold from the hinterland for export to Rome.

Archaeological work that has been done at Axum suggests that in size, and in grandeur, it may even have rivalled many of the classical cities of the Mediterranean. Through a variety of other towns and staging posts—whose ruins have also been discovered—it was connected to the coast by a paved highway. Its streets were paved, too, for the horses and chariots of the rich. The palaces of its kings and princes were vast constructions of stone, measuring up to 130 yards long by 90 yards wide. It had a coinage system of its own, mining cash in gold and other metals. And about the town were monumental statues, probably of kings, which—judging from the pedestals that remain—were cast in metal and possibly twenty or twenty-five feet high.

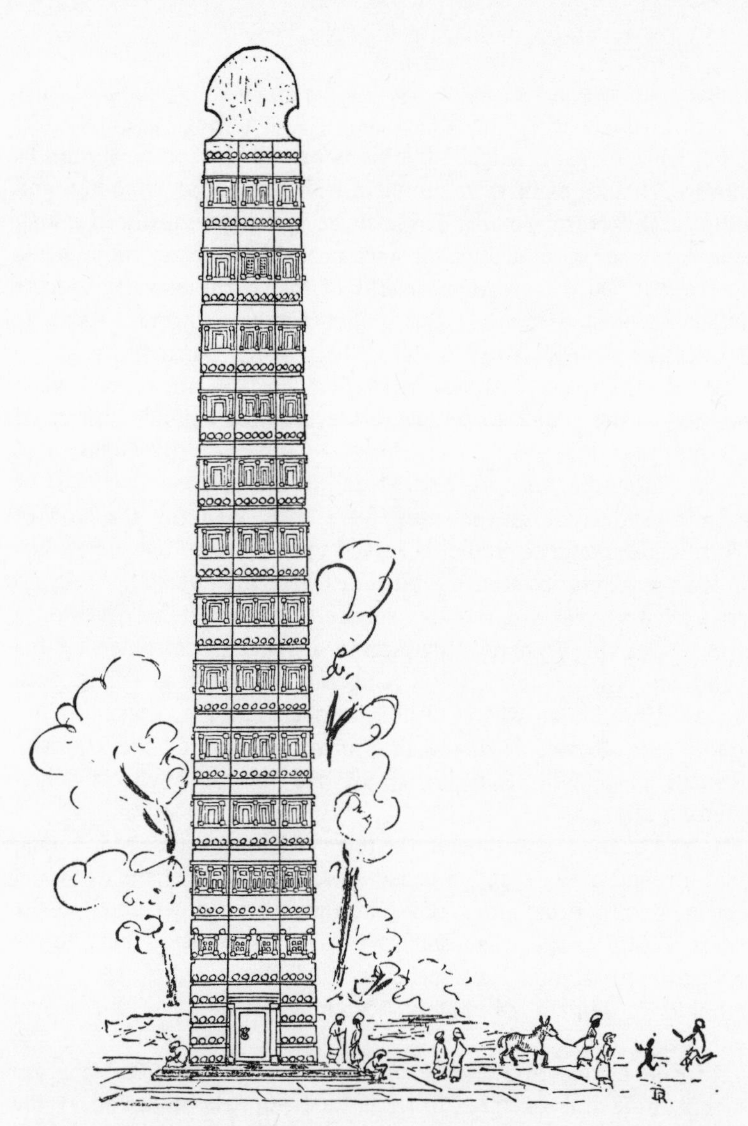

But the most amazing relics of ancient Axum are the colossal monolithic stelae for which the city has doubtless been renowned far and wide throughout the past two thousand years. The largest of these enormous stelae, which now lies fallen and broken into several huge chunks, was originally one single piece of granite that stood well over a hundred feet high. This was larger than the greatest obelisk of ancient Egypt, and was in all probability the largest single piece of stone ever to be erected by mankind anywhere in the world. The tallest stele still standing is seventy feet high. Like its giant neighbour, this is carved to represent a multi-storeyed palace of its day, complete with false door, windows, and other architectural details. These stelae, arranged mostly in a long line down one side of the city, were probably funerary monuments to royalty. Once there were dozens of them; but now many have fallen or been destroyed. Those that remain, however, stand as impressive memorials to a long forgotten age of pagan glory.

When these giant stones were first erected, they must have seemed to the people to be the very symbol of Axum's power. Of all the gods the people worshipped—Ashtar, or the Goddess of Love; Bahr, the Sea-god; and Medr, the Earth-god—the focus of their most fervent prayers must have been Mahram, the God of War, whose crescent symbol is carved upon some of the stones. For in the first centuries after the birth of Christ the city-state of Axum controlled a great and war-like empire. Early in the fourth century A.D., under the Emperor Ella-Amida, its boundaries extended beyond the Nile, to include the Kingdom of Meroe in the modern Sudan. Ella-Amida was even able to challenge the power of Constantine in Rome, seizing and destroying ships of the Imperial Roman navy in the Red Sea, which had come to attack a neighbouring ally.

It was at about that time, in the reign of Ella-Amida's son, Ezana, that a remarkable thing happened. Two young Christians of Syrian origin, named Frumentius and Aedesius, were shipwrecked off the coast of Ethiopia; and being picked up and saved were taken to the Emperor in Axum. There, being intelligent youths, they were allowed to remain, ultimately becoming members of the Royal entourage.

In due course Frumentius so impressed Ezana with his arguments in favour of the Christian God—of whom doubtless the Emperor had already heard rumours from foreign merchants—that Ezana renounced Mahram; and in about 324 A.D. became converted to Christianity.

Thus it came about that after centuries of pagan worship, during which time the great city-state of Axum had developed and flowered, it became one of the first nations in the world to accept the teaching of Christ as its official religion. And since that day, over sixteen centuries ago, up till modern times, the Christian tradition of Ethiopia has remained unbroken.

Axum as a city-state fell into decline in the seventh century A.D. With the rise of Islam, the Ethiopian coastline—and consequently access to the outside world—came under the control of the Muslims. Between the seventh and the fifteenth centuries, as Gibbon put it, "encompassed on all sides by the enemies of their religion, the Aethiopians slept near a thousand years, forgetful of the world, by whom they were forgotten". With trade brought to a sudden halt the days of wealth and splendour passed into history, and Ethiopia withdrew into itself, a nation in retreat, with little more than its Christian religion upon which to live. But that religion lasted; and though we know practically nothing of what took place during those "thousand years of sleep", when the first Europeans arrived in Ethiopia early in the sixteenth century, the church was seen to have been the main support upon which the nation had rested.

Today, apart from the giant stelae, a few subterranean tombs, and a remarkable reservoir carved into the side of a hill, little remains of ancient Axum; for upon the ruins of the old city others have been built, each more degenerate and uninspiring than the last. Modern Axum is but a hotch-potch of tin-roofed shacks thrown up around a market square where local farmers sell lentils and tomatoes, beans and flour, amid the hubbub and din of clacking mules and hooting motor coaches. The lines of stelae—once the greatest pride of this noble city—are today used as a forest of trees might be, as a public lavatory;* and the stones of ancient palaces are callously incorporated into the mean shacks of the peasants.

When Chris and I arrived in Axum we found the city preparing for one of its greatest annual celebrations, the Feast of St. Mary. The town was crowded with visitors from all over Ethiopia, and the only hotel was already full. But we had with us a letter of introduction to the local Governor who very kindly allowed us to pitch our tent in a copse of tall gum-trees at the bottom of his garden. The Governor was a lordly-looking gentleman in his fifties, easily recognisable among his ever-present entourage by the homburg hat and heavy overcoat that he wore more for prestige

* Since we were in Axum, I understand that the Ethiopian government has made strenuous efforts to clean the place up. Despite the filth we found, a visit to Axum was well worth while.

than necessity. Despite the fact that he was busy entertaining many important civic guests he treated us hospitably and saw to it that we had all we needed. As we planned to make several excursions from Axum, and to be in the area for two or three weeks, one of our most urgent needs was a good interpreter. And this the Governor said he would arrange.

Very early the next morning, whilst we still lay in bed, we were aroused by a mild, polite voice outside the tent calling "Getuch! Getuch!" ("Sir! Sir!") Chris got up and flung back the flap, and from where I lay I could see a tall young fellow of no more than twenty, neatly dressed in trousers and open neck shirt. Maybe the young Ethiopian was frightened by the sight of the chaos in the tent, or of Chris, with hairy chest and balding head, in his Javanese sarong; but for a time he stood nervously looking at us without saying a word. Though we repeatedly asked him what he wanted, the only information he seemed willing to impart was that his name was Shifarau; and it was some time before we gathered that he had been instructed by the Governor to act as our interpreter.

Shifarau, like all other Ethiopian children, had learned his English in school, and spoke it quite well. In the next few weeks he proved to be an extremely useful companion. One day, later on, he came out with a strange story about his family. He was talking with Chris, and having heard that he had been working in the Persian Gulf, asked him if he knew the best way to get to Riyadh in Saudi Arabia. For a young Ethiopian Christian to want to visit this city in the heart of the Muslim world struck us as being very strange, and we asked him why. He was, so he told us, the youngest of eleven children. His eldest brother who was now a man nearing fifty, had been stolen from his home when he was a small boy, and taken to Saudi Arabia where he was sold as a slave. When he grew to adulthood he was freed, and his master had set him up in a small business. He had never forgotten his home, and now, having done well in business, he came back to Ethiopia every few years to visit his family. On these visits he invariably brought with him substantial presents; in fact, he seemed to be far better off in Arabia than he would ever have been in Axum. And Shifarau wanted to join him.

We spent our first day wandering among the remnants of the ancient city, returning to our tent in the late afternoon. We had had little to eat or drink during the day, so as soon as we were home we set up our primus to brew some coffee and cook a meal. We were about to start eating when we saw the Governor approaching through the gum-trees with his usual retinue of hangers-on trailing obediently behind him. We assumed that he was now off duty, for he had discarded his overcoat and homburg hat in favour of a spotlessly clean white shamma; and whilst he lazily flicked his ivory-handled fly-whisk back and forth with one hand, he played incessantly with a little silver object in the other. The Governor plainly wished to speak to us; but as it seemed somewhat impolite to sit eating and drinking whilst he watched—and as we were too thirsty to watch our coffee spoil before our eyes—we invited him to join us.

Unwilling to part with either of his playthings, the Governor was momentarily at a loss what to do when he was handed his cup of coffee. This problem was quickly solved, however, by one of his attendants who took the fly-whisk from him, thenceforth keeping it moving solemnly back and forth above his master's head. It was only when he had settled down that we were able to see what the silver object was. It was an ear-pick—a prized possession among Ethiopians—shaped like a tiny spoon. And as he noisily gulped his steaming coffee from the cup in his left hand, his right hand was busily engaged upon a sanitary expedition into his ears. Scarcely any conversation ensued as he downed first one cup of coffee, then a second, and a third—instant coffee being something new, and apparently delectable to him. And only when he had finished did he mention the purpose of his visit, which was to invite us to a banquet he was giving later that evening for all the visiting dignitaries. We accepted with pleasure, hoping that he would provide something as exotic to us as the instant coffee had been to him.

The Governor's residence was one of the few old houses in the city, a three-storey stone dwelling built many years ago in a style reminiscent of the crenellated castles of Gondar, near Lake Tsana. It reminded me of a semi-derelict castle in Ireland I had once

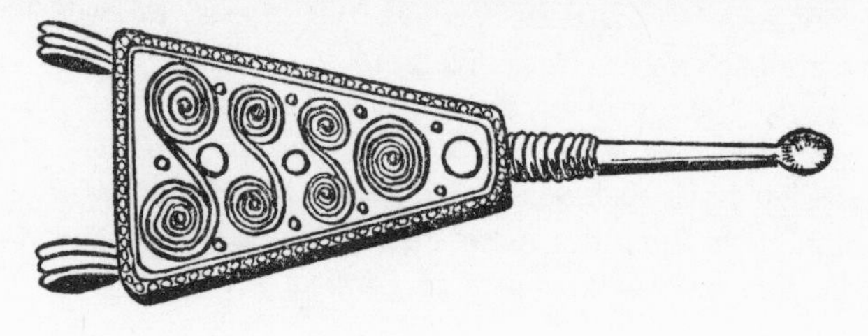

visited, reflecting an age of splendour that had long since passed. At the top of a grand staircase was a long, high-ceilinged baronial room. It was this sort of place that the explorer Bruce had described when he visited Ethiopia in the eighteenth century; but whereas in his day the walls of the hall might have been lined with Venetian mirrors carried painstakingly over the mountains on mules, today the room was bare apart from several benches and long wooden tables.

The meal was a haphazard sort of affair, table manners in our sense not being considered of much importance in Ethiopia. Several large round dishes of curried meat, baskets of the unleavened, crêpe-like Ethiopian bread called "njera", and various other delicacies were strewn over the tables, and small carafes of "tej" (honey wine) and "talla" (beer) stood opposite each place. The guests seemed to come and go as they pleased. With a degree of thoughtfulness that we found typical in Ethiopia we were supplied with knives and forks; but we preferred to eat, as the others did, with our fingers. Servants wearing breeches and off-white shammas about their shoulders scurried to and fro in answer to gruff requests; and such was the atmosphere of a medieval binge that I had an almost irrepressible desire to hurl my bones over my shoulder where I suspected large hound-dogs lay ready to carry them off into dark corners. The other guests were cordial, and many seemed greatly amused by our presence; but some, in a lordly way, took no notice of us whatsoever. The feast being more of a diplomatic dinner than an orgy to enjoy, within an hour people had already started to leave; and we ourselves did not remain long.

Feasting played a large part in our life in Ethiopia. We found the local food on the whole palatable; in fact months later when we returned to England both of us missed an occasional dish of a njera folded around a mouthful of spicy wat, or dipped into hot lentil sauce. In Axum, soon after our secular feast with the Governor, we were invited to another, this time with the priests. The food here was simpler (though the priests' tej was better); and the atmosphere was very different.

The party was given by the Chief Priest of St. Mary of Zion, whose small two-storey stone house lay at the end of a crooked alley of high walls in the cathedral precincts. His house not being large enough to entertain more than half a dozen guests comfortably, he had erected a shelter of grass in his backyard, through which the sun shone as through a sieve casting flecks of light over the ground beneath. And here, when we arrived, we found about fifty priests and monks from all over Ethiopia squatting on mats on the ground, waiting for the food to be brought. The scene was in complete contrast to that in the Governor's house. Gone were the swashbuckling manners of the Fitauraris and Blattas and other titled lords, and in their place was the sort of polite peace that one would expect from a gathering of churchmen. The guests—all male—ranged in age from their early twenties to what seemed to be their late hundreds. Some were dressed in white robes, others in black, and yet others, from the Tigrean monasteries near Axum, in brilliant saffron yellow. All wore hats, either white turbans or upturned flower pots like those of Greek archimandrites. They sat now in a quiet hum of conversation, the younger ones occasionally risking a chuckle of laughter, the older ones mostly silent as if praying to the Lord for time enough at least to taste the Chief Priest's tej before He called them. We refused the offer of chairs, to everyone's childlike delight and amusement, and squatted with a group of priests who chatted to us animatedly notwithstanding the fact that we were totally ignorant of what they were saying, for Shifarau the interpreter had not been invited. By and by the food was brought in circular baskets with conical hats, and a forest of fingers began to tear the njera into delicate pieces to be dipped into the lentil wat. Our host, the Chief Priest, hurried up and down like a vicar at a village bun-fight, grinning benignly, chatting here and there, generally making sure that all were happy.

Apart from the immediate enjoyment we derived from these two parties, they were interesting as they gave us a chance to see under similar conditions two of the most important facets of Ethiopian life . . . the Church and the State. Constitutionally, the Church and the State in Ethiopia are one, the Emperor being also the head of the Church. Though in the last resort the State may overrule the Church, the latter has always been, and still is, extremely powerful, being one of the largest landowners and having an influence that pervades many aspects of secular life.

The Ethiopians are members of the Eastern Church along with the Egyptian Copts, the Syrians and Armenians. The fundamental difference between the Eastern—or Monophysite—churches, and the Greek Orthodox, Roman, and other Western churches turns upon a piece of theological hair-splitting that first became the cause of controversy in the fourth and fifth centuries A.D. Whereas the Western churches regard Christ as uniting within Himself two natures, divine and human, the Monophysites (as their name implies) assert that the two natures were actually fused into one. To demonstrate this rift on a profane level, it is almost as though the Bartender's Association were to divide into two irreconcilable, bitterly opposed, factions over an argument as to whether a Dry Martini consists of Gin and French or Ginandfrench. To all but a few lofty philosophers the result tastes much the same.

From its very earliest days until as recently as 1948, as a result of a forged document produced at the Council of Nicaea in the fourth century, the Ethiopian church was officially looked upon as the "daughter" church, or a diocese, of the Coptic church of Alexandria. And except for brief periods the head of the Ethiopian church, or the Abuna, has always been an Egyptian Copt nominated by the Patriarch of Alexandria. This has led many people to believe that the Ethiopian church is the same as the Coptic church; but in fact this is far from true. The Abunas of Ethiopia have all too frequently been men ignorant of the country, and often unable to speak any Ethiopian language, and their influence on the active life of the church has been small. Throughout the "thousand years of sleep" that followed the decline of Axum, the Ethiopian church developed very much along its own lines.

To a European their church life is hard to understand. Apart from theological arguments, there are many differences in ritual and daily practice. Though some elements of pre-Christian, pagan worship can still be observed in most Western churches, pagan traditions are more noticeable in Ethiopia than elsewhere. Pre-Christian worship of the sun, of genii, and of serpents, finds expression in early Ethiopian church decorations; and the siting of pagan shrines on tops of hills and mountains gave rise to similar practices after conversion to Christianity. Also, as one might expect in a country shut away from outside influence for so long, many things about their church life are probably nearer the practices of the primitive church soon after Christ's death, than are those in other parts of Christendom where there has been continual interchange of ideas. For instance Epiphany, the twelfth day after Christmas, when Christ was manifested to the Magi at Bethlehem, is of far greater importance to the Ethiopians than Christmas Day. They set greater store by the Old Testament than the New, and some of the most noticeable differences between their church and ours are the outcome of early Jewish influences that have persisted down the centuries. They recognise the Jewish Sabbath as well as Sunday. In place of the altar in their churches is the Ark of the Covenant—supposed to be a representation of one of the tablets of Moses—heavily shrouded from view by hanging cloths. Much of the dancing and singing that we later witnessed is said to be a relic of Jewish tradition, in the remembrance that David himself danced around the Ark; and the layout of Ethiopian churches, being divided into three main sections, owes much to the design of the Jewish synagogue. But apart from differences of this nature many aspects of Ethiopian church life are basically similar to those elsewhere. For example, when Holy Communion is celebrated, as in other Eastern churches, consecration takes place within the sanctuary which is hidden from view, and which no layman may ever enter. Communicants (whose numbers are limited by severe church laws that result in many people being partial ex-communicants) receive the sacraments in the middle portion of the church that approximates to the nave. Here, as elsewhere in the church, the congregation stands, or squats on the floor, since, apart from occasional T-shaped pieces of wood like outsized shooting-sticks, the Ethiopian churches have no pews or chairs.

The language of the church is an archaic Ethiopian language called Geez, the use of which is comparable to Latin in the Roman church. Up to the present century the Bible was only available in Geez, and as all copies were handwritten they were few and far between. Thus the ordinary people's knowledge of the Scriptures, even if they were literate in their own modern language, was until recently limited to what they heard secondhand from priests.

The priesthood of the Ethiopian church is vast, though many of those often looked upon as priests are in fact "debterras". There is no equivalent to a debterra in our church, though he might be looked upon as being something between a chorister and a lay reader. There is an anomaly here, however, for a debterra's training of seven years is longer than that of a priest. In the church's "rule book" the pattern of life is so designed that priests might live a godly, clean, and wholesome life, whilst at the same time it recognises the normal human urges. Priests *must* be married; though divorce for them and other communicants married by the church is out of the question. But also they may marry only once; thus, after the death of their spouse, widows and widowers from among the priesthood, rather than forsake the church, generally seek the peace and quiet of monasteries and nunneries for the remainder of their days. Deacons of the church are chosen from among young boys, who have to give up their position at time of puberty lest, in a moment of weakness, they commit a sin that cannot be countenanced by the church.

In theory this looks fine. But from it one should not get the impression that all priests, or for that matter all Ethiopians, are saints. The great majority of Ethiopians avoid a church marriage, thus allowing for easy and frequent divorce without sinning in the eyes of the Lord. Fornication is almost the national sport, the illegitimacy rate is astronomical (but was not their first king the bastard son of Solomon and the Queen of Sheba?); and venereal diseases, mostly endemic syphilis, are the scourge of the country. And in a great many people's view there is little to be said for the priests themselves in respect of sexual morality or, for that matter, in other aspects of their life. The priests have been described as "drunken", "lazy", "lecherous", and "clerical drones that fatten in idleness on the labour of the working classes".

We were not in Ethiopia long enough to see how true these criticisms were. For my own part I would say that the great majority of priests that we encountered on subsequent journeys seemed good people. Sometimes they appeared to be woefully ignorant and simple-minded, and at others, they were suspicious to a point that nearly drove us round the bend. Doubtless also there is some truth in that they are lazy. One early traveller to Ethiopia told the story of how an idle Archbishop overcame the difficulty of ordaining deacons in some distant village by sending them his breath of ordination in a leather bag!

But making due allowances for the different cultural background, for the almost total isolation of the people from many of the mind-broadening influences of the modern world, and for the lack of facilities for a general education, my own feeling when I left Ethiopia was that the church, for all its faults, has done an astonishing amount of good in the past—even if today it is a drag on modernisation. I am far from being a deeply religious person myself; but I could not escape the feeling that the higher plane of civilisation that one encounters in Ethiopia compared with other

African countries is in large measure due to its religion rather than to any effects of racial origin or even ancient history. In Ethiopia, Christianity has often proved to be a unifying influence, and without it the nation would undoubtedly long ago have been overrun by its Muslim neighbours. They are a volatile lot, the Ethiopians, and were it not for their fervent, if not deeply spiritual, following of Christ, God knows what state their country would be in now.

In the Ethiopian church calendar over two hundred fast days are listed. Only the most devout Christians observe them all; the rest make do with roughly two mornings of fasting each week. There are certain annual festivals such as Easter and Epiphany that are observed by everyone; and large celebrations are arranged in all churches on the days of the Saints to which they are dedicated. St. Mary's day being the great day for the Cathedral of St. Mary of Zion in Axum, and this in any event being the oldest and holiest shrine in the land, it was hardly surprising that on the day of the festival one could barely move in the city.

The great rock-brown rectangular edifice of St. Mary of Zion, built in its present form in the seventeenth century, stands on a high earth mound with broad stone steps rising to it in two terraced flights. Around the cathedral are two enclosures, the first crenellated, like the cathedral itself, the second enclosing a much greater area where sheep normally graze, surrounded by a high wall with access through a gate-house opposite the western end of the sanctuary. When we arrived there, both enclosures were already packed tight with several thousand white-clad, turbaned men, women and children. Even the space beyond the enclosure was thronged with people, waiting for the one aspect of any Ethiopian church festival that the people most enjoy—the ceremonial entrance of the priests. There was an atmosphere about the place similar to the Mall on Coronation Day. Several women, making a "bit on the side", shuffled amongst the crowd selling saffron yellow cakes, much like ice-cream vendors in London; and had they had periscopes to sell as well, one feels they would have made a small fortune. To while away the time a number of hermits and troglodytes who had come out of hiding for this great occasion attracted small crowds of attentive listeners as they harangued them with their extreme views on the Christian life; and lines of uniformed police stood ready to keep back the crowds once the procession began.

When at last the Bishop arrived on the scene, forcing a way

through the crowds in a chauffeured car to join the other waiting priests, the procession did not even then immediately begin. For a while, bedecked in magnificent robes and golden crown, the bishop, with the chief priest and other dignitaries, remained beneath a huge fig-tree to read aloud passages from the gospel appropriate to the day, and to bless the Ark of the Covenant that had been brought out from the cathedral on this special occasion. This was a great event; for the Ark, shrouded in fine cloths, only leaves the cathedral on two occasions each year, on this, the Feast of St. Mary, and again at Epiphany. When the short preliminary service was complete, the procession now formed and slowly began to move through the crowds towards St. Mary of Zion.

There can be few more colourful sights than an Ethiopian religious procession. On this occasion seventy or eighty priests and musicians were involved, forming a long, slowly moving line in a riot of vivid reds, purples, and streaks of blue and green, their garments embroidered in dazzling gold and silver filigree designs. Many of the priests and deacons bore large silver and copper crosses, elaborately worked; and behind each of these came a bearer with a brilliant umbrella held near the cross for symbolic protection from the elements. The Ark itself was borne upon the head of a priest, above whom was held the father of all umbrellas, bright crimson with golden tassels hanging from its sides. The procession was led by the musicians; first there were flautists; and then came an orchestra of "masenkos", one-string fiddles that emitted a delicate drone only audible at close range in the clamour and noise of the crowd. Behind the masenko players were two trumpeters, blowing brass trumpets about four feet long with an ear-splitting cacophony of tuneless hoots. Amongst the priests were drummers, too, with colourful double-ended drums, beating out a deep-pitched rhythm that throbbed through the clamorous atmosphere with primitive African resonance; and young deacons clanged brass bells.

The procession moved gradually through the outer yard, and up the steps to the inner enclosure. Now, with the Ark borne aloft, the priests circled the cathedral three times before finally going inside and disappearing from view.

We had, all along, been struggling to film this impressive scene, being jostled to and fro whichever way we moved. But when it came to entering the cathedral, filming proved to be impossible. The building, large though it is by Ethiopian standards, was already a solid mass of sweating bodies, standing on every available inch of floor. We were, however, able to squeeze our way into the porch at the west end where we found an assembly of debterras singing and dancing, oblivious of the hubbub in the main body of the church; and so we stayed for a while to listen to them.

There were amongst them several drummers like those we had seen outside; but most of them, dressed in deep Prussian blue cloaks, and white turbans, were singing the strangest dirge—almost a wail—forced from their throats, swaying back and forth as though in an agonised trance. In their hands they held instruments called "sistra"—little metal discs on a wire that clashed together with the sound of a gently beaten tambourine as they shook them to the sombre rhythm of their dance. Their chant was a special chant for the feast day of St. Mary; but what they said there was no way of telling. For verse after verse they went on like this, glorifying God and the Virgin, clashing their sistra, beating their drums, and shuffling their bare feet back and forth in dreamy repetition. Would that churchmen back home might institute performances like this, I thought. Perhaps then they would draw the crowds!

The crowds dispersed as mysteriously as they had come. One by one and in small groups, the people filtered away and moved to the town where they filled the bars and public places. And that evening there was much drunkenness and fornication in the ancient city of Axum.

Wherever we travelled in Ethiopia, whenever possible, we carried letters of introduction to Chief Priests, and local Governors, from important people in Addis Ababa. We had been told by friends that this was not merely useful, but sometimes absolutely essential for overcoming fears and suspicions in distant parts of the provinces, and getting the co-operation that we needed. In Addis Ababa, before leaving on our travels to Tigré, we had been fortunate enough to meet Dedjazmatch Zewde Gabre Selassie, a highly cultured Oxford graduate, who, besides being an important landowner in Axum, was also a relative of the royal family, and a grandson of Ras Seyum, the Governor-General of Tigré. Zewde's friendship and help was invaluable, and it was largely because of him that we had been so well received in the north. The word had got around rapidly that we had the patronage of the Governor-General, and its effect snowballed. At the Chief Priest's party, we had met several monks from an ancient monastery called Debra Damo, which we planned to visit next, and by the time we left Axum we had been able to make a number of important arrangements for our journey.

Debra Damo is a few hours' drive to the east of Axum, and an easy afternoon's mule ride north of the road from a point in the middle of nowhere. One of the main problems for a visitor travelling to Debra Damo is that of hiring mules; for to hire the mules one has first to go to Debra Damo. But for us this was easily overcome as at Axum we were able to make a firm date with the monks to meet us with mules by the roadside.

Our reasons for wanting to go to Debra Damo were three-fold. Firstly, the monastery is situated in a fantastic position on a flat-topped hill, the summit of which can only be reached by means of a rope; and we wished to experience the masochistic pleasure of scaling the impregnable cliff. Secondly, its church is the oldest building in Ethiopia, and has possibly been in unbroken use for longer than any other church in Christendom; and this we felt was reason enough on its own for a pilgrimage. Thirdly, it contains amongst other treasures a finely carved panelled ceiling, each panel depicting various animals woven into interesting designs; and we wished to photograph these for our film on Ethiopian art.

We waited at the appointed meeting place for an hour, and though we began to fear that the monks had let us down, they were as good as their word, and came personally with mules to show us the way to the monastery. We drove the car off the road as far as we could to hide it from potential wheel-stealers, and having loaded our baggage on to the mules we set off across broken red hills into a landscape dotted with candelabra euphorbia, a few farmsteads and rocky infertile fields. Almost immediately we came over a ridge, and there before us, on the other side of a huge valley, we saw Amba Debra Damo rising out of a conical mountain, the grey walls of its cliffs gleaming against the blue sky. But if the first sight of Amba Debra Damo was impressive, it became even more so the nearer we got. As we wound our way across the valley the cliffs rising above us began to look frighteningly precipitous. The last two hours of the journey involved a slow drag up a twisting path with steps cut into it here and there, until finally we were right beneath that terrible wall.

For the most part the sheer face of Debra Damo's cliff rises above the surrounding hill from about a hundred to three hundred feet. But at the spot at which we stood, which was where the cliff was at its lowest, a fault in the rock had enabled the monks to clear a narrow pathway from the top to a point almost half-way down. So in fact, the climb that we were faced with was only about fifty feet. At the top of the climb was a neat little doorway through which visitors from outer space would first enter the monastery precincts. From a thick peg imbedded in the rock near the doorway, a plaited leather rope as thick as a wrist hung down to the ground below; and beyond the door several monks were waiting to greet us. Twenty or thirty yards behind them, up a flight of steps cut in the rock, was a larger gate-house; and between this and the smaller one, on the lip of the cliff above us, was a row of rough-hewn stone seats. The seats reminded me rather of some corporation benches that had been set up near my childhood home at a particularly dangerous cross-roads. There, every Sunday, all the old pensioners of the town would gather like vultures to watch the cars stream by, waiting for a spectacular crash. And now, in the seats, a row of monks sat silently, waiting for one of us to make a spectacular death plunge to the rocks below.

All of a sudden I began to take fright. I have a terrible head for heights, and in the normal course of events I would no more climb up the face of a five-storey office-block for the sheer hell of it than fly. The whole venture—all in aid of a few carved bits of wood—suddenly seemed utterly lunatic.

While several monks who had accompanied us ran up the main rope like heavenly commandos, I watched the baggage being hauled aloft piece by piece on a subsidiary cord. But soon I was beckoned over to the cliff. It was my turn. Thankfully, I noticed that all visitors were tied into a safety harness; but this looked frail and thin and I doubted whether it would take a man's weight if he slipped. But there was no turning back now, and I started up the cliff.

At first it was easy going. There were several indentations worn by centuries of use, where it was possible to get a grip with one's feet. About twenty feet up there was a narrow ledge, and here I stopped for a few moments for a breather. Just as I was about to start climbing again some psychological genius at the top shouted down to me to be careful when I reached a certain outward-hanging ridge. Several people had lost their grip there, he added, and fallen to their death. I tried to pretend I hadn't heard, and struggled on. At about forty feet I glanced down, and was smitten with a wave of vertigo. For a few seconds I hung, unable to move either way: and at that moment I recollected a picture I had seen somewhere of Takla Haymanot, an Ethiopian Saint. He was climbing to the monastery once when the Devil sneaked up and cut the rope. But the Lord had come to his aid, and blessed him with six wings, I wished that God might do the same for me.

But the wings were not necessary. As I struggled up the last few feet, arms appeared from above, clutching me about the shoulders, and dragging me over the lip to the firm rock. Chris followed me with less fear. He is the sort of person who enjoys hanging over precipices.

The top of Amba Debra Damo is a flat oval about half a mile long and almost as wide. Nobody seemed to know precisely how many monks and novices lived up there; but there was quite a size-able village of flat-roofed stone houses, sufficient for two or three hundred inmates at a pinch. When we arrived there were no more than forty or fifty men and boys on the plateau. The rest, so we were told, were down in the valley on the monastery's farm, or tend-ing the mechanised flour mill that the monks run as a business in a village not far from where we had left the car. There were a few very small cultivated fields on the plateau, little more than gardens, behind some of the houses; and there were half a dozen bullocks. These, though fully grown when we saw them, had been hauled up on the rope when they were young. There were, of course, no cows with them, for as in all other Ethiopian monasteries, nothing of the opposite sex is allowed to enter at any time. The monks even went so far as to assure us that there were no female rats, or fleas even. Impossible, they said.

The monastery's water supply consists of a number of deep rectangular catchment wells cut into the rock. These appear to be filthy stagnant pools, but in fact the green weed that covers them oxygenates the water, keeping it fresh. Soon after our arrival I nearly committed an error to end all social errors. Traditional Ethiopian houses do not have lavatories, it being the custom to use any convenient patch of grass, or stone wall. Being in desperate need, I was about to follow local form upon the outer wall of a monastic dwelling, when I was arrested by a shout of horror from a group of attentive monks. Though many yards from the nearest well, they pointed out that I was just within the catchment zone. As we planned to spend two or three days on the plateau drinking their water, it was good to see such attention to hygiene.

We had brought with us our tent and other camping gear, but when we arrived we were told that the Memhir, or Abbot (whom we had met in Axum) had sent word that we were to use his house. From its outward appearance this was the same as any other on Debra Damo, and inside it was one of the most charming little places I have stayed in. Within the encircling walls of the house were several tiny courtyards. Inside there were some dark rooms downstairs, and up an unlit flight of wooden stairs was our bedroom, with floorspace about nine feet by four. There were three little windows, two about a foot square, and the other half the size; and into one wall, two feet six above the floor, was a sleeping-alcove into which we were just able to fit a camp bed. The room was furnished with a table and a chair, and covering the floor and bedspace were Persian rugs. In the mud-plastered wall were even smaller alcoves for candles, and from hooks on the wall hung several small handwritten books in wooden covers. It was austere; but in its Lilliputian compactness it was enchanting.

When we arrived we were taken to the refectory for a meal. There are two such refectories on the plateau, all the cooking being done communally by the young novices under the guiding eye of one of the monks. The storerooms were interesting and had obviously been built with the capacity to withstand a siege of some duration. Grain was kept in several huge chambers moulded in mud, each of which would have held at least a ton of barley or tef (an Ethiopian grain from which they make njera). Near the bins was a line of stone querns, and it was not difficult to visualise seven or eight young boys busily grinding away for hours on end in the days when the monastery (according to tradition) had six hundred inmates. One of the monks was repairing the refectory walls when we arrived, happily slapping on mortar with the confidence of a professional bricklayer. Apart from tasks such as this, the monks spend their days mostly in prayer and contemplation.

After our meal we went for a stroll across the plateau. The day was already drawing to a close as we sat down upon a ledge of rock

near the lip of the western precipice. From where we sat, as though perched high upon a cloud, we looked out into a gigantic void. Far below, the stream we had crossed that afternoon was a pencil-thin trickle of silver barely visible in the gloaming. Across it, on the other side, the red hills rose one upon another in gentle folds, fading into the distance where the purple thumb-like mountains of Adua and Yeha stretched against the sky like a twisting serpent. As we sat, the sun sank fast, and the heavens in the western sky began to glow. It was a coppery fire at first, the orange streaked with aquamarine; but rapidly the firmament expanded into an explosion of red and orange that burst across the sky sending tongues of flame through the feathery clouds to the very limits of the heavens. When the flames had reached their zenith, a great quantity of storks came flying from the south. They circled above us once, sweeping and gliding, their slender bodies sleek and black against the orange sky. Then, gathering together, they flew off into the setting sun, leaving us alone in peace to contemplate. One of the monks who sat with us, hushed by the intensity of the moment, muttered a prayer. The sun died beyond the hills; and the fire withdrew.

Early next morning we were taken to the largest and oldest of the two churches on the plateau. The architectural style of this building was reminiscent of that depicted on the largest of the Axumite stelae. Between courses of stones there were layers of timber, inset slightly, giving the appearance of a multi-layered sandwich cake. And protruding at intervals of about two feet round each narrow layer were the stub ends of wooden beams, or "monkey-heads", a typical feature of Ethiopian architecture over many centuries.

Having taken off our shoes, as is customary in all Ethiopian churches, we entered. First we came into a porch, or narthex, from which a second door led into the nave. The church was dimly lit, and our vision was further hampered by cloth hangings strung across the nave at intervals so that they obscured most of the interior from view. The division between the nave and the sanctuary was recognisable from a wooden cross on the beam from which the curtains hung. It was a plain cross—carved crucifixes as we know them being unknown in Ethiopia, the Crucifixion being depicted only in paintings. Above it my eye was immediately caught by a wonderful wooden arch, superbly carved in symbolic, geometric, Christian designs. This, together with most of the rest of the building, is very probably part of the original construction dating from the reign of the Emperor Gabra Maskal in the middle of the sixth century A.D. For over fourteen hundred years Christians may have gazed upon it as they have entered this citadel of Christ to pray.

But what we had come to see was the roof of the narthex. This was made up of three rectangular sections, each about nine feet across, and comprising twelve, or fifteen, smaller carved panels. These depicted a fantastic array of beasts, real and mythical. There were goats fighting, does suckling their young, a camel standing by a palm tree, lions, elephants, and winged dragons breathing fire. Each was portrayed in a simple but forceful design. One of the animals that particularly caught our attention was a beast with antlers. This was a strange thing to find, as, so far as is known, no

antlered stags have lived in Africa since prehistoric times when, judging from cave paintings in the Sahara, they lived in parts of north Africa.

The style of the carving at Debra Damo is typical of early Coptic work in Egypt—so similar, in fact, as to suggest that the work might have been done by craftsmen from Alexandria. The antlered stags might not have been observed in Africa at all, but in Syria or Turkey. As we found later, animals of every variety feature often in Ethiopian art. Their precise significance is hard to understand; but such a menagerie as that at Debra Damo may relate to Noah and his Ark as it does in some of the superb mosaics of fifth-century churches in Cilicia (Turkey) in which, incidentally, antlered stags also appear. Although the human image predominates in Ethiopian art especially in later centuries, work such as that at Debra Damo seems to reflect the same primitive preoccupation with the animal kingdom that was so strongly noticeable amongst the pagan people of the Cameroons.

We spent most of that day in the church, photographing; and early the next morning we prepared to leave. A deacon was sent to fetch some of the monastery's mules from a hamlet near the foot of the cliff, and many monks came down with us to see us off. When I looked through the doorway, and down the perpendicular rock face, I almost wished that I might spend the rest of my days on the top of the plateau. But finally, with fear and trepidation, we launched ourselves into space, and descended once more to the less holy world below.

Whether to encourage asceticism or for purposes of defence, the Ethiopians, from the very earliest days of Christianity, had a habit of building their churches and monasteries in the most inaccessible places. My own feeling is that originally they did this for ascetic reasons, for Debra Damo was founded in times of relative security, before the country was cut off and threatened by Islam. Nevertheless, in later years, the isolated positions of the monasteries and churches served them well, for there were occasions when Ethiopia was temporarily overrun by Muslims who destroyed every Christian sanctuary they could find. Debra Damo was one of the few that escaped these ravages. Another was a monastery called Gunda Gunde.

Gunda Gunde, however, is not built on the top of a mountain;

but at the bottom of a valley so inhospitable and remote that it was never discovered by the Muslim hordes. The Valley of Gunda Gunde, known locally as the "Valley of Hell", lies at the eastern edge of the Ethiopian highlands where they begin to break up and tumble away in a series of jagged ridges to the arid Danakil desert thousands of feet below. We particularly wanted to visit Gunda Gunde as it was said that the monastery's collection of manuscripts, saved from Muslim destruction, was unsurpassed in Ethiopia. We were unable to find out much about the place in advance as we understood only four Europeans had been there before us, an Italian, who died on the journey; two French antiquarians; and an Englishwoman who, having reached the monastery, was then unable to enter on account of her sex. As it turned out, we found several other interesting antiquities apart from manuscripts.

To reach Gunda Gunde we drove east from Debra Damo, to the small market town of Adigrat. There, with the help of our letters from Ras Seyum and Zewde, we had the local Governor's co-operation in finding mules and donkeys for our two-day journey to the monastery. The guide we were supplied with was an upstanding Tigrean named Walda-Selassie (Son of the Trinity), lean and gaunt like many Tigreans, with a face like a buzzard, and firm twinkling eyes. Poor fellow, we gave him many scares. In Adigrat he was a man of some authority, and he had been sent with us to guard us as much as to guide us. The journey was not without hazards either from the precipitous paths we had to trek over, or from bandits, or "shiftoich", who lurk in these inhospitable regions, and who, not many weeks before our journey, had waylaid and murdered some Ethiopian travellers. If one of us strayed beyond his hawk-eyed gaze for more than a moment, even to go behind a bush, he scolded us fiercely as though we were children; but he was a proud and admirable person who commanded our greatest respect.

The journey was not as terrible as we had been led to believe; but it was tough going. We had taken donkeys as pack animals, as the last part of the journey was too steep and rough for mules, sure-footed though they are. We ourselves had to walk the last part; and as it turned out it was too hard even for the donkeys; it was our armed guards who finally had to carry our gear. The final stretch was fantastic. It seemed as though the earth had been subject to a sudden cataclysmic upheaval that had tilted the plateau into jutting ridges. The hillsides were devoid of earth, and vast slabs of stone, brought down by frequent landslides, were strewn across the path.

We wondered how anyone managed to survive at all down here. From our track it seemed to be an arid bowl, encompassed on all sides by these treacherous mountains. But when we came near the bottom we saw that in fact there was a small clear stream winding out of a deep gully, hidden from view. The monastery was not immediately in sight, but following the stream down its gorge for two or three miles past hamlets perched precariously on narrow ledges, we at last found Gunda Gunde sprawling over a spur of rock above the stream. The monastery consists of a settlement of about twenty houses, flat-roofed and built in stone, in the Tigrean style, in the centre of which, surrounded by an encircling wall, is the church. It is a rectangular building nearly forty feet long, with an unusual roof. Over the narthex, which is rather larger than most, it is vaulted and thatched; whilst over the nave it rises in two square tiers like a small stepped pyramid. We were unable to discover the age of the monastery. It may not be older than the fifteenth century; but as with most Ethiopian antiquities, it is impossible to give it a precise date, and it could possibly be older. The houses climbed up the hillside in tiers, one leading to the next up alleyways and steps. Though again we had brought our tent, we found this unnecessary, being shown to a house built above a large paved courtyard, looking directly out over a sheer cliff that fell away to the stream. The house had considerable character and charm, and was by no means primitive.

Far from being a "Valley of Hell", once we had reached the bottom we found it in many respects a haven of peace. Shut away far from the world, life here was completely self-contained. In the valley by the stream were cool groves of oranges, bananas, coffee bushes, and limes. A little way up the stream were the monastery's fields where they grew ample millet and maize. These fields were ingeniously irrigated, water being carried to some along trenches built on high stone walls, carried over gullies by wooden aqueducts propped fifteen and twenty feet above the ground. There were cows in the valley, too, being watched over by small herd-boys one of whom we found sitting high up on the rocks playing a delicate tune on a home-made flute, as he watched his cattle grazing below. And the quiet, sun-drenched valley was teeming with bird-life.

The monks were slightly suspicious of us at first. But as soon as they learnt that we were carrying a letter of introduction from Ras Seyum, the suspicion fell away, to be replaced by enthusiastic hospitality. First thought, as always, was to provide the weary travellers with food. Tumblers appeared as if by magic, and having been washed in front of our eyes to dispel any qualms about their cleanliness (though certain brown stains seemed permanently established on the glass), these were filled to the brim with smoky flavoured sour milk—the idea of which at first I found to be repulsive, but which later I realised was a very refreshing drink. A basket of wat and njera was brought for Chris, Shifarau and me, which, when we had had all we needed, was taken over to the guards who customarily eat after the guests of honour. As they tore the njera to pieces I was surprised to see two of them feeding each other, stuffing their food into each other's mouths with amusing vigour. This, we were told, was a traditional way of showing their happiness in this part of the world.

The Chief Priest of Gunda Gunde was not a pretty-looking fellow, being afflicted with a cataract in one eye. Like many of the others he looked as though he might also be suffering from malaria which they say is prevalent in the valley; and having once been given aspirins by a previous traveller, he repeatedly pressed us to give him more. But he made every effort to see that we had all we needed, and willingly showed us the monastery's manuscripts.

Most of the manuscripts were illustrated with full-page and double-page paintings on parchment in the traditional style. The precise history of the development of painting in Ethiopia will doubtless never be known. The style is essentially borrowed from that of Byzantium and Syria; but it has many characteristics that are the products of Ethiopian imagination and invention. The colouring is always forceful—strong primary reds, greens, blues and yellows predominating—and much about its primitive simplicity in outline reflects the impact and strength of other African art. At the same time many manuscript paintings bear an astonishing resemblance to medieval religious paintings in Europe, such as those in the eighth-century Irish Book of Kells.

One of the most striking double-page paintings that we saw at Gunda Gunde depicted Christ riding into Jerusalem on an ass (John XII, v. 12 onwards). On the left-hand page rigid crowds stood above and below Christ, bearing palm fronds and pointing towards the right-hand page. Here, in the centre of the page, was a

symbolic doorway with the words "The Gateway to Jerusalem" written above it. More crowds stood to the left of the gateway pointing to it as though saying "This is the way in", and on its right stood an old man holding out his hand as though inviting Christ to enter. Above was a picture of Our Lord with angels on either side.

Other manuscript paintings that we saw depicted the Crucifixion, the Virgin Mary, various Saints, and other Gospel stories told in strip form. One amusing peculiarity in the Ethiopian style is that all good people are depicted full face, whereas only the devil and bad men are shown in profile. Some of the "devils" are really fiendish-looking creatures with ugly faces and grotesque horns. The writing in the manuscripts is of almost equal interest to the paintings. On one occasion we saw a scribe copying out a religious book using reed pens of a type that has been used for centuries.

He was using inks made from earth, red for the capitals and black for the main bulk of the lettering, taking infinite pains to form the beautiful characters, which were derived originally from Himyaritic and Sabaean scripts in Southern Arabia long before the time of Christ. Owing to the fact that manuscripts have always been in constant use in Ethiopian churches, many of the older ones have deteriorated badly. It has been the custom, when a book has got beyond use, to copy it—copying its paintings also—and then to destroy the original. Thus there are very few really ancient manuscripts in existence still, the earliest known being of the fourteenth century. Dating these manuscripts, however, is difficult; for frequently, in copying, the date of the original is reproduced, but not that of the copy. Thus the safest ways of putting a date to them is by the character of the script and the style of the art-work; but both these methods have obvious drawbacks as styles in such a region as this tend to change so slowly.

One of the finest manuscripts that Chris and I found was shown to us under somewhat shady circumstances when we returned to Addis Ababa. Getting into conversation with a post-office official one day, I learnt that a friend of his—a clerk in the Ministry of Defence—claimed to have a very fine old book in his possession. With some difficulty, as he was obviously reluctant for the authorities to hear about this, we were eventually able to arrange a meeting and see the book. It was a large copy of *The Lives of the Saints*, bound in wooden covers and beautifully illustrated with more than a dozen dazzlingly colourful paintings. One painting which I took to be the Holy Trinity, but which we were told was of three saints together, was of particular interest as at some time or other it had been over-painted in a totally different style that was not Ethiopian. This gave us a clue as to the possible date of the manuscript.

Long before Ethiopia became known to Europe from the reports of the Portuguese embassy in the sixteenth century, a number of individual Europeans are known to have visited the country. One or more Florentine painters were in Ethiopia in 1402, and fifty years later a Venetian artist named Brancaleone is known to have travelled throughout the land working on manuscripts, and even introducing characteristics of Graeco-Italian iconography. The style of the over-painting in our manuscript was akin to that of fifteenth-century Europe, and may thus have been the work of

Brancaleone. This would date the manuscript at the latest to the mid-fifteenth century, and if it was in need of renovation at that time, it may well be that the original work was done considerably earlier, sometime in the fourteenth century. This would mean that it is one of the oldest known Ethiopian manuscripts in existence.

According to a note in the front of the manuscript it had at one time belonged to a famous monastery called Debra Work. As it is unlikely that the monks would have sold such a masterpiece it had probably been stolen; but our questions about its recent history were never fully answered. We were interested in buying the book if we could, as it was obviously of great value. But its owner was asking the price of $U.S. 400,000! He had recently been reading about the sale of a Rembrandt, and having a shrewd idea as to the rarity of his own manuscript, he could see no reason why it should not command a similar sort of price. Having tried to point out to him the strange ways of the art market, we persuaded him to come down to $50,000; but as our maximum offer was £50, we were never able to clinch the deal.

Gunda Gunde was the only place in the whole of Africa where I have ever seen people eating with forks of an indigenous design. I cannot imagine where they got the idea, or why it never spread elsewhere, for the long, two-pronged wooden forks that several of the monks used were both elegant and extremely practical. Apart from these we found a number of other strange things in the monastery. There was a wooden bier, for instance, that stood on four short legs, and had cross-shaped holes in the bottom to allow the putrefying liquids of the deceased to escape. Then there were some interesting bells. The main church bells were "phonoliths"—sounding stones. There were three of them hanging together beneath a small shelter, each one a rod of basalt about a yard long that, when struck with wooden sticks, emitted clear ringing notes of different pitch. Such phonoliths are quite common in Ethiopian churches. Also I found an iron gong, basically similar to many that I had seen in other parts of Africa, but the only one of its type that I ever saw or heard of in Ethiopia. Elsewhere on other journeys we found yet other types of bells. In a monastery on Lake Tsana we had seen a finely cast bronze bell. In the same monastery there was an interesting double wooden clapper-bell that stood about three feet high. And in a church in Lasta province we later saw some locally made cast-iron bells shaped like medieval witches' hats.

But the most curious of all the antiquities we found in Gunda Gunde was a wonderful old lectern standing on four wooden wheels so that it might be trundled up and down the vestibule. A real old war-horse, it was, from behind which one could well imagine a steely-eyed monk with a flowing beard booming out the teachings of our Lord to a fearful audience of simple peasants from up the valley. The platform that held the book could be raised and lowered on a central threaded axis like the seat of a Victorian piano-stool. It was an immensely ancient Heath-Robinson device, crudely and heavily built; and though its design was surely not of local origin, there was no way of telling from where it had come.

We spent two days in Gunda Gunde before embarking on the frightful climb back to the modern world. At Adigrat we said good-bye to Walda Selassie, and also to Shifarau whom we put on a bus back to Axum. We never heard whether he achieved his ambition to visit his brother in Saudi Arabia, but having learned a certain amount about that part of the world from Chris, about the severe penalties for having anything to do with alcohol or girls, for both of which he had a taste, he probably dropped the idea. Then we ourselves departed on the long drive back to Addis Ababa where we were due to stay with friends in the British Embassy. Though this journey should have taken us only three days, owing to repeated mechanical troubles with our ancient Volkswagen, we were on the road for more than four, and finished up limping into the Embassy compound early one morning, dirty and unshaven, just in time for breakfast.

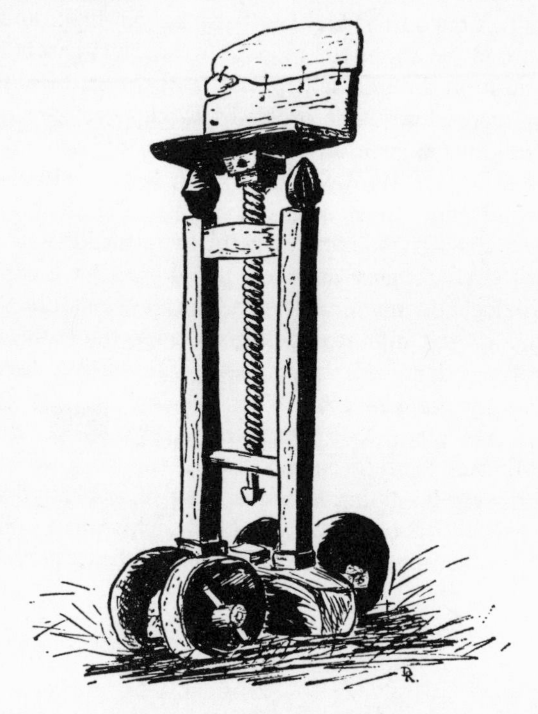

CHAPTER NINE

The Hidden Sanctuaries of Lasta

On our brief mule journeys in Tigré we had discovered, to our cost, some of the many snags in this form of transport. The mule saddles provided in the country districts, for instance, were nothing more than two boards, like sharply pitched roofs, that cut disastrously into our backsides. And the stirrups we had been given were tiny iron rings, large enough only for our big toes, which meant that for most of the time we were riding through the mountains with our shoes strung round our necks. On our next journey we were going to be away from civilisation for at least a month, travelling on mules the whole time. Therefore much of our time in Addis Ababa was spent taking advance precautions against these, and many other maddening inconveniences. To guard against the clouds of flies that hover perpetually around the mules we bought fly-whisks. To urge on our lazy beasts we bought hippo-hide whips; and we scoured the shops for proper stirrups, and sheets of sorbo-rubber to cushion the pile-driving effects of the saddles. But apart from these there were other problems to be overcome before we set out on our final expedition to the mountains of Lasta.

Before leaving for Tigré we had written home to England for a fresh stock of film to be sent out by air. This had long since arrived in Addis Ababa; but by one of those maddening quirks of bureaucracy that so many travellers in Ethiopia have experienced, this was still locked, unattainable, in a bonded warehouse.

The story of our film stock clearly demonstrates the best way of getting things done in Ethiopia. That is to make a direct appeal to His Majesty the Emperor. When we had first arrived in the country we had made a firm agreement, through Amde Mikael, the Vice-Minister for Information, that, as the work we were doing would ultimately be giving Ethiopia a lot of publicity, we should be allowed to import our film free of duty. This was a considerable advantage, as the normal duty on film was astronomical. But now, with the arrival of this fresh consignment, the Customs had taken it into their heads to go back on the arrangement, and were suddenly insisting that duty be paid. They had no grounds for this volte-face, and I was adamant that they should honour the original agreement. Amde Mikael was naturally on our side as he had made the arrangement in the first place; and one day, when discussing our Customs troubles with him, I tentatively suggested that we might ask His Majesty to intervene.

The Emperor, having given his approval for our venture in the first place, had followed our travels with interest. He himself had confirmed the agreement on our film, and I felt sure he would disapprove of the Customs' action if he knew of it. Amde Mikael plainly agreed with me, though he was visibly nervous about bringing His Majesty into the dispute. After a while, however, seeing no other solution, he picked up the telephone and rang through to the palace.

For a time I had no idea what he was saying as he lolled back behind his vast ministerial desk chattering volubly in Amharinya. But suddenly I realised that he was being put directly through to the Emperor. For, leaping out of his chair and hastily straightening his jacket, he began bowing respectfully into the telephone as he unfolded my problems to the invisible Majesty at the other end.

As he replaced the receiver and sat down, he beamed at me delightedly, and as though I might not have already gathered, said with awe:

"*That* was His Majesty!"

When he had fully recovered from the magnitude of the occasion he told me that I was to go directly to the Customs office where the necessary arrangements would be made for me to collect the film.

On arrival at the Customs office the English Adviser (with whom I had been dealing) greeted me with a look of dismay.

"My God, what have you done to us," he said. "We've had Tiger Tim on the 'phone about *you* . . ." His recent altercation with an angry Emperor had obviously put him into a complete flap and the Customs office was in a state of uproar and confusion.

I still had to wait over four hours while the bureaucratic mesh that had been woven around the package was disentangled. But once we had got the film, we were able to think about getting on the move again.

One of the most remarkable things about the churches of Ethiopia, apart from their inaccessibility, is their extraordinary variety of design. Those that we had visited in Tigré are all straightforward rectangular buildings constructed of stone. Elsewhere, however—and especially in the province of Lasta where we were now heading—there are some of the most peculiarly conceived buildings on earth. Some churches are hewn into the peaks of mountains with only their doorways visible on the outside; others are ordinary buildings, but constructed deep inside vast caves; and yet others, such as the famous group at Lalibela, are carved both inside and out—with scrupulous attention to architectural detail—from the living mountain itself. Some of these extraordinary churches house frescoes and other works of art as ancient as the buildings themselves. It was both the buildings and their works of art that we now set out to find and film.

The first part of the journey involved a drive of a day and a half through fantastic scenery along the edge of the Great Rift Valley to the little town of Waldia, situated in the plains below the mountains of Lasta. At that time the Governor of Lasta, who lived in Waldia, was a Shoan named Dedjazmatch Berhane Maskal. We had met him once, with Zewde, in Addis Ababa, and before we left town we had cabled to warn him of our arrival.

Berhane Maskal lived in a long, slightly dilapidated, white bungalow set back from the teeming main highway of Waldia behind a broad expanse of grass. Like most titled Ethiopians, his establishment consisted of a sizeable retinue of servants and hangers-on who spent much of their time loafing around his house waiting for something to happen. It was these gentlemen, dressed in their breeches and off-white shammas, whom we encountered when we arrived. And like faithful watch-dogs that growl at any stranger—friend or foe—their greeting was not at first particularly friendly. But once we had persuaded them that the Dedjazmatch was expecting us, their manner changed, and we were ushered into a waiting-room furnished with heavily upholstered European chairs, and tables.

The Dedjazmatch and his wife were about to have lunch in a back room; but as soon as they heard we had arrived, they joined us in the "parlour" and instructed servants to bring food for us all. His wife, a motherly woman dressed in traditional white, with her black hair bundled up in a net, Ethiopian style, wore the kindly expression of a dedicated social worker. She spoke no English at all, and a visit from a couple of young Europeans seemed to be something of a novelty for her. She was brimming with coy laughter as she pressed us to more wat and njera, and quietly beckoned the servants to refill our glasses with tej. The Dedjazmatch himself, a middle-aged man dressed in a dark suit, was not unlike her. He was quietly spoken but his English was excellent, and he wasted no time in turning the conversation to our journey.

Berhane Maskal knew the mountains intimately and gave us a lot of advice; but, of particular interest, he told us how to get to several churches that he believed had either never been seen by "Ferengis" (as Europeans are usually called), or never before been photographed. As he had promised us when we met in Addis Ababa, he had already arranged the hire of five mules, with two muleteers; and he had also selected half a dozen armed militiamen to accompany us on the first leg of our journey into the mountains. This was more out of courtesy than necessity, as shiftoich, or bandits, are few and far between in that particular region. He had also found an interpreter for us, a local schoolmaster named Ato Haile Mariam, a sturdy fellow in his mid-twenties who made no effort to hide his annoyance at being dragged away from his duties.

Berhane Maskal suggested we made a start into the mountains that same day, and sent one of his bowing, scraping servants to call the muleteers. By and by we heard a dreadful commotion outside, and looked up to see three wild-looking men chasing five unruly beasts about the "paddock" in front of the house. Two of the men were our muleteers: Fantau, gaunt and wiry, who was always good for a laugh; and Tadessa, shorter and older with a rather disturbing glint of cunning in his eyes. The third man, an enormously fat, jovial, Sancho Panza type, was the owner of the mules. Apart from the fact that I doubted whether he would have been able to keep up, I rather wished that Sancho Panza was coming with us, as he looked as though he would be an amusing companion. As soon as he could get me on to one side with the interpreter, he broached the question of money. The hire fee, forty-five pounds for mules and muleteers for one month, had been agreed between him and Berhane Maskal, and half of this I now paid him in advance.

As soon as the mules had been quietened down, our baggage was strapped on to them—so tight that I wondered how the wretched creatures could breathe. And having said good-bye to everyone, we departed. The first half-mile took us through the town, down muddy avenues of tall gum-trees, past the tin-roofed dwellings of priests and prostitutes, rich men and poor men. Like the Pied Piper, as our cavalcade ambled through the outskirts, we gathered a huge crowd of shouting, delighted children, who ran along beside us in wide-eyed wonderment that two ferengi should be travelling in this way. But soon we came out into a broad expanse of fields, ablaze with yellow Maskal daisies, and our young escort gradually faded away. Ahead of us, ten or twelve miles to the west, loomed the impressively rugged Lasta mountains, a soft grey-purple wall, rising in places to twelve thousand feet or more.

Though I must admit that on occasions the flies and the heat led to outbreaks of ill-temper that were treated with contempt by our imperturbable Ethiopian companions, I found travelling on mules a pleasant experience. It was slow; but the tempo of life was slow, and my heart-beat by then being regulated to the gentle throb of Africa, this was no longer a worry. Except now and then, on the less frequented trails, the paths down which we trekked were worn deep into the earth by countless centuries of use, meandering through fields of barley and peas and tef, and up twisting rocky ascents to mountain passes sometimes ten thousand feet high, where the air was cool and crisp. Fantau and Tadessa, the muleteers, ran and walked alongside us, urging the mules on with guttural cries of "Murk . . . Murk . . ."; and the armed guard, looking more like a band of brigands than soldiers, ambled ahead and behind, occasionally shattering the peace with piercing war-cries, and hardly less savage Ethiopian love-songs.

Sometimes a pack-mule would stray from the path and start chewing a crop of peas, and the muleteers having chased him off with swinging whips and threatening shouts would then tear out an armful of plants for themselves, giving us a few, laden with pods, to pick at and chew as we went. Frequently we passed other travellers on the path; perhaps a local carpenter head-loading his box of tools far inland; or a caravan of donkeys carrying slabs of rock-salt from the Danakil deserts many days' ride to the east; or sometimes, upon richly caparisoned mules, a finely dressed nobleman and his wife would ride past us, bowing low, as we did also, muttering friendly greetings "Teneisterling . . . Teneisterling", but otherwise unsurprised by our presence.

The country was wild and beautiful, the mountainsides descending thousands of feet in huge terraces sometimes a mile wide, to rock-strewn river beds. Often as we crossed these rivers we stopped to water the mules, and regardless of who was coming and going stripped off for a swim in the icy waters.

The hillsides of Lasta are mostly devoid of trees, but here and there, seen from far off, a large clump of gums, grey in a haze of smoke in the early morning, would herald a village of round stone houses thatched with grass. Sometimes, upon a hill-top, or crouching thickly in a deep hillside gully, a grove of dark green junipers, which once covered the barren hills in profusion, would mark the hiding place of a church. Mostly these were round churches of a recent type, and we would pass them by; but sometimes we believed the trees might shelter a cave or rock-church of more ancient date, and we would go off our path to investigate.

One such church we visited, which had not hitherto been described or photographed, was the tiny sanctuary of Wallé Jesus hidden in a huge cave high up in the mountains to the right of our path, only a few hours from Waldia. After a stiff trek up a twisting path we came into a narrow gully, and climbed steeply through a grove of junipers. Here we met two old priests who showed us the way to the church.

Only in the last few yards were we able to see the cave in which the church was built. But even then we were unable to see the

building itself, which was hidden behind a high wall and wicker fence obscuring the entrance to the cave. It was magnificently situated half-way up a precipice over which a small stream tumbled, spattering its waters on the rocks below. And from it there was an impressive view far out across a landscape of rugged mountains and flat-topped plateaux. The church was approached by crossing a narrow ledge behind the waterfall and entering a doorway at the far end of the wall. This led down a narrow incline into the cave, the floor of which was strewn with trampled hay.

Wallé Jesus, only about nine feet high, fitted easily into its

cavernous home. In construction it reflected the Axumite pattern of alternating recessed courses; but it was built of well-cut blocks of pink volcanic stone. Apart from its ceiling, which was painted with geometric patterns and a representation of the sun and the moon over the west door, it contained no works of art, so far as we could see. Most remarkable were its pierced wooden windows, beautifully carved in a series of interwoven zigzag lines forming a repeating pattern of the Star of David, and in other similar designs. By tradition this church was almost as old as that of Debra Damo; but there was no way of verifying this, and from comparison with others we felt it was unlikely to be older than the tenth or eleventh century.

The day after we visited Wallé Jesus, Haile Mariam suggested that we visit another church that he himself had never seen. This was the church of Stefanos, carved inside a mountain peak, three hours off our track to the south of Kulmask. Here we discovered some fine wooden stools constructed in the form of boxes in which prayer-books were kept. One, that was marked in Geez with the words "The Four Evangelists", depicted four winged saints exquisitely carved in a style similar to that of many fifteenth-century manuscript paintings, and probably of the same date. These the priests allowed us to photograph after we had donated a few shillings to their church.

It was the time of the harvest, and sometimes, as we rode along a high ridge, we could look down upon a vast panorama of fields and see the farmers, like midgets far below, gathering their crops. No sight more than this gave us the feeling of living in medieval times. Painstakingly, sheaf by sheaf, the corn was cut with sickles, and stacked in stooks, which were later piled high in conical ricks to be threshed and winnowed. Threshing was done by oxen, driven round and round by small boys in dizzying circles, trampling the grain from the ears. Winnowing was done upon a small round patch of earth, beaten hard and swept clean. With long wooden shovels, a harvester rhythmically threw the grain high against the blue sky in a graceful arc, so that the wind caught the chaff, blowing it away in shimmering yellow clouds. Often we would come upon such a scene on a ridge where the wind blew steadily, and the farmers would invite us to stay and share a meal of coarse njera and rough talla beer, brought out from the farmsteads by the women and girls. And we would stop for a while, resting in the ricks, until Fantau and Tadessa grew impatient, wanting to hurry on to the next night's resting place.

On the steeper hillsides it was sometimes hard to find a piece of flat ground near to a stream on which to pitch our tent. Usually we made camp near a settlement of one kind or another—a church, or a farmstead—and Haile Mariam would go off to find a bed with a friendly stranger. Otherwise, having no tent of his own, he would bed down beneath the "verandah" flaps of ours. Fantau and Tadessa slept in the open near the tethered mules, and we would find them in the mornings huddled together beneath their blankets, warming each other against the biting night air that often, in the higher places, came near to freezing.

On the fourth day out from Waldia we arrived in Lalibela, an ancient village known as Roha until its name was changed seven hundred years ago. This was to be our base-camp for the next few weeks, and we were therefore in no hurry to see the rock churches for which it is famous. Instead we went directly to the house of the Memhir, or Chief Priest, which stood with several others upon a hillside overlooking the village and the twenty-mile-wide gorge of the Takazi river beyond.

The Memhir's house was a rectangular stone building of two storeys, with a door in the upper storey like that of a flour loft in an old English bakery. As we approached, we saw that there was a small gathering of debterras in the grass yard beneath, presumably discussing matters of the church. Huddled in the doorway up above, like an eagle in his eyrie upon the roof of the world, squatted the Memhir himself wearing a deep blue cloak and hat, answering questions being put to him from below. When he saw us approaching he asked the debterras to stand aside and invited us to come close.

Perched aloft as he was, in a village so ancient and holy, we might well have expected the Memhir to be a wizened Old Testament prophet with a long flowing beard. But Abba Amsalu was a young man, no more than thirty-five, clean-shaven, and educated in the ways of the modern world. He even spoke sufficient English for us to converse without an interpreter—a rare thing amongst Ethiopian priests. He spoke with a gentle, ethereal voice, and moved in the graceful unhurried way that befits a man of godliness. He was a man of totally different character from other priests we had met, reminding me in a way of a scientist friend of mine who had given up a well-paid job to go into the church. He was an intellectual; a master in the art of "kene", a type of poetry set to music that has its origins in the Hebrew world of the pre-Christian era. Yet he was a man of the world, with his feet set firmly on the ground.

Abba Amsalu welcomed us well, and honoured us by inviting us up to his eyrie where we sat on rugs for some time drinking glasses of thick, milky tea, answering his questions about life in Addis Ababa, about his friend Berhane Maskal, and many other things of the "outside world" that we felt he greatly missed. He told us he enjoyed having us with him, as it was nice to speak with "intelligent" people. He had little in common with the rough-hewn locals of Lalibela, though he was patient with them as he realised their isolation and lack of education. Truly we felt he was their "father" as the word "abba" means.

We pitched our tent on the grass terrace in front of Abba Amsalu's house. Though noisy at times, when chattering locals gathered outside to speak to the Memhir, it was a convenient site, as we were never without people to fetch our water for us, and could always buy wat and njera and eggs.

The day after we arrived, Abba Amsalu took us on a conducted tour of the churches in the village below. The rock churches of Lalibela have often been called the "eighth wonder of the world". The first European to see and record them was a certain Father Alvarez, a Portuguese priest who accompanied the first European embassy to Ethiopia in 1520. He was so worried that people in his homeland would not believe his descriptions that he forebore to say as much about them as he wished; and when one sets eyes upon them for the first time one can readily understand his anxiety.

There are eleven churches in all, each one carved from the deep red volcanic rock of the mountain. The largest of them, and surely the largest single carving in the world, is Bieta Medhanie Alem, the church of the Saviour of the World. It is over one hundred and ten feet long, and nearly forty feet high. This huge church, like many of the others, emerges from a deep pit, excavated in the rock; and to all appearances, it seems to be constructed in the normal way from bricks and mortar. A colonnade surrounds it, supporting the eaves of the gently sloping roof, and its basilical interior is hewn immaculately into columns and arches. A tunnel through the rock connects Medhanie Alem to another church courtyard; in fact the whole spur upon which they have been created is a maze of tunnels and furrows in the rock so that it is difficult to tell at first exactly where one is. There may be a church or a chapel a few feet through the rock to one side, or even underneath where one is standing; but to reach it, it may be necessary to walk some distance by devious passages.

The church of Abba Libanos is hewn into the *side* of the mountain, just as though it were constructed in a cave. Only the façades of some of the smaller ones are visible, as at Petra. None of the churches is the same size as another, and all are of different design. In one church in particular the form of architecture derived from that of ancient Axum can again be seen quite clearly—the "layered cake" effect that we had seen also at Debra Damo and Wallé Jesus.

The most beautiful of all the churches is that of St. Mary, or Bieta Mariam, a basilical building with three porches set in a wide sunken courtyard. To us this was of particular interest as it houses many delightful frescoes. In a frieze round the nave we were able to pick out paintings depicting various biblical stories, the miracle of the loaves and fishes, the story of the man who was told to take up his bed and walk, and Christ meeting the Samaritan woman at the well. These biblical paintings were mixed with others that seemed to have no religious connection. In one corner, there were two bulls and a splendid giraffe, and also two cocks fighting. And between two of the beautifully carved and painted pillars there was a fine representation in the Byzantine style of a two-headed eagle.

The church of St. Mary may yet hold many other mysteries. There is, for instance, one pillar perpetually shrouded in cloths that

has never so far been seen by any foreigners. Who knows what paintings lie beneath? Again, although even on close inspection the church appears to be of only two storeys (having a gallery above the nave), it is in fact of three storeys. Beneath the floor there is a crypt which we were only able to discover from a hidden air-vent that rises into the nave. Few people know how to get into this crypt, and under no circumstances were we allowed to enter. It could be that it houses many important relics from very ancient times, of which no outsider yet knows. Like most of the churches, Bieta Mariam was dark inside, too dark for us to consider filming; but we spent considerable time taking still photographs of the works of art around its walls, which we could later enlarge and transfer on to film.

These churches of Lalibela were built by a king of the same name towards the end of the twelfth century and at the beginning of the thirteenth. Although their architectural style is undoubtedly Ethiopian, being derived at least in some cases from that of pre-Christian Axum, the work was in all probability done by foreign craftsmen. Some believe that stone-masons came from Jerusalem; but the common theory is that they were Copts from Egypt, or even Nubians who had come overland up the important Nile tributary, the Atbara, or Takaze, which rises just near to Lalibela. Certainly there is striking similarity between the art of Nubian churches of about the same period and that of Ethiopia. Though none of the actual tools used for constructing these rock buildings had ever been found, it was known from a manuscript painting showing a priest at work, that the tools used were adzes like those of craftsmen elsewhere in Africa.

We spent several days visiting all the churches of Lalibela, photographing them from every angle. Then we set out on a two-day journey across the valley to the Takaze to visit a monastery about which very little was known up till that time. This was the monastery of Debra Abuna Aaron. Our militia-men had returned to Waldia as soon as we reached Lalibela—so now, apart from the three Ethiopians, we were on our own.

The journey was one of the roughest we ever made. Much of the valley was parched and scorching hot; and the Takaze gorge, famous for its fantastic hills further downstream, was rugged and steep even in these upper reaches. Few people lived near the gorge; but so beautiful did we find it that we decided to spend the first night on a shelf half-way down. When we suggested this, Fantau and Tadessa were horrified.

"Shiftoich! Shiftoich!" they cried, drawing their hands across their throats and pointing fearfully at the massive rock cliffs around us. And indeed, the hundreds of caves that riddled the cliff-face would have made an ideal hiding-place for bandits. Abba Amsalu, however, had assured us that none lived along here, and being determined that this was where we would sleep, we pitched our camp despite their vigorous protestations. Poor devils, they were genuinely frightened, and haunted by visions of sudden death or at very least emasculation, and I don't think either of them slept a wink that night. But in the morning they were still alive.

When we arrived at the gorge that evening, I went for a walk along the cliff, in the course of which I very nearly had an accident that could have brought the expedition to a sudden end. Had anyone been watching, it must surely have looked like some grotesque scene from a Chaplin film. I was walking down a very narrow path at the time—along a forty-five degree slope falling away to a sheer precipice that dropped down to the river. Suddenly I lost my footing and began to slither, quite out of control, down the slope. The hillside was covered with short grass, with nothing to stop my fall; and as I gathered speed, clutching vainly at loose stones and grass, I caught horrifying glimpses of the vast chasm rapidly approaching. There appeared to be nothing between me and a pile of ugly, jagged rocks far below—except one small, solitary bush clinging precariously to the very lip of the precipice. Just as I was about to launch into space I was able to grasp the bush which, for one horrible moment as it took the impact, seemed as though it would come flying over the top with me. But, with my fervent prayers to a host of Ethiopian saints, it held fast; and I was able, slowly, to scramble back to safety.

For half an hour or so I was completely shaken, but no damage had been done except for several deep grazes down my legs. I cleaned these off in a stream, and thought nothing more of the incident—until early the next morning, when I woke up with a deep throbbing in my groin. Like an idiot I had not put antiseptic on the scratches, and, as wounds are inclined to in Ethiopia, they quickly began to go septic. Throughout the next day, as we climbed up to Abuna Aaron, the pain grew worse, until eventually it became difficult either to ride or walk.

Despite the pain, I could not but appreciate the strange and beautiful situation of Debra Abuna Aaron, and our memorable arrival. The monastery itself, like the church of Stefanos, was hewn out of the inside of a rocky mountain peak jutting from one end of a long, gently sloping plateau. To approach it we rode across this plateau, over broad, fertile fields of barley and tef, shimmering in the evening light like acres of yellow and purple silk.

As we neared the monastery the path led us by an old fig-tree, under which were gathered thirty or forty men holding a meeting. The men looked up as we passed. One or two of them muttered a polite "Teneisterling" which we acknowledged; but mostly they took no notice of us whatsoever as though the sight of foreigners on mules was an everyday occurrence. At the time we had no idea who they were, and so rode straight past; but a short way further on we stopped at a house to ask where we might find the Abbot and the other local dignitaries. The woman we spoke to pointed back to the fig tree telling us that we would find them there. This seemed strange, as one would have thought they would have asked us who we were as we passed; but back we went, and interrupted the meeting.

As soon as it was realised that we had actually come to visit Debra Abuna Aaron—their monastery—a surge of excitement went through the crowd, as they rose to their feet and came over to greet us, each one shaking our hands, and laughing with delight.

"You are the first ferengis that have ever come to Abuna Aaron!" the Abbot announced with tremendous excitement. "Even the Italians never found our monastery! Welcome, welcome!" And the Balabat and the Headman, too, told us the same tale.

It would have been exciting to feel that we were the first Europeans ever to have visited the place, but sadly, we knew that it was not true. Stephen Wright, an English friend in Addis Ababa, had passed that way several years before; and it was he who had suggested that we visit it in the first place. However, we did not disillusion our hosts; and as we knew that we had at least explored a new route across the Takaze (having taken a wrong track) we pretended that we were as delighted by the event as they were. (Stephen Wright had only spent a short time there, and had not had time to explore the monastery thoroughly.)

By now my leg and groin were swelling up alarmingly, and were extremely painful. I had been dosing myself throughout the day with aureomycin which, following my experience in the Cameroons, I had fortunately brought with me. But this had as yet had very little effect. All I really wanted to do once we had pitched the tent was to lie down and go to sleep; but this proved impossible.

Many of the younger people at Debra Abuna Aaron had never before seen a ferengi; and barely anyone there had seen a tent or a camp bed. No sooner had we put these up than word got around, and we were inundated with curious visitors. Whether it was just their local breed, or the fact that they lived in such a supremely beautiful piece of country isolated from the world, I do not know; but the people here were all exceptionally good-looking, good humoured, and polite. Though at first they formed in a mass round the door of the tent, they quickly organised themselves into a queue so that each in turn could have a look. One of them asked if he might try the bed; and from then on there was bedlam as one by one they came in, laughing their heads off, to bounce up and down upon a camp bed.

Almost immediately messengers appeared from the Headman, the Balabat, and the Abbot, each bringing us a huge jar of talla beer and a basket full of wat and njera—enough to last us a week. These three were quickly followed by yet another jar of beer from the farmer on whose land we had pitched our tent. Then the Headman himself came along to present us with a choice white ram from his flock. Having been given to us with much bowing and thanking on the threshold of our tent, it was thereupon slaughtered on the spot. Boys were sent scurrying for firewood; a large fire was lit a few yards from the tent; and after being skinned and butchered, the ram was put in a pot to cook.

When the initial excitement had subsided, and the young children had been chased away to a corner of the field from where they could watch, all the notables came down and cordially invited us to a banquet on our own front door-step.

For half an hour I was forced to excuse myself and lie down. My groin was swelling more and more, and the pain was excruciating. I lay on my bed trying to rest, reflecting on the fact that we were now five days from the nearest road, and six days from the nearest hospital; and I prayed that the antibiotics would soon have some effect. The sun had now gone down, and with the darkness the party began to get going. I had hardly had any rest when the Abbot himself came to commiserate—and drag me out to the binge. There was nothing for it but to go.

Shortly after I joined the party, two minstrels suddenly appeared and began to play upon their "masenkos" singing gentle love-songs. The crowd fell absolutely quiet as they sang, listening to them intently. It was beautiful and moving, far up in these mountains, as their voices rose and fell upon the cool evening air, flickering light from the fire falling upon their rapt faces. When they had sung for a while they were invited to join us; but they thanked us and departed.

As we had been sitting round the fire waiting for the meat to cook, I had noticed a priest sitting slightly to one side busily engaged cutting up pieces of meat into inch-long bits, and dropping them into a bowl of sauce. At the time I had no idea what he was up to; but Chris and I were soon to discover. The meat, cooked by now, was handed round, but not to us. We watched in silence as, piece by piece, it was cut up and offered around until all was gone. By now the priest with the bowl had finished his work, and bringing it over to the fire, he gave it first to the Balabat, who then handed it on to us. This, we were told, was the *specialité de la maison,* the ultimate in delicacies reserved only for the most honoured guests. On one side of our dish were the two testicles of the ram, roasted in the embers like potatoes—but to these we had no objection, they were excellent. It was what was in the bowl that worried us. There was no doubt that we had to eat it, whatever it was. It would have been the height of ill-manners to have turned it down. It was in fact the guts of the goat that had been cleaned out in hot water and cut into short lengths like macaroni; the stomach lining; and the liver. None of it had been cooked. With some trepidation we began to eat it; and, thank God, the peppery sauce in which it floated was sufficiently hot to take away much of the flavour. But it was the feel of it that was unforgettable—the grating roughness of the stomach-lining, the leathery toughness of the guts, and the slimy sensation as one sank one's teeth into the jelly-like flesh of the liver.

I don't know whether this delicate dish had curative powers beyond imagination, or whether in fact it was my aureomycin. But the next morning my leg had considerably improved.

During our "banquet" I particularly noticed one of the guests who received much attention from everyone and was given all the choicest bits of meat. This was a young boy of only sixteen who was deaf and dumb. Despite his affliction it was easy to understand why he was everyone's favourite. For not only was he extremely good-looking, but he was obviously very intelligent. The only noises that he could make were a series of strange squeaks, some of which seemed to be intelligible to those around him. It would be easy to say that he was unnecessarily spoiled by everyone; but—having heard so much about the callousness of Ethiopians towards cripples, and for that matter, human life in general—it was rather delightful to see how well he was treated. Maybe it was his distressing predicament that had made him, also, extremely emotional. When things went well he laughed louder than anyone and looked astonishingly happy; but if things were against him he quickly collapsed into tears.

Having never before seen a European, he was fascinated by everything we did. During the next two days he accompanied us everywhere. Before we left Abuna Aaron Chris gave him one of his old shirts, and I have seldom seen anyone so utterly overjoyed with a present. For hours he danced around, squeaking and grunting as he showed off his new possession to his friends, as happy as a pea in a whistle. But when we finally left, he was a pathetic and sorrowful sight. He desperately wanted to accompany us back to Waldia to see cars and lorries and all the other things he had been told about but never seen; but unfortunately this was not possible, and as we rode away we left him sitting by the wayside, weeping bitterly.

Early in the morning after the feast the Abbot and the Balabat came to our tent to take us to the monastic church. As we were camped more than two miles along the plateau I rode on a mule for most of the way; but with still half a mile to go I had to leave this at the foot of a precipitous hill. From the hill the path led away across the face of a barren rocky slope which had been worn into a deep groove by centuries of use. The church itself was situated at the end of a spur with a sheer drop of several hundred feet down the far side. It was not visible until we were within a few yards of a doorway that led into the rock. Having entered and passed through one tunnel we came out into a tiny natural courtyard, open to the sky, and from there passed directly into the main body of the church. This was rough-hewn when compared with many of the rock buildings of Lalibela, but seemed to be laid out on much the same basic plan as any other church with a narthex, the floor covered with sweet-smelling grass, a nave, and a sanctuary. As is customary in all Ethiopian churches the sanctuary and parts of the nave were shielded from view by hanging cloths. For some reason we were not permitted to go far into the nave. We were, however, conducted down a long dark tunnel leading off the nave by the light of waxed tapers, to a minute domed chapel buried in the heart of the rock. This had been built on the very edge of the outer precipice, with small windows looking out into space.

Everything seemed to go on in the narthex, which had one very peculiar feature. Carved right through the rock above, eight or ten feet thick, was a slanting hole, so placed that at certain times of the day sunlight streamed through, falling upon a lectern below. In the minds of the superstitious priests the most remarkable thing about this hole was that, no matter how hard it rained, water never came through into the church. This fact they attributed to the "holiness" of the hole. But to us it seemed more likely to be due to the fact that half-way down it there was a shelf that appeared to have been carved for the express purpose of catching rain!

Whilst we were in Lalibela, Abba Amsalu had told us that we should ask the monks of Abuna Aaron to show us one of their prize possessions—an ancient adze, said to have been used by Abuna Aaron himself in the construction of his monastery eight hundred years ago. As no such adzes had hitherto been recorded, I was most anxious to see this instrument. We did not ask for it outright, but, when we had apparently been shown everything, we

asked the monks if they were sure there was nothing else for us to see. Deep in thought, they all seriously shook their heads saying, "No, there is nothing more in the church apart from what you have seen."

"Are you quite sure?" I asked again.

"Yes," they replied, they were quite sure.

"What about Abuna Aaron's adze with which he built the church?" I asked. And for a moment they looked at me in astonishment not knowing quite what to say or do. But the Abbot came to their rescue.

"Aah!" he said, as though it had suddenly occurred to him. "The adze! Yes, of course, the adze!" And a monk was sent off with a taper into the deepest gloom of the sanctuary to fetch it.

We now gathered outside the church waiting for the adze to be brought. There was some delay as several of the monks tried hard to think of some reason why we should not see it; but finally it came, wrapped in a dirty red and blue cloth. Slowly, and with great care, it was unwrapped, and, the cloth having first been laid over a rock, it was put down upon it for us to see. It was a finely made tool about twenty inches long. The haft and the blade were of iron, fitting snugly into a bronze junction from the back of which protruded a small bronze cross. At the top of the haft was a bronze orb, indented with a simple design, like the seams on a football. Both the haft and the blade had at one time been elaborately inlaid with bronze filaments in alternating circular and chevron patterns; but much of the inlay had long since fallen out. Everything about it suggested that this was a ceremonial tool that had probably been used for making the first cut into the rock, just as a ceremonial trowel might be used in Europe today for laying the foundation stone of a new building.

I stepped forward to pick it up and take a closer look. But as I did so, a forest of arms shot out barring my way, and the monks let out a horrified gasp.

"*You* cannot touch it!" they said firmly. "It is holy!" So with one of them twisting it and turning it to my directions I inspected it as best I could. Now having seen it, we wished to take some photographs of it. To this the monks agreed, but told us to go ahead quickly, as they could not keep it out much longer. But it had been laid on the dirty red and blue cloth in which it had been wrapped—hardly the best background for a photograph; so we asked if it could be put on a piece of yellow cloth that we carried around with us to use as a background on just such occasions as this.

"No, no, no! Your cloth is not sanctified!" they protested. But by then their illogical superstition was beginning to make me rather peevish, and I asked firmly if they would please put it on a piece of sanctified white cloth for us. They said there was no white cloth in the church and that this was impossible. But eventually they agreed that one of the monks should take off his white shamma for us. This, they said, was sufficiently holy cloth on which to lay the adze. And so finally we were able to get the photographs we needed before the tool was re-wrapped and hastily hidden away again beneath the mountain.

We spent two enjoyable days at Debra Abuna Aaron before setting out on the long haul back to Lalibela. We were told that if we took a short cut we could cross the Takaze valley in a day, though this would be a long ride. I was a bit worried about the condition of the mules. The standard of animal welfare in Ethiopia would send the R.S.P.C.A. up the wall; and two of the baggage animals had sores on their backs where the saddles had chafed through to the flesh. But Tadessa dismissed this as being nothing out of the ordinary, and as he and Haile Mariam were keen to get back, we decided to try the supposedly quick route.

Like most short cuts it had its disadvantages, and on one occasion we had to unload the mules and head-load the baggage up a particularly steep path. One of these wound through an avalanche of gigantic boulders worse than anything on the road to Gunda Gunde, and it was only by scaring the life out of the animals that the muleteers could get them to scramble up at all. The way they treated the mules was horrifying, and frequently we nearly came to blows with them when their goading became torture. But as we were dependent on them, and as nothing we did in the short time we were with them would make any lasting difference, there was no alternative but to turn a blind eye, and hope that the wretched creatures survived.

As we came down into the plain at the foot of Mount Abuna Joseph, from which Lalibela is hewn, we suddenly saw a most incongruous sight. Far out in the wilds, so we thought, and in an area that was in every sense unchanged since medieval times, we came upon an aeroplane parked at the end of a field, as though it were the most natural thing on earth. It was a DC–3 of Ethiopian Airlines; but as there was no one anywhere in sight we were unable at first to discover why it was there. It was only when we reached Lalibela late that night, having been on the road for twelve groin-aching hours, that we were enlightened. The Alexandrian Patriarch of the Coptic Church, with a large following of priests, was paying a visit to the sacred town.

Despite Lalibela's "isolation" from the world, these days it is possible to fly to within three hours of the town. The building of Lalibela's airstrip involved a remarkable feat of aviation. A bulldozer was necessary to level the strip; but as the only way in which they had any hope of getting this to the site was by air, Ethiopian Airlines were faced with a difficult problem. This, however, was ingeniously solved. First, sufficient space was cleared by hand in which to land a 'plane carrying a small bulldozer, which then cleared a large enough runway to enable the 'plane to take off again. There are no regular commercial flights to Lalibela airstrip, which is used only a few times a year for tourist charter flights, and visits from the Emperor and other V.I.Ps. A rough road connects the strip with the town, and there is also a Land Rover track from Lalibela to the main road near Waldia.

The visit of the Coptic Patriarch, despite the fact that he was no longer the head of the Ethiopian church, was an event of importance, and Lalibela had over-night become something of a humming metropolis with at least four Land Rovers bouncing over the rocky road from one end of the village to the other. The Patriarch had arrived only a few hours before our return from Abuna Aaron, and the following morning we were able to witness his remarkable public welcome as he came in from his encampment to visit the rock churches.

Bieta Mariam being considered the most important church, it was this that he visited first. The track that led down to the church, and the quarry-like courtyard around it, were thronged with a seething mass of men, women, and children. Priests, some with painted wooden crosses, others with smaller ones finely worked in silver and iron, milled around blessing people; and, as at Axum, hermits had come down from their hiding-places and were busily preaching the words of God to little groups of listeners. Along the top of one of the walls stood a single line of debterras in dark blue cloaks, with staves and sistra ready to break into a mournful religious dirge for the occasion. And on either side of the Patriarch's route stood hundreds more, holding fronds of spiky palms gathered from the mountain-side. Suddenly from the village beyond the church, the air was rent by the thrilling sound of hundreds of women ululating in high shrill voices wavering up and down in a minor key. LiLiLiLiLiLi. LiLiLiLiLiLi. LiLiLiLiLiLi. The Patriarch was approaching; and a stir went through the crowd. Suddenly the Great One came into view, slowly moving through the ranks; and as he came, the debterras bowed low and laid their palms on the ground before him in a carpet of green.

At once I was reminded of the ancient manuscript of Gunda Gunde depicting Christ's entry into Jerusalem, in which serried ranks of bearded people held out "branches of palm trees" to lay in His path; indeed it could not fail to bring back vividly the gospel story itself. And maybe, too, besides cries of "Hosanna, Hosanna in the highest" the outskirts of Jerusalem that day thrilled to the sounds of ululation.

But if the priests and people of Lalibela gave to the Patriarch the honours that might have been reserved for Christ Himself, the Coptic priests tended to treat the Ethiopians like dirt. High-ranking members of the Coptic church in Alexandria are generally regarded as wealthy, highly sophisticated people. And not without justification. Indeed, amongst the Patriarch's followers we met one who spoke perfect English, having finished his education at Balliol. However, some of the priests gave the impression that the whole trip was a nuisance, a rather tedious diplomatic necessity, and blastedly uncomfortable to boot. Whereas we would never have dared to enter the churches without first taking off our shoes, as this would have caused great offence, the Coptic priests blandly disregarded such niceties, and blundered around the churches disgusted by the "primitiveness" and "filth" of everything. When poor wizened old Ethiopian priests, trying their hardest to please, offered tins of "holy" water to the Copts to sip as they entered a church, they were waved away with signs of horror at the thought of having to drink from such rusty vessels. Maybe there was some justification for their attitude to many things, but there was none for the way in which they expressed it. And when all was done I felt a greater sympathy than ever with the Ethiopians for having finally broken their ties with their Mother Church in Alexandria.

A day or two after the Patriarch's visit we left Lalibela for good, and embarked on a roundabout journey to film some other cave and rock churches. We were sorry to leave Abba Amsalu as he had been so hospitable and helpful to us throughout our visit. Later we heard that Abba Amsalu himself had had to leave Lalibela soon after; the reason being apparently that his modern outlook towards church affairs aroused too much controversy and conflict among the priests. This, in its way, was a tragedy, and was typical of the problems that Ethiopians are facing in bringing a "new look" into their church. Abba Amsalu had been sent to Lalibela expressly by the Emperor, this being an important shrine, and one visited more and more frequently by foreign visitors, and His Majesty felt that it should be able to give a lead to other church groups. But conservatism and tradition, especially when so deeply rooted as it is in Ethiopia, make a damnably hard nut to crack; and maybe not even the next generation of priests in the country districts will have a sufficiently broad education to overcome the superstitions that bind this African church so firmly to the past.

The route that we now followed took us over the high mountains behind Lalibela to the cave church of Imrahana Kristos, or Imraha as it is commonly called.

Having crossed a deep gorge behind Lalibela, we came out upon a lush green shelf, above which climbs the thirteen-thousand-foot peak of Mount Abuna Joseph. Here herds of horses, from which mules were bred, gallivanted on the banks of gentle streams, and from these slopes there was a magnificent view stretching almost across to Lake Tsana, eighty miles to the west. Across the shelf the scenery changed suddenly as we began to descend through a beautiful forest of junipers that climbs up the hillside for a thousand feet above Imraha. This church is one of the most famous of all in Ethiopia, and since 1520, when Father Alvarez first set eyes on it, it has been visited by quite a number of foreigners. It is a cave church like that of Wallé Jesus, but far more beautiful. It was built early in the twelfth century, and considering its great age, its superb construction and interior decoration is in a remarkably good state of repair. Most of this decoration takes the form of symbolic geometric designs; but on the ceiling are a number of small paintings showing a ship, and various beasts set in painted medallions reminiscent of the carved panels in Debra Damo.

We spent one night with the priests of Imraha before moving on to several rock-carved churches, poorly made in comparison to those of Lalibela. Then making a wide loop through the mountains we joined the track that would take us back to Waldia. There was, however, one more church that we wanted to visit. This was the tiny little church of Mechena Medhanie Alem, built in a cave about ten thousand feet up, near the top of Mechena mountain. The church had been visited only once before, by an indomitable Englishwoman named Beatrice Playne. But although she had made several sketches, no photographs as yet existed of the church, or the frescoes it contained.

We had been on the move now for a month, and we were all growing tired—Tadessa and Fantau especially. And when we announced that we wished to climb Mechena mountain to visit Medhanie Alem, they absolutely refused. First they said it was impossible for mules to reach it; but this we knew was not the case. Then they said it would take too long; but we did not really mind how long it took. Then they said that they had to be back in Waldia by a certain date; but this was plainly a lie. Having argued some time they finally agreed, or so we thought, and led us off across the side of the mountain. But suddenly I realised that they were going right past the church and had no intention of climbing the mountain at all. We called a halt, and once again we started to argue. It was obvious that Haile Mariam had no desire to climb the mountain either, and he was little help to us. Nothing would make them change their minds.

Having circled the hills from Imraha we were now back within three hours walk of Lalibela where I knew we would be able to get muleteers to take us up the Mechena if need be. So as Tadessa and Fantau refused to go, we decided to send them straight back to Waldia, and to hire fresh mules from Lalibela for the remainder of the journey. With this in mind, Chris and I started to unload our baggage. Tadessa and Fantau looked on bewildered, but did nothing. Only when all the baggage was on the ground did we announce our plan, angrily telling them to beat it—that we wanted nothing further to do with them—and that they could tell their master when they got back to Waldia that he could expect to forfeit the rest of the hire fee, owing to *their* stupidity.

As we expected, this did the trick! They were terrified at the thought of what might happen to them if they arrived back in Waldia without us—both from Sancho Panza and from Dedja Berhane Maskal. And now their tune suddenly changed, and realising that the tables had been turned they became as docile as lambs. So once again, as soon as the baggage had been strapped back on to the mules, we set off up the mountain.

This was our last big climb, and one of the steepest. But as is so often the case in this land of gigantic views, it was rewarding when we reached the top. Medhanie Alem still lay two hours off, round the far side of a spur, so we spent that night in a cold but pleasant pasture, on the fringe of a forest.

Early the following morning, arranging to meet Haile Mariam and the muleteers on the path at midday, Chris and I set off alone to visit Medhanie Alem. We had by now grown accustomed to the seclusion of these churches, and it did not surprise us that we were unable to see it until we were within twenty yards. But when finally we clambered over some boulders and looked down into the mouth of a vast cave, the sight that greeted us was the most beautiful of the entire expedition. The roof of the cave must have been forty or fifty feet high, and was shaped like the vaulted roof of a huge cathedral. And there, squatting on the floor of the cave—its vaulted roof precisely echoing the angles of the rock above it—was, to my mind, the most beautiful of all the Ethiopian churches. It was not

its grandeur, nor even its architecture, that gave it its beauty; but a combination of its fantastic setting and a sort of homely warmth.

There was no one in sight. But there was a large iron bar that served as a church bell, and this we beat in the hope of attracting the attention of some priests in the hamlet many hundreds of feet below the cave. Still no one came, and it seemed for a moment that our luck would be out and that we would be unable to see inside the church. But walking round to the west end we found that the priests had failed to lock the door securely; so cautiously, knowing that we would be very unpopular if the priests found us inside, we went in and looked around.

All the walls, the pillars, and the sanctuary dome were profusely covered with mellow frescoes. There was Saint Theodore slaying the dragon; and St. George behind him. There was a splendid primitive scene of Daniel in a quaint den, with even quainter lions on either side. There was Raphael, with wings swooping down like the wings of a swift; and Makarios seated upon a horse, staring balefully down with wide, dark eyes. Over the west door were two pairs of cockerels apparently in conversation—for they looked far too naïve to fight—and humanised representations of the sun and the moon. Beneath them was an extraordinary hunting scene in which three doleful-looking gentlemen with clubs and bows and arrows were chasing three skittish buck. This hunting scene, that looked more like a cave painting than anything else, was in surprising contrast to the rest of the biblical scenes.

Beatrice Playne, when she visited this church, suggested that Medhanie Alem might date from the tenth century; though as she rightly mentioned, it is impossible to be sure of the date of any of these antiquities. By tradition it dates from the sixth century, which would make it, with Debra Damo, one of the oldest buildings in Africa that is still in use. Certainly, from the character of the script that accompanies the paintings, and the delightfully primitive style of the paintings themselves, it seems to be older than any others that we saw; and two points make me feel that it could be as old as tradition claims. In the sanctuary, incorporated into the writing above the painting of Makarios, we noticed a "chi-rho" cross, which looks like the letter X with a P superimposed on it. This type of cross (of which I know of no other examples in Ethiopia) was in common use in the earliest days of Christianity, examples appearing on fifth-century tombs as far away as Scotland.

This alone may suggest an early date for the paintings; but judging from the fact that two of the original windows in the tiny dome have at some time been plastered over to form a continuous painting-surface, it would look as though the building itself is of an even earlier date than the frescoes.

Though I think most ethnographers who have studied Ethiopian churches—and these are few and far between—would disagree with me, I can see no reason why some churches which were traditionally founded in the misty era soon after Christianity came to Ethiopia should not in fact be of a very early date. Not enough is known about Ethiopian architecture to prove anything to the contrary; and situated as many of them are, in great caves, protected from wind, and rain, and even light, there is no reason why they should not have survived for centuries.

Ethiopian priests are said by foreigners to take no care or interest in antiquities. In some cases this is certainly true—many manuscripts are in a shocking state of preservation—but so far as we could see most priests have tremendous pride in their churches; and even though they do not now have the knowledge to repair them in the original style, they would rather die than see their sanctuaries desecrated.

We spent the whole morning in Medhanie Alem taking photographs with both still and cine-cameras by flashlight, before emerging into the bright sunlight to find, after all, that we had not been alone. A small boy sat silently on a rock, peering at us; probably sent by the priests to see who was ringing the bells.

So our month in Lasta came to an end. Two days after leaving Medhanie Alem we arrived back to Waldia where we paid off the muleteers and said good-bye to Haile Mariam. The atmosphere in Waldia was, for some reason, tense, though we did not then understand why. Berhane Maskal and his wife were not at home, though no one would tell us where they were, and there appeared to be far more people in the streets carrying guns than we had previously seen.

We set off almost immediately for the nearby town of Dessie where we had previously been invited to spend the night as guests of the Crown Prince. We had not driven far when rounding a bend we suddenly found our way blocked by several tree trunks dragged across the road. At first we thought the road was being repaired; but suddenly two brigandish-looking men appeared with rifles, and waved us to stop. Without a word they opened the car doors and beckoned us to get out. Then, at gun point, we were marched off up a low hill on the crest of which we could see a stockade, built of sharpened wooden posts with a menacing portcullis over the entrance.

As we were pushed through the gate—not roughly, but brusquely enough for us to be thoroughly alarmed—I noticed four men lying behind bren-guns that were pointed directly at us. In the centre of the large enclosure was a single hut with, a short distance from it, a table round which sat a dozen important-looking men in earnest conversation. Our guard nudged us towards this group where one, named Blatta Gabriel, who spoke English, asked us who we were, where we were bound for, and various other personal questions. No one smiled; no one but he spoke; but all their eyes were trained suspiciously on us as though we were blackguards of the worst order. Neither of us had the slightest idea what it was all about, and as soon as we could get a word in we asked for some explanation from the Blatta.

"You have not heard?" he said gravely.

"Heard what?" we said.

". . . that there is a rebellion in the land, and that we have overthrown His Imperial Majesty the Emperor?"

And this was the first we heard of the attempted military take-over in 1959. The tragic, bloody coup had occurred three days earlier; and though we still did not know it, our benefactor Ras Seyum, with whose letters of introduction we had been travelling in Tigré, and our friend Ato Amde Mikael, were dead—shot down in cold blood in the Emperor's palace. Later we heard that Amde Mikael, whom I had at first acquaintance thought to be a cowardly man, had died the most honourable death of them all, when, though riddled with bullets and mortally wounded, he had fought the rebels to the last, until he fell with a battered, broken chair still gripped in his hands. But this part of the story we had not yet heard.

Now, it seemed, we were being held by a rebel band; and for several minutes we were anxious about the outcome. But we had no need to fear. For as soon as the Blatta was convinced that we were ignorant of the events and obviously had nothing to do with them, stools were brought up for us, and in a suddenly more cheerful atmosphere we were plied with glass after glass of tej. After half an hour we were allowed to go on our way; but this was not the end of our problems. We had decided, now, to drive through the night, direct to Addis Ababa; but several times more we were stopped for questioning, never quite knowing whether our hosts were Royalists or rebels. But with equal hospitality lavished upon us by both sides, we were soon beyond caring as we followed an unsteady course south through the darkness of the Ethiopian night.

Within a few days of returning to Addis Ababa Chris and I left Ethiopia and came home to England.

Several years had now passed since my first foray into the field of African art, and during those years I had learnt a great deal about *sanamu* and their creators, besides deriving considerable enjoyment from trekking through the African bush.

My various safaris had not been limited in dimension to distance alone, for in addition to the thousands of miles I had covered, I had also been able to travel through a period of thousands of years. Having started in Kenya, in the modern age of "airport" art, I had then had the chance to capture glimpses of the few remaining traditional craftsmen at work in Moçambique and the Congo. Later, in the Cameroons, I had been able to extend the search a few centuries back, and had found works of art produced in the years immediately preceding the art-stifling era of European colonialism. Down the Nile, and on the Ethiopian lakes, I had been able to compress nearly six thousand years of time between the tombs of Saqqara and the *tankwas* of Lake Tsana; and finally, in northern Ethiopia, I had lived, to all intents and purposes, in the splendour of medieval Christian Africa.

Quite apart from the adventures involved in reaching them, these fleeting visits to some of the studios and workshops of Africa had been tremendously stimulating. But at the same time they had been sad. For the further I travelled, the more evident it became that the arts in Africa today are at their lowest ebb. Except in a few small, isolated communities the traditional arts are dead; and these can never again be reborn. In a number of countries sporadic efforts are being made in schools and universities to grope for new art forms that symbolise modern Africa—but Africa today is a bewildered continent, and consequently its modern art is seldom convincing. No doubt, in some future, less materialistic age, when the continent has found its own level, Africa's artists will again recapture some of the power of their ancestors. It may be a long time before this happens; but when it does there is no reason why the *sanamu* of later generations should not be as vital and exciting as those of the countless generations that have passed.